48

Social History of Canada

Allan Greer and Craig Heron, general editors

Riots in New Brunswick:
Orange Nativism and Social Violence
in the 1840s

During the mid to late 1840s, dramatic riots shook the communities of Woodstock, Fredericton, and Saint John. Irish-Catholic immigrants fought Protestant Orangemen, with fists, clubs, and firearms. The violence resulted in death and destruction unprecedented in the British North American colonies.

This book is the first serious historical treatment of the bloody riots and the tangled events that led to them. Scott See shows mid-century New Brunswick roughly awakened from the slumbering provincialism of its post-Loyalist phase by the stirrings of capitalism and by the tidal wave of Irish immigration that followed the potato famine. His main focus is the Loyal Orange Order, the anti-Catholic organization that clashed with the immigrants, many of them impoverished exiles.

See presents an extraordinary profile of the Orange Order and concludes provocatively that it was a nativist organization similar to the xenophobic groups active at the time in the United States. Unlike other recent works on the Order, his book emphasizes the importance of the organization's specifically North American concerns, and questions the significance of its connections to Old World sectarianism.

SCOTT W. SEE is a member of the Department of History, University of Vermont.

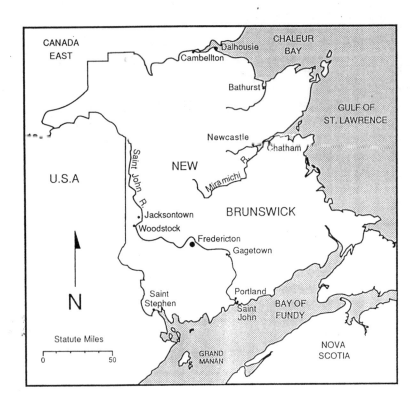

CANADA
EAST

CHALEUR
BAY

Dalhousie
Cambellton

Bathurst

GULF OF
ST. LAWRENCE

Newcastle

Chatham

U.S.A

NEW

Saint John R.

Miramichi R.

BRUNSWICK

Jacksontown
Woodstock

Fredericton
Gagetown

N

Saint
Stephen

Portland
Saint
John

BAY OF
FUNDY

NOVA
SCOTIA

Statute Miles

0        50

GRAND
MANAN

SCOTT W. SEE

# Riots in New Brunswick:
# Orange Nativism and
# Social Violence
# in the 1840s

UNIVERSITY OF TORONTO PRESS
Toronto  Buffalo  London

ISBN 0-8020-2944-2 (cloth)
ISBN 0-8020-7770-6 (paper)

Printed on acid-free paper

---

**Canadian Cataloguing in Publication Data**

See, Scott W., 1950–
   Riots in New Brunswick : Orange nativism and
   social violence in the 1840s

   (The Social history of Canada : 48)
   Includes index:
   ISBN 0-8020-2944-2 (bound)   ISBN 0-8020-7770-6 (pbk.)

   1. Orangemen – New Brunswick – History – 19th century.
   2. Nativism.  3. Riots – New Brunswick – History –
   19th century.  4. Irish – New Brunswick – History –
   19th century.  5. Catholics – New Brunswick – History –
   19th century.  6. New Brunswick – Social conditions –
   19th century.  I. Title.  II. Series.

   FC2500.A1S4 1993        971.5'102        C93-094298-1
   F1045.A1S4 1993

---

**Social History of Canada 48**

To the memory of my mother,
Nathalie Leighton See

# Contents

**PART FOUR: THE PERSPECTIVE**

# Acknowledgments

Many years in the making, this book has been profoundly shaped by numerous individuals and organizations. This project started as a dissertation at the University of Maine under the direction of Robert Babcock, who deserves tribute for his rigorous standards and unerring guidance. Jane Pease, Alice Stewart, and William Baker asked probing questions and offered insightful criticisms that greatly improved my work. Over the years, as the project developed and broadened, I accumulated more debts. I gratefully acknowledge the criticisms and suggestions offered by Peter Toner, David Frank, Phillip Buckner, Bill Spray, and Greg Kealey. They will no doubt disagree with some of my conclusions in this book, but their fertile minds moulded and strengthened my research in various ways. My colleagues in the History Department and Canadian Studies Program at the University of Vermont have been unfailingly supportive. Jim Overfield, Jerry Felt, and Denise Youngblood have been particularly helpful in providing sage advice. At the University of Toronto Press, I owe a special thanks to Allan Greer, who encouraged me to submit the manuscript for inclusion in the Social History of Canada series. His provocative criticisms on earlier drafts vastly improved my writing and sharpened my arguments. I acknowledge another important debt to Gerry Hallowell, who did not waver as he masterfully guided the book to fruition. John St James did an exceptional job with the copy-editing. Thanks are also in order to Susan Kennedy and Jesse Sheridan of the University of Vermont's Geography Department for designing the map and the graph in appendix B. Having cited the individuals above, I hasten to point out that the deficiencies that remain in this work cannot be attributed to any of them.

Various institutions deserve special mention for their service as well. The University of Maine's Canadian-American Center, Graduate School, and Sigma Xi Society generously funded my earlier research. The History Department and the Canadian Studies Program at the University of Vermont were instrumental in providing research funds. Finally, this book has been published with the help of an extremely generous grant from the Canadian Embassy in Washington, DC. I owe a special debt to Dr Norman London, who has tirelessly supported my research over the years. Portions of the accounts of the Saint John and Woodstock riots have appeared in articles in *Acadiensis*, and some of my work on the Orange Order has been presented in a chapter in Peter Toner's *New Ireland Remembered*.

Scores of librarians and archivists generously donated their time and shared their expertise while I was researching this book. Thanks are in order to the staffs of the Public Archives of New Brunswick, the New Brunswick Museum, the Harriet Irving Library at the University of New Brunswick, the National Archives of Canada, and the Saint John Regional Public Library. Several other research centres yielded important sources, including the Legislative Library in Fredericton, the Public Archives of Nova Scotia, the Woodstock Public Library, and the libraries at the University of Toronto, Dalhousie University, and Mount Allison University. The staffs at the University of Maine and the University of Vermont merit special mention, especially the individuals in the interlibrary-loan and microfilm departments.

Most important, I am deeply indebted to my family for cheerfully living with this project for many years and for tolerating with great equanimity my sometimes erratic behaviour. My wonderful daughters, Hadley and Hilary, have been remarkably understanding, especially when it concerned weekends spent in the library rather than engaged in play. Finally, words cannot possibly do justice to articulate the admiration and respect that I have for my wife. Mylese's patience and support have been truly extraordinary; indeed, they are immeasurable.

# PART ONE: THE CONTEXT

# Introduction

On 12 July 1847, the anniversary of the historic Battle of the Boyne, nervous magistrates and a small detachment of British garrison troops from Woodstock, New Brunswick, inserted themselves between two hostile crowds. Approximately three hundred Irish-Catholics and a roughly equal number of Orangemen, members of an ultraloyal and Protestant fraternity, surveyed one another menacingly as they clutched an assortment of arms that included muskets, axes, pitchforks, and wooden bludgeons. After ignoring repeated commands to disperse from the authorities, who then expeditiously withdrew from the immediate line of fire, the two groups resorted to their weapons and commenced hostilities. Following an initial salvo the Irish-Catholics broke ranks and fled, pursued by a spontaneously formed coalition of troops, magistrates, and Orangemen. Many died on that sultry summer day. At least ten bodies lay on the soil of one of Britain's North American colonies, lives shattered by tensions borne of the reciprocal antipathies of natives and immigrants, Protestants and Catholics. Scarcely three months later over five hundred Orangemen gathered to dedicate the cornerstone of an Orange lodge on the battle site, an event that symbolized the hegemony of New Brunswick–born and immigrant Protestants as they successfully protected their economic and cultural interests in the mid-nineteenth century.

Exactly two years later, in the squalid, predominantly Irish-

Catholic enclave of York Point in the coastal city of Saint John, two crowds – at least twice the size of the Woodstock contingents – confronted one another with hostile intent. Orangemen, marching behind their mounted leader, approached an evergreen arch that spanned the procession route. City officials and units of the local British garrison arrived at the scene but refused to defuse the impending clash by positioning themselves between the opposing forces. Hurled rocks led to gunfire; shots whipped the summer air, killing at least a dozen combatants and wounding countless others. After a few minutes of furious battle, the Orangemen emerged from the Irish-Catholic bastion and the troops sealed off the main thoroughfare. With a symbolism analogous to the construction of Woodstock's Orange hall, the troops hastily drew up cannon and pointed their muzzles at York Point. Behind them Orangemen continued their procession with impunity. The battle capped a bloody decade of struggle between the Orangemen and Irish-Catholic immigrants and their descendants; it also heralded the triumph of nativist ideology and proved the efficacy of vigilante tactics.

If riots are considered a fair standard for judging social disorder, the decade before mid-century stands as the most tumultuous period in New Brunswick's history. Waves of disturbances between crowds of Irish-Catholics and Orangemen broke over the colony, all concentrated in three communities: agrarian Woodstock in the northwest hinterland; Fredericton, the provincial capital; and Saint John, New Brunswick's largest municipality and principal port. Woodstock and Fredericton each endured a major conflict in 1847, while Saint John and neighbouring Portland experienced several disturbances that increased in intensity during the 1840s. In the main this work seeks to understand those riots and the complex forces, including community and provincial, that shaped them.

Questions framed to broaden this understanding focused on what caused the violence and why rioting appeared to be concentrated in the second half of the 1840s. The pursuit of answers to those questions led to an intellectual meandering along some well-marked channels, but as was more often the case, it coursed through essentially uncharted waters. On the one hand, the riots have long been recognized; they receive various degrees of treatment in the standard works that students of nineteenth-century New Brunswick history typically consult at the outset of their endeavours.[1] Indeed, in several cases the riots have attained a sort of mythical stature in the province's oral traditions and collective folk memory: the great 'Woodstock Riot of 1847' and the 'York Point Battle of 1849' are the two most notable cases.[2] And yet these explosive and often bloody encounters warrant for the most part only anecdotal treatment; with the exception of the scholarly sources cited above, they hover precariously on the fringe of historical inquiry.

On a broader scale, the assessment of violence, including rioting, is certainly not unheard of in Canadian historiography; indeed one of Canada's foremost scholars broke the silence with a clarion call many years ago. Kenneth McNaught sensibly entreated scholars to engage in the painful process of understanding indigenous violence, unrestrained by the tendency of historians, many of whom are prone to articulating only the country's unique contributions to North American history, to overlook episodes that do not make the Procrustean fit into late twentieth-century nationalistic agendas.[3] Despite pervasive interpretive models based upon the axiom 'peace, order, and good government,' violence infused the Canadian past, as did racist behaviour. Contrary to the notions of popular defenders of Canadian mythology, the weak and strong waged their battles on British North American soil with a fervour that matched that of their southern neighbours.[4] Violent popular disturbances erupted with surprising regularity in the nineteenth century, a point made compellingly by Michael Cross when he too challenged historians to scrutinize social violence in the Canadian context.[5]

Arguably Saint John, Woodstock, and Fredericton suffered violent and traumatic episodes that equalled in magnitude and spawned a legacy as profound as those riots that rocked American, English, and Irish communities. In fact, if the analysis is telescoped, it becomes clear that dramatic forces buffeted the Western world in the decades before and after 1850. Countless tensions, simultaneously frightening, cathartic, and seductive, simmered and often reached the boiling point during these years.[6] As many scholars have painstakingly pointed out, people throughout Europe and North America perceived it as their 'right' to take to the streets, protest injustices, and collectively pursue their goals. As a result, members representing virtually all social groups were inclined to confront change or injustice collectively; be they of a cultural nature, such as the ethnic riots in Ireland; of an economic nature, such as the innumerable bread riots in England and France; of a denominational nature, such as England's Gordon Riots; or of a political nature, such as the grass-roots Chartist movement that sought to effect deep political reforms.[7]

In the context of nineteenth-century New Brunswick, crowds emerged as strikingly utilitarian, or in the lexicon of crowd specialists, purposeful. Echoing resoundingly the conclusions presented recently by European and North American scholars, this study finds that New Brunswick's crowd members pursued identifiable and even pragmatic agendas.[8] As the research unfolded, it rapidly became apparent that the Orange Order habitually engaged in crowd activity and often rioted to protect what its members perceived to be its 'essential' rights of Protestant pre-eminence and loyalty to the Crown. Similarly, the Irish-Catholics often used crowds to pursue a clearly defined, yet more sketchily articulated, scheme of either gaining or maintaining a foothold in the local economies, social milieux, and political structures of the communities under study. Quite simply, Irish-Catholics in the 1840s often struggled to achieve a sense of place through collective efforts. Significantly, the protagonists of this study turned to a common modus operandi for prosecuting their agendas.

While the riots undoubtedly lay ripe for historical re-creation and assessment, questions remained as to why one should devote the effort to explore these phenomena and grapple with them historically. In other words, why is social violence important? And are riots merely anecdotal anomalies that appeal, as Lawrence Stone observed, to the 'voyeuristic instincts in us all'? To some extent, the answer to the latter question is yes. Violence captures our attention; we dwell upon the horrible examples of our mistreatment of fellow humans in both our present and our past. We remain morbidly fascinated that humans can indulge in violent activities that frequently appear to be anathema to our survival. Yet with this dynamic acknowledged, there are compelling reasons for the serious study of violence. As Stone goes on to argue, 'violence [is] an integral part of all human experience,' and it is therefore 'reasonable and defensible to explore [its] impact on individuals in the past.'[9] The study of collective violence in the context of the period in which it occurred can provide important insights. In short, disturbances are valuable signposts for social historians.

The search for this study's documentary grist led to a variety of provincial sources, colonial-office papers, court transcripts, Orange Order records, immigration documents, manuscript collections, and newspapers. The path wound through a veritable morass of literature on crowds and collective violence. The relatively value-free term 'crowd' was deliberately selected in lieu of such appellations as 'mob' and 'rabble' to refer to both the Orangemen and Irish-Catholics as they gathered in processions or counter-demonstrations. 'Mob' connotes an unstable, extremely volatile gathering with a minimum or absence of leadership. The distinction is of critical importance in historical perspective; contemporaries used the pejorative 'mob' and 'rabble' as they condemned actions or goals of aggressive gatherings.[10] Similarly, semantical problems can be created at the other end of the spectrum by labelling gatherings as the 'people,' which tends to carry positive or virtuous implications.[11] Crowd is the most neutral term and hence will be used to describe the collectives of protagonists in this analysis; it is intended to transmit neither pejorative nor defensively apologetic messages.

The step from the literature on crowds to sources on rioting proved to be a short one. 'Riot,' a term that lies at the heart of this book, deserves to be understood in its nineteenth-century context. New Brunswick statutes defined riot as three or more persons who 'wholly, or in part, execute[d]' any act of force or violence. This statute, borrowed almost verbatim from English penal codes, clearly blended a prior intent to intimidate or hurt others with a measure of success in doing so.[12] Although the contemporary interpretation sounds a trifle legalistic, it serves this analysis admirably. Riots thus occurred only when crowds gathered with the intention of intimidating or harming others, and violence, in any degree, resulted.

And whom did the crowds comprise? The swelling tides of Irish-Catholic immigrants who disembarked in New Brunswick's ports and filtered into the hinterland in the decades before mid-century triggered a virulent social reaction. Irish-Catholics and their progeny quite literally found themselves stuck in the lower rungs of New Brunswick's socio-economic ladder by a combination of mutually sustaining forces, including a nativistic ideology and its physical manifestation of vigilantism. A fraternal organization, the Loyal Orange Order, embodied both of these operative principles and galvanized native-born and immigrant Protestants to parry what they believed to be an inundation of Irish-Catholics. This 'invasion' triggered skirmishes on several fronts, including cultural and religious institutions, the workplace and market-place, and ultimately local and provincial politics. Orangemen forged powerful linkages between their organization and political leadership at both community and provincial levels. Entrepreneurs, businessmen, and social leaders – men of prominence – joined the organization in droves.[13] Simply put, many Orangemen involved in the social violence led their communities; other Orangemen and Protestants supported the activists for a variety of ideological, social, political, and economic rationales. Patronage and power interceded and shaped the riots.

The exploratory paths thus followed the fortunes of the riots' principal protagonists, the Orangemen and Irish-Catholics. But rather than compartmentalizing into tidy mini-investigations, conveniently intersecting only when the groups confronted one another at periodic contentious gatherings, the story took on variegated hues. For example, a portrait of the Orange Order defies a monochromatic characterization. In the best sense of nineteenth-century organizations, it provided its members with an array of social services and forums for comradeship. Similarly, the roughly 150 local lodges that mushroomed by mid-century resist a universal definition thanks to their strikingly different membership pools, especially when factors such as ethnicity, occupation, age, and social standing are taken into account.

Many of the obstacles to providing a simplistic description of the Orangemen surfaced in the analysis of their counterparts. Most fundamentally, the generic rubric that historians have applied for generations – Irish-Catholics – tends to obscure important variations within the group.[14] Substantial numbers of Irish-Catholics populated New Brunswick long before the tragic famine migrations of the late 1840s. Moreover, even a superficial assessment of the riots clearly indicated that recent arrivals and entrenched Irish-Catholics sought different goals in their collective behaviour, depending upon their locality. They used the urban streets of Saint John and the dusty roads of hinterland communities such as Woodstock to confront their enemy. Badly outnumbered, they relied upon their culture as a survival tool for facing the rigours of the new world.[15] In both metaphorical and concrete terms, they used their religion, kinship networks, and sometimes their Gaelic language to combat hostile ideologies and vigilante forces.

After exploring the riots, identifying and assessing the agendas of the protagonists, and delving into provincial issues, the crucial task remained at hand to trace the complex linkages between the rioters and the socio-economic and political realities of the host communities and the entire province. Undeniably a full understanding of the riots' timing, causes, and legacies would be impossible without a firm anchoring in the histories of Saint John, Portland, Fredericton, and Woodstock. Furthermore, while the riots were not inherently 'caused' by sweeping changes, they signalled a series of profound transitions and might be usefully interpreted as manifestations of structural tensions in New Brunswick's society.[16] Perhaps most fundamentally, the colony grappled with the beginnings of a wrenching conversion from pre-industrial to industrial capitalism during the 1840s. A series of severe depressions, brought about by a decline in the staple timber economy, touched the lives of virtually all New Brunswickers and brought scarcities of jobs, goods, and services.

Many ambiguities emerged as the research unfolded, the most important of which subdivide into three complex problems. First, the Loyal Orange Order and Irish-Catholics were clearly ensconced in New Brunswick long before the tumultuous decade. Irish-Catholics had migrated in significant numbers since at least the turn of the century, while the Orange Order held organizational meetings in several communities before 1820. Therefore, the facile assumption that the two groups combined to form an inherently volatile mixture would have to be modified; certainly the dynamic between the groups shifted dramatically during the 1840s.

Moreover, while some New Brunswick communities experienced social violence, most did not. The rate and intensity of collective violence in those communities that did witness riots clearly suggested that those events should not be characterized as anomalous or aberrations, but the fact that many other New Brunswick communities with similar admixtures of groups remained quiescent bore serious contemplation. If nothing else, the argument's counter-factual dimension should cast more illumination on the factors that triggered the riots. For example, some regions with substantial Irish-Catholic populations, such as the Miramichi, witnessed no collective violence during the late 1840s on the scale of those covered in this study.[17] Similarly, other Loyalist bastions with emerging Orange organizations, such as Sunbury, Queens, and Kings counties, remained essentially unscathed by the waves of tumult. While this book does not explicitly assess the absence of violence in various New Brunswick localities, a consideration of the demographies and economies of relatively peaceful communities implicitly shaped the research and analysis.

A third challenge emerged as a direct outgrowth of the preceding. Why was social violence so neatly confined to the decade before mid-century, almost as if preordained by historical forces? Dated and deficient theories, based largely upon the interrelationship between economic factors and violence at critical junctures in history – some even purporting to predict when social turmoil is most likely to occur – seemed poor vehicles for sharpening an understanding of the New Brunswick experience.[18] For example, other periods in the province's history brought dramatic economic, political, and social problems without collective violence. Moreover, riots have materialized at seemingly paradoxical moments, such as during the relatively secure 1870s in Caraquet.[19] Unquestionably, a variety of explanatory tools would be required to identify and explain the factors that linked the protagonists to certain communities during the 1840s.

For several of those methodological implements, this work borrows unabashedly theories that have to date been infrequently applied to Canadian history, most notably the ideology termed nativism and the behavioural pattern labelled vigilantism. Nativism, most often encountered in the nineteenth-century American experience, is a deceptively rudimentary concept for describing what in fact are complex systems of beliefs.[20] Nativism describes in general the response of established groups, which need not be monolithic in ethnicity, religious beliefs, or political persuasions, towards other groups. Often those alienated include recent immigrants whose race, religion, or culture represent a sharp departure from the host society's. Burgeoning nationalism fostered nativism in the United States; thus, on first glance the term might seem poorly suited for understanding the history of a British North American colony.[21] However, this book will argue that the native-born and Protestant community in New Brunswick articulated and defended a British colonial nationalism. Within broad imperial parameters, this form of nativism embraced both native- and foreign-born individuals. Thus, it serves as a useful paradigm for assessing the intersection between immigrant and native; it is a value system in which the dominant group typically espouses racist ideas, employs negative rhetoric, and overtly seeks to prevent immigrants from gaining access to virtually all avenues of political, economic, and social power.

If nativism characterizes a system of beliefs, vigilantism describes a system of behaviour. As with nativism, vigilantism has most typically been identified and assessed in regions comfortably removed from the Canadian landscape. Yet the dynamic applies well to this study. The Orange Order emerged, at least in the 1840s, as an extra-legal organization that routinely buttressed the legally constituted arms of authority in New Brunswick's communities. Acting as a paramilitary group, it sought to ensure colonial order, Protestant ascendancy, and Loyalist principles during a bewildering period. In this Canadian case, therefore, vigilantism propped up the state and reinforced those who held the reins of community and provincial power. To contemporaries it represented a defence of the Old World during a decade rife with economic uncertainty, shifting immigration patterns, and social chaos. Vigilantism in New Brunswick spawned social violence as virulent and historically significant as episodes found in comparable European and North American communities.[22]

Yet episodic rioting did not represent a simple transfer of Old World struggles to the New. This is neither to deny nor obfuscate the obvious and powerful linkages between the European and North American continents. The migration of ideas and populations shaped and often gave direction to the actions of Irish-Catholic and Orangeman alike in New Brunswick. The province comprised a heterogeneous mixture of ethnic groups and denominations, including various Protestant denominations and Roman Catholicism, Celts and Anglo-Saxons, Loyalists, ex–New Englanders, English, Scots, Irish, and Acadians. Considered alone, however, this mosaic did not create the problems, for most of the participants in the riotous episodes subordinated Old World concerns to more compelling indigenous forces, including local settlement patterns, job availability, and political environments.

Finally, by definition this work touches on class issues.[23] Orangemen and Protestants jealously guarded the socio-economic order to the deliberate, and often patently illegal exclusion of minority groups such as Irish-Catholics. The analysis will fall well short of characterizing these riots as conflagrations in a expansive 'class war' ignited by the transition between merchant and industrial capitalism. Yet undeniably class issues underpinned these riots, most notably at the community level. Elites and their 'enablers,' typically Orangemen, artisans, farmers, merchants, and even labourers, sought to protect the privileges of the state as an act of self-interest. In the course of doing so, they alienated the largest ethnic and religious immigrant group. Throughout this struggle, of which these riots illustrated merely one phase, the doors to virtually all of New Brunswick's socio-economic, judicial, and political corridors remained firmly shut to Irish-Catholics. Thanks largely to the withering effects of the mid-century disturbances, élites retained virtually total control over magisterial positions, police and constabulary forces, provincial offices, and, with rare exceptions, New Brunswick's economy. Viewed from the perspective of these individuals, nativism proved a useful ideology and vigilantism a devastatingly effective tool.

This work thus represents, quite deliberately, a parochial exercise. As Donald Akenson recently pointed out with his customary blend of a scholar's eloquence and a zealot's sense of the unshakable correctness of his interpretive path, case studies serve as handy historical tools.[24] The bulk of the evidence, as well as the historical messages, emerge from the contexts of the towns and cities under scrutiny. Admittedly, New Brunswick serves as a convenient geographical label, for this study actually focuses on several communities scattered along the reaches of the Saint John River. It does not explore the unique textures of Madawaska with its Acadian population, the North Shore region, the towns hard by the Bay of Chaleur, the southwestern counties rich in Loyalist traditions, or the lively timber-processing communities along the Miramichi River. The reason should rapidly become apparent to the reader: all of them lacked riots and socio-economic confrontations that achieved the drama and magnitude of those addressed below.

# 1

# New Brunswick in mid-century

Loyalist fervour provided the guiding ethos for the British colony of New Brunswick. From its earliest political beginnings as an excised appendage of Nova Scotia, New Brunswick drew its population from Loyalist regiments and their families who fled the rebellious colonies after the preliminary peace settlements of January 1783 that concluded the American Revolutionary War. Although these Loyalist immigrants from the eastern seaboard claimed primary responsibility for New Brunswick's official detachment from Nova Scotia in 1784 and the creation of a new government the following year, they did not find the colony empty when they arrived. New Englanders occupied farmsteads in the Saint John Valley following the Seven Years' War; along the northern and eastern shores, Acadians clung tenaciously to the land in defiance of the deportation of 1755. Yet while New Brunswick was never homogeneous, its political roots can be clearly traced to the expelled American Loyalists.

Loyalist principles motivated many New Brunswickers for the first half-century and, with the exception of a Roman Catholic Acadian population far removed from the enclaves of Loyalist and New England descendants and a modest number of Irish-Catholic immigrants, various Protestant denominations predominated. Emigration from Great Britain buttressed these trends. English, Scots, and Irish-Protestants made their way to the colony in search of an improved life within the British imperial frame-

work. Moreover, New Brunswick retained strong economic linkages to the Mother Country; a timber colony, it depended almost
entirely on a single export staple. Britain 'farmed' the rich New
Brunswick hinterland. A system of preferences and taxes on
foreign imports protected the raw material and allowed the
fledgling colony to compete with closer and more sophisticated
European competitors. In short, New Brunswick's political, economic, and social eyes remained firmly focused on England. The
population concentrated on timber exports and attempted to
establish a viable agricultural economy, the descendants of Loyalists and New Englanders ran the political institutions based upon
the English model, and modest numbers of immigrants from
Great Britain reinforced the relatively homogeneous Anglo-Saxon
and Protestant population.[1]

Yet as the mid-nineteenth century approached, New Brunswick
found itself immersed in a tumultuous period that rocked its
economic and social foundations. The forces that shaped this part
of the colony's history came largely from outside the province.
New Brunswick's timber staple economy, never a passive child,
grew to maturity and faced severe exploitation and a withdrawal
of preferences in the 1840s as Britain embraced free trade. Moreover, the colony grappled with the transition from a pre-modern,
staple economy to merchant capitalism and diversification. These
economically oriented problems, thoroughly intertwined by mid-
century, created the arena for social upheaval. The dramatic
increase in the numbers of Celtic-Catholics in the 1840s provided
the catalyst for social conflict.

New Brunswick's economic existence during its first fifty years
can be attributed primarily to the cutting, processing, and shipping of a single staple commodity – timber. Prior to mid-century,
the province might be best characterized as a pre-industrial hinterland with a few modest urban centres. Processing and moving
a badly needed product to Great Britain became its primary
function. Although farmers gamely settled the most promising
regions, the generally poor soil and short growing season handi-
capped agricultural diversification. Thus, during the 1840s the
colony remained married to the staple trade, and as a result it

continued to be a pawn to British commercial markets. New Brunswick's pecuniary star rose and fell according to fickle British trading patterns; one historian observed that the boom-and-bust economy of England forced the province to dance like a 'gigantic bandalore' to the tunes of unpredictable mercantilism.[2]

New Brunswick entered the 1840s as a scarred veteran of the timber trade wars. As early as 1800 the colony provided masts and spars to the voracious English navy. Wartime tariffs helped the province stay afloat during the Napoleonic conflict, and afterwards a series of preferences supported the industry until 1842.[3] Overall, New Brunswick enjoyed moderate growth during this period. Yet its economy was not immune to cyclical swings; 1819, 1825, and 1837 brought sharp downturns due to bankruptcies and financial panic in Great Britain. From 1825 to mid-century, New Brunswick's timber trade struggled against a mounting danger of collapsing.[4] Entrepreneurs scrambled to protect their investments and stake out regional monopolies. Tragically, their myopic practices contributed to a general economic 'retardation.'[5] By the 1840s agricultural output stagnated and alternative export markets remained essentially unexplored. A half-century had witnessed negligible changes in New Brunswick's economy; it still depended on the farming of timber stands, which fell prey to the lumberman's ax at an alarming pace, the rough sawing to make the product portable, and the shipping of stocks to destinations in the British Empire.

An increasingly sharp delineation between employers and employees contributed to New Brunswick's general lack of economic diversification. A select group of entrepreneurs emerged in the 1830s as the dominant force in the staple economy. Aided by rising costs, a fragile market-place, and prohibitive licence fees, large operators squeezed out smaller and poorer individual cutters. Lumber titans such as Northumberland County's Joseph Cunard and Alexander Rankin actively exploited their political connections to protect their interests. This helped to intensify and solidify the colony's focus upon a single staple. Except for providing the capital for forward linkages such as an indigenous shipbuilding enterprise, New Brunswick's entrepreneurs contributed little to the colony's economic diversification.[6]

Eighteen-forty ushered in New Brunswick's worst economic decade. The 'hungry forties,' as some Western Europeans and North Americans sardonically dubbed the decade, became a grim reality for tiny New Brunswick. Moderate gains accompanying the late 1830s dissipated in a few short years. Bad news loomed on the horizon in 1841 as Great Britain's investment capital shifted from the lumber industry to the more lucrative cotton trade in the United States and southern colonies.[7] England's prime minister, Robert Peel, exacerbated the situation in 1842 when he altered Britain's course towards free trade in an attempt to combat soaring deficits. England's legislators responded by lowering or dropping tariffs on foreign square timber and increasing colonial duties. News of this policy implementation rocked New Brunswick's financial community. Fear of the ramifications of such a move led to a severe loss of confidence among investors and triggered a deep depression in 1842–3. High unemployment, bankruptcy, outmigration, legislative indebtedness, and abysmal provincial credit characterized the downturn. To add to the pall, the important port communities of Saint John and Portland suffered from devastating fires in their business districts in 1837, 1839, and 1841.[8]

Panic spread among New Brunswickers during the 1840s. It ran to epidemic proportions, touching indiscriminately financiers, entrepreneurs, merchants, and labourers. Ignoring the voices of calm, and even those who predicted that free trade would ultimately be a boon to the colony, most New Brunswickers doubted that they could compete in an independent market-place without the advantage of protective tariffs.[9] Although the province enjoyed a slight recovery from late 1843 throughout 1844, prompted by a railroad boom in Great Britain, mid-decade found New Brunswick's economy still severely troubled. Glutted international timber brokers scaled back their orders, while virgin forest stands virtually disappeared at an alarming rate. Decades of indiscreet cutting practices, caused by timber barons who sought short-term profits, had undermined the very source of New Brunswick's life-blood.[10]

The second half of the 1840s, rather than bringing relief, compounded the financial turmoil. The years from 1845–50 were marked by an anemic economy; further reductions in England's foreign tariffs forced New Brunswick's timber merchants to compete in a progressively free market-place. The worldwide surfeit of timber continued apace. In addition, a general economic depression in trade forced prices down in Europe and North America. As a result, New Brunswick's 'prophets of doom,' pundits and businessmen alike, predicted a total collapse of the staples trade. A series of poor harvests from 1845–8 only served to lend credence to their arguments. The failure of the massive Cunard enterprise in the Miramichi, once one of the reigning timber operations, powerfully symbolized the economic malaise.[11]

Financial gloom reached its zenith in 1849 when a severe commercial depression struck New Brunswick's chief port at Saint John. The year marked an important transition in the colony's economic history. As food prices rose and exports dropped, bankruptcies and financial collapse followed among merchants and traders. Unemployment also rose dramatically as sawmill owners replaced their labour-intensive operations with newer steam-driven machinery.[12] To the chagrin of colonists, the 1840s went out in much the same fashion as it had come in – marked by financial distress. Except for a brief respite in mid-decade, it proved to be the most tumultuous period in New Brunswick's political history.

New Brunswick's severe economic problems in the 1840s touched the lives of virtually all its inhabitants. Countless investors, tradesmen, and entrepreneurs suffered ruin and bankruptcy as they panicked and withdrew their investments. But at a more fundamental level, the decade proved disastrous for much of the colony's labouring population. Contemporary observers noted a stubborn pessimism even among the employed workers, particularly in urban areas. Long hours, typically from sunrise to sunset, coupled with the ubiquitous policy of payment 'out of shop,' meaning in goods rather than in specie, led as one contemporary observed to a certain 'non-chalance' among day labourers.[13]

Many workers in troubled industries sought relief from their plight. Budding unions and associations struggled throughout the decade for higher wages and shorter working hours.[14] In May 1842, for example, Saint John building workers struck for wage increases. Violence erupted when strikers pelted one of their co-workers with stones and bricks when he attempted to report on the job.[15] Seven years later a public meeting in Saint John drew over four hundred disgruntled labourers, primarily stevedores. Their resolutions pointed to endemic problems; they demanded a minimum wage of four shillings a day for unloading ships as well as shorter working hours to bolster the ranks of the employed.[16] Saint John sawyers gathered one month later to condemn the 'evil' introduction of steam machinery which they claimed had already 'disemployed a multitude of mechanics.' Like their stevedore brethren, they wished to counter unemployment and dislocation by raising wages and increasing the number of shifts.[17] Clearly, New Brunswick's labouring population grappled with dramatic adversities during the 1840s. Confronted with low wages, long hours, high unemployment, and displacement, they coped with the 'hungry forties' by banding into trade unions and friendly associations.

Together with merchants and financiers, some New Brunswick labourers sought more radical solutions to their economic plight. Among the most disenchanted, the panacea of annexation to the United States appeared the only viable alternative to total financial collapse. The small but vocal annexation movement flared and quickly died after having peaked during the misery of 1849. Ultimately, New Brunswick's Loyalist population provided an infertile ground for sowing republican seeds. Though never a serious threat to New Brunswick's colonial status, the annexation movement illustrated the severity of economic distress.[18]

A movement for reciprocity with the United States represented a more substantive attempt to solve the economic problems accompanying the British shift to free trade. In May 1848, a large public meeting including mercantilists, manufacturers, and mechanics met in Saint John to discuss the idea of a reciprocal trade agreement with their southern neighbours. While lamenting the demise of Britain's preferential system, the group enthusiastically resolved to seek trading arrangements outside the colonial system.[19] The following year a New Brunswick delegation attended an intercolonial conference at Halifax and boldly recommended giving the Americans substantial concessions in order to secure reciprocal trade. After several years of debate, New Brunswick signed a reciprocity treaty between the United States and British North American colonies.[20] Though the Americans abrogated the treaty in 1866, reciprocity contributed to a redirection in New Brunswick's trading patterns away from the British Empire. Undoubtedly reciprocity helped to alleviate the province's economic distress of the late 1840s.

Some New Brunswickers coped with the problems of the 1840s by seeking more cooperation among the British North American colonies. They sought to remain British, counter the annexation movement, and improve trade. In July 1849, Saint John merchants and businessmen gathered at the Mechanics Institute to form the New Brunswick Colonial Association.[21] Delegates noted that the province wallowed in an 'extreme depression' and resolved to band together with other anemic colonies to develop new markets, especially outside the timber industry. Desperate tones infused the language of these 'respectable' citizens: one delegate called New Brunswick a 'sick child' of England. The delegates, who would receive the enthusiastic support of Fredericton's businessmen a month later, prescribed economic diversification to diminish their dependence on England. By encouraging more agricultural settlers, they hoped to negate the catastrophic fluctuations attendant upon the staples trade.[22] Although little came of the Colonial Association, the concepts outlined in 1849 anticipated colonial unification that would become a reality in the British North America Act of 1867.

All the above schemes sprouted from the fertile soil of economic distress in the 1840s. The decade marked by panic and bankruptcy closed with all sectors of New Brunswick's economy searching for solutions: entrepreneurs, merchants, small businessmen, and labourers. Their attempts to cope underscored the severity of the problems they faced. The decade found the colony in the midst of a painful transition from a dependent timber exporter to a more mature province that could chart its own course in the world of North American commerce.

But to almost everyone's surprise, the 1850s brought a significant recovery. New Brunswick's economy rebounded in virtually all sectors. Improved crops in 1849 and the following year signalled agricultural recovery. Plans to develop railroads linking the eastern colonies and the United States sparked interest among investors who saw a potential market for local materials. In the traditional lumbering sector, shipbuilding began in earnest, and wages increased as deal and log prices recovered handsomely. By 1851 timber exporters commanded double the price that their goods had obtained two years earlier. But perhaps most importantly, the 1850s brought a restoration of confidence in the colony's viability. The 'prophets of doom' found their arguments eclipsed by a new breed of industrious investors and workers. People began to predict a bright future for New Brunswick in the competitive cauldron of free trade. And when reciprocity became a fact in 1854, even the sceptics grudgingly admitted that the colony's chances for survival were infinitely better than they had been five years earlier.[23]

Yet New Brunswick at mid-century remained pre-industrial; it hovered on the brink of modernity. Vast and relatively undeveloped stretches of hinterland beckoned. Only in larger towns and urban centres had aspects of merchant capitalism become firmly entrenched. For example, a chasm already separated labourer and entrepreneur. The large enterprises that dominated the timber trade by 1850 succeeded in driving smaller competitors out of business. Still, the 1849 crisis of confidence marked an important transition in the province's history. Several paths lay open, including annexation to the United States, a colonial association, or reciprocity. New Brunswickers chose the latter and so passed into a new phase of economic development. Though it was still a backwater colony in Great Britain's vast imperial network, New Brunswick had by mid-century made the first tentative steps towards diversification.[24]

Clearly, New Brunswickers faced formidable economic problems in the 1840s. A series of severe depressions, especially from 1842–3 and 1845–50, ravaged financiers, merchants, and labourers alike. Coupled with the wrenching transition from a pre-industrial economy to merchant capitalism, the cyclical downturns cast an important foundation for social problems among the colony's inhabitants. Economic and transitional turmoil, while not the only causes for collective violence between Protestants and Catholics, created a favourable climate.

However severe and concentrated the riots of the 1840s would appear, episodes of collective violence had marred New Brunswick's history since its political inception. Basically, incidents involving crowds prior to 1840 can be categorized by cause; political or economic factors underscored virtually all of them. Scores of exceedingly warm election campaigns serve as perhaps the most conspicuous example. Crowds of supporters often followed candidates to block the polls from opposing parties. Enthusiastic voters established a precedent for violence during the first provincial election in 1785. Strong political divisions, mainly between the older New England stock and newer middle-colony Loyalists, led to a disturbance at a Saint John tavern during polling hours. British garrison troops from nearby Fort Howe finally quelled the riot after civilian authorities failed to bring it under control.[25] Similar disputes often erupted in the first half of the nineteenth century, culminating in the province-wide riots during the 1842–3 election campaigns. Northumberland County, Saint John, and Fredericton experienced the worst disturbances.[26]

Some of New Brunswick's collective violence, while shaped by political issues, did not focus on election campaigns or polling. During the 1840s, a series of clashes broke out on Grand Manan between Wilford Fisher, a powerful magistrate, and the rector of the Church of England. In the course of the disturbances, incendiarism claimed stores, homes, and church buildings. Though the incidents involved adamant followers of the Anglican church, religious issues did not kindle riots. Islanders waged a battle for magisterial control, and thus Grand Manan's disturbances fell into the realm of political collective violence.[27]

Economic motivations accounted for the second major category of collective violence. For example, competing timber cutters engaged in countless small skirmishes along the Miramichi. The most severe of these broke out from 1822 to 1826 between rival gangs of Irish immigrant labourers and itinerant American lumbermen. Garrison troops from Fredericton appeared on two occasions to quell the disturbances. Though rival ethnic groups orchestrated the main clashes, economic competition created the antipathy. Riots flared only when groups encountered one another in disputed cutting areas. Ultimately the Irish were successful in driving out their American foes, and a tenuous peace returned to the Miramichi in the late 1820s.[28]

A series of riots at Dalhousie and Campbellton during the summer of 1841 also fell under the rubric of economic conflict. Approximately two hundred lumbermen, claiming that they had been cheated, attacked and destroyed the stores of several merchants. When constables arrested a handful of the offenders, a crowd assaulted the tiny county jail and liberated the inmates. A 'large number' of men, 'impossible to identify,' rallied in an attempt to rescue jailed prisoners, triggering the organization of a 'sort of police force ... under the direction of a respectable militia officer.'[29] Economic issues clearly underscored the disturbances; poor lumbermen found themselves hopelessly locked into a system of 'borrowing' goods from merchants until the end of the season when they could repay their debts. In a classic example of workers being hamstrung by a shortage of capital, the lumbermen rarely made enough in a season to clear their debts. As a result, the frustrated woodsmen rebelled against the merchants who held lien on their goods and property.[30] The riots at Dalhousie and Campbellton typified the severity of New Brunswick's economic distress in the early nineteenth century – problems that affected not only the large merchants of Saint John and Fredericton, but the common labourer in the hinterland as well.

Thus New Brunswick experienced sporadic, disconnected, and limited episodes of collective violence by mid-century. Only when appropriate factors coalesced – when economic hardships, coupled with fundamental changes, provided a fecund ground for socially defined disturbances – would social violence on a large scale be possible. Social violence necessitated a catalyst for shape and definition, and in the 1840s, a substantial immigration of non-Anglo-Saxon Catholics provided the missing ingredient. The destitute Irish famine victims that flooded into the colony's ports would provoke a nativist response among fervent Protestants. These immigrants, thrust upon the scene during a depression, would threaten New Brunswick's fragile economic structure. The Irish also arrived during New Brunswick's transition from a pre-industrial to a capitalistic economy, prompted by Great Britain's effort to withdraw colonial preferences and chart a course for free trade. This would be the milieu for collective violence between native and immigrant Protestants and Irish Roman Catholics during the 1840s. Social violence would occur in the matrix of economic depression and transitional disarray, and a conceptualization of the riots will best be achieved in the contexts of their community settings.

# 2

# Communities in transition: Saint John, Fredericton, and Woodstock

The riots erupted in three localities that, on a superficial level, shared little in common other than the fact that they bordered the stately Saint John River and served as important service communities to their respective hinterlands. Saint John, Fredericton, and Woodstock differed vastly in population, economic orientation, and ethnic composition. While they shared similar cultural groups and religious denominations, they diverged dramatically in the relative proportions of those groups in the decade prior to mid-century. Moreover, each comprised a socio-political élite roughly moulded by provincial dynamics, yet given final form and hardened in the kiln of regional determinants such as geography, economies, demographics, and social institutions.

Saint John gained modest stature as New Brunswick's most populous city in the nineteenth century. As its most cogent historian recently pointed out, the anglophone community mushroomed and outpaced provincial growth in the years between the War of 1812 and Confederation.[1] From the 1820s to 1861 its population quadrupled, while that of the entire province increased by a less impressive factor of two and a half.[2] Settled by Loyalists in 1783 and incorporated two years later, Saint John rapidly developed into the province's primary port for both the exportation of staple timber goods and for the importation of manufactured products and foodstuffs. Situated at the mouth of the Saint

John River on both sides of a fine natural harbour, the city comprised distinct sectors. A peninsula bordering the harbour's eastern shore contained the bulk of the city's population, while across the bay to the west lay the section known as Carleton in the mid-nineteenth century. Portland Parish, technically a distinct administrative unit prior to its amalgamation with the city, ringed Saint John directly to the north.[3]

The decade before mid-century witnessed dramatic transformation in Saint John and its immediate environs. As T.W. Acheson observed, a series of 'ward villages' eroded and reformulated under the control of a centralized civil bureaucracy by mid-century. While a tone of lament underscored Acheson's argument about the realignment in power structures, which he attributed largely to an 'intrusion' of 'new social and ethnic groups,' his carefully reconstructed image of transformation provides a useful contextual model.[4]

Mid-century found Saint John the bustling locus of New Brunswick's timber trade. Sawn timber and deals left its wharves destined for the British Isles. Sawmills and iron foundries, as well as numerous brick works and grist mills, dotted the skyline. Fishermen and farmers brought their products to the city's docks and market-places to be processed and sold. Along the narrow streets and wharves sailors rubbed shoulders with tradesmen, merchants, lawyers, mill workers, and itinerant labourers. Distinguished by its working classes, perched at the estuary of New Brunswick's lifeline, Saint John dominated the province's economy.[5]

Its socio-economic character, while appearing monolithic when viewed at a distance, takes on important nuances upon closer inspection. Indeed, each ward carried distinctive demographic and economic signatures. Sydney Ward lay farthest to the south, surrounded by the waters of Courtney Bay to the east and Saint John Harbour to the west. Populated by lower classes, many of whom made their livings by providing services to British soldiers garrisoned at the head of land, Sydney was the city's smallest ward. Adjacent to and north of Sydney lay Dukes Ward. Its population of artisans, merchants, and mechanics constituted

Saint John's Loyalist heart. Farther to the north one encountered Queens Ward, also an established Loyalist enclave, and home to the city's largest percentage of businesspeople. The most diversified section of the city, Kings Ward, reached to the north and west. Protestant artisans congregated in the ward's eastern streets, closest to Courtney Bay. To the west, packed in dilapidated structures within sight of the bridge to Portland, resided most of Saint John's Irish-Catholic population.[6] Finally Guys and Brooks Wards, generically termed Carleton in the years before mid-century, nestled along the western reaches of Saint John Harbour. The distinctive characteristics of each ward irrevocably shaped the turmoil of the 1840s, for the tensions most often flared in the more diversified Kings Ward and its neighbouring community of Portland.

Cast in the city's northern shadow was Portland Parish. With roughly one-third the population of Saint John, Portland became the shipbuilding centre of the bay region. Several roads connected the localities, the busiest thoroughfare being a dilapidated bridge spanning an inlet on the harbour's northern extremity.[7] Numerous shipyards and timber docks, as well as an assortment of foundries and small manufacturing plants, dotted its shoreline. Like its populous southern neighbour, Portland drew its strongest identity from labouring residents.[8]

In the 1840s city governance fell to a Common Council, comprising an appointed mayor and an equal number of aldermen and assistant aldermen elected by the freeholders in each of the six wards. The mayor, a personal appointee of the lieutenant-governor until the early 1850s, chaired the Common Council and acted as chief magistrate.[9] During the decades before mid-century, élites dominated the Common Council. While Acheson asserted that it comprised a petite bourgeoisie, including shopowners, artisans, and captains of small fishing boats, in fact an impressive array of influential male citizens, especially those from Saint John's 'proper families,' served terms on the council during the 1840s. Overwhelmingly Protestant and middle-class, most of these guardians of the moral order traced their lineage to Loyalist and English immigrants. As will be established later, Orangemen and Protestants openly sympathetic to Orange tenets accounted for many of them. Their community positions, as well as their political appointments, rested on an intricate web of kinship and business allegiances. Irish-Catholics and Scots-Presbyterians, with a few notable exceptions, grappled unsuccessfully with formidable barriers to achieving power through mid-century.[10]

In addition, Fredericton's executive government appointed dozens of justices of the peace who possessed formidable legislative, executive, and judicial powers. They variously controlled and appointed county and parish officers; they acted as justices of the Court of General Sessions, presiding at local trials; they regulated education, poor relief, parish roads, and ferries; they also licensed taverns and collected an impressive array of local surcharges from poor relief to timber taxes. While many of New Brunswick's justices would not fairly be characterized as wealthy, even by nineteenth-century standards, they inevitably constituted the highest echelons of both the social and economic classes of their respective communities. A palpable element of patronage accompanied the position. Locals doffed their hats to them and called them 'squire'; many took advantage of the customary right to affix the grandiose title 'esquire' to their correspondence. In more concrete terms, they routinely presided over their constituents as moral watchdogs.[11] Their role mirrored that of magistrates in other British North American colonies, perhaps most closely those of Upper Canada, later Canada West. In short, they represented an established, centralized group. Often devoid of formal legal training, these 'men of prominence' exercised substantial responsibility that included keeping the peace and dealing with petty criminals and debtors.[12] As in Woodstock and Fredericton, the magistrates simultaneously defined and protected Saint John's moral order.

Significantly, the mayor and justices of the peace were appointed functionaries throughout the years of intensified social violence. Of all the political and judicial representatives covered in this work, only Saint John's aldermen owed their positions to the electorate. Yet thanks to a severely restricted franchise, they too essentially represented the élite.[13] Throughout the period only freemen and freeholders held the franchise in Saint John; by 1851 this translated to an estimated one-quarter of the male population and a handful of females. Freeholders, defined as those owning real estate, assuredly represented the entrenched and propertied elements of Saint John society. Freemen, by contrast, included those who purchased the status at a price set by the mayor, which ranged in this period from £1 to £5, depending upon the economic standing of the individual. Acheson determined that by 1851 freemen comprised one-fifth of the city's male residents over twenty-one years of age. When freeholders are added to the cohort, an estimated one-quarter of Saint John's male population enjoyed the franchise. Acheson carefully noted that this represented a favourable percentage compared to contemporary British cities, less so when measured by American standards; none the less, a rarified group of individuals served as Saint John's aldermen during the 1840s.[14] Notions that the city resembled even a crude model of egalitarian self-government must surely dissipate when the equation's missing three-quarters is considered. Saint John's legislative, judicial, and executive powers reflected almost exclusively established, Loyalist, English, and Protestant elements.

Community order fell under the jurisdiction of a sheriff, several constables, and a paid night watch. As the judicial centre of Saint John County, the city housed the court-house and jail. Moreover, permanent detachments of British military troops on the city's peninsular tip and at Fort Howe just across the city line in Portland Parish buttressed, in both psychological and realistic terms, the civilian constabulary. As in the two other communities under analysis, the military profoundly shaped Saint John's history in the pre-Confederation period.[15] It also played an important role in quashing the disturbances in each of the communities.

Despite distressing fluctuations in the timber trade in the first half of the nineteenth century, Saint John cultivated an expanding import trade. Starting with a limited base of regional domination, it aggressively rolled back the periphery of an expansive hinterland. By mid-century the port's facilities controlled one-half to two-thirds of New Brunswick's wood products. As a forward linkage to its indigenous staple, shipbuilding expanded to the point where Saint John boasted the largest fleet in British North America. In addition, Saint John served as the financial capital of the province; for example, political and commercial leaders chartered in 1820 the Bank of New Brunswick.[16] Poised at the epicentre of economic growth, approximately two hundred merchants presided over the ebb and flow of goods. Native-born made up approximately one-half of the total, while Scots, English, and Irish-Protestants accounted for the remainder.[17] As in the case of governance, a small percentage of citizens, over-representative of those with correct religious and ethnic backgrounds, set the city's economic course and maintained responsibility for its fortunes.

The economic prognosis appeared dismal. Panic and depression rocked virtually all of New Brunswick's communities as a result of a slump in the timber market when Great Britain lurched towards free trade. As a result, Saint John experienced a relative decline after 1825. A pessimistic outlook concerning the ramifications of free trade, news of the equalization of preferential rates with Scandinavian timber suppliers by 1846, and the 1849 repeal of navigation acts that had insulated New Brunswick shippers from direct competition with Americans collectively spelled economic doom to many Saint Johners. While the province ultimately survived the crisis of confidence in far better shape than the pundits had predicted, fear of a catastrophic erosion of provincial markets permeated the citizenry throughout the 1840s.[18]

While merchants struggled to maintain control, the decades before mid-century witnessed the rise of an articulate and organized artisanal class. Often working in tandem with their merchant counterparts, especially as a disproportionately large component of the Common Council, artisans built a powerful socioeconomic base by the early 1840s.[19] Those years brought a premium for labour, with concomitant high wages that attracted American workers. A labour depression, beginning in 1842, precipitated what one historian termed a 'hiatus' in the record of the city's working classes.[20] Faced with the twin evils of economic malaise and increasing numbers of Irish immigrants, who represented a willing – if not desperate – workforce that would accept marginal wages, Saint John's established and politically powerful artisanal and merchant elements felt themselves under assault in the 1840s. For example, the rate for sawyers dropped by one-half between 1841 and 1849.[21] An improving economic climate by 1849, however, watered the soil for more fruitful labour activity. Three unions organized in the space of seven weeks during that year: the Longshoremen's Labourers' Society, the Saint John Ship Carpenters' Society, and the Saint John City and County Sawyers' Society.[22] Importantly, the emerging working classes characterized themselves according to occupation, ethnicity, religion, and provincial longevity. Faced with aggressive competition for limited jobs, whether it came in the form of feisty Yankees or desperate Irish-Catholics, Saint John's protean working classes and organized labouring groups closed ranks with the governing and social élite to ward off aliens.

Steadily mounting Irish-Catholic immigration rapidly relegated American competition to a bitter memory. While Saint John and Portland each absorbed thousands of immigrants prior to the 1840s, primarily Scots, English, and Protestant-Irish, the waves of increasingly destitute Irish-Catholics placed a tremendous strain on the communities' resources. The sickest emigrants faced quarantine on Partridge Island in the harbour; the poorest filtered ashore and depended on public relief. By the spring of 1847, the city gained legal permission to prevent ships carrying Irish-Catholics to discharge their passengers when the captains failed to post bonds ensuring that their charges would not become a burden.[23] While this tactic rapidly foundered owing to the unrelenting Irish diaspora, it illustrated Saint John's and Portland's attempt to cope with the problem of absorbing thousands of sick and impoverished famine victims.

Ultimately the inundation of immigrants profoundly altered the ethno-religious compositions of both Saint John and Portland. The Irish-Catholics entered communities whose history had been shaped by Loyalists and Protestant immigrants from England,

Scotland, and Ireland. By 1851 the city had the largest Irish-born community in the province; Acheson determined that the Irish-born accounted for fully three-fifths of the head of households of four central wards in Saint John's 1851 census. By the mid-1840s Roman Catholics equalled and probably surpassed all the Protestant denominations.[24] St Malachy's Chapel, constructed from 1815 16, became a beacon for the city's Roman Catholic faithful.[25] When the 1861 census appeared, the first to include religious data, both localities had populations almost 40 per cent Catholic. Since Acadians, who were New Brunswick's only other substantial Catholic population, were practically non-existent in the Saint John region during mid-century, the Irish accounted almost entirely for the increase.[26]

The Irish-Catholics settled primarily in two sections of Saint John and Portland. They clustered in overcrowded squalor in York Point, a district of north-western Saint John bounded roughly by Union Street to the south, George's Street to the east, Portland Parish to the north, and the bay to the west.[27] In Portland they huddled in the busy wharf area on the harbour's northern shore. The two districts, connected by the 'Portland Bridge,' grew into twin ethno-religious ghettos during the 1840s.[28]

These districts were so strongly identified with Irish-Catholics that they hosted virtually all the major episodes of social violence between Orangemen and Irishmen. Indeed, to alarmed Protestants and natives, York Point and Portland became synonymous with poverty, disease, crime, and Roman Catholicism.[29] Elites typically drew distinctions between the worthy and unworthy poor, a centuries-old British custom, and between the few virtuous Roman Catholics and the 'disorderly' and 'infernal' masses.[30] Class boundaries, as well as ethnic and religious lines, etched deep moats around the Irish-Catholic enclaves in Saint John and Portland.

A measure of truth underscored this fusion, for crime rates rose precipitously in the ghettos during the 1840s. But sociological factors, rather than cultural idiosyncrasies, explain most of these increases. Overcrowding, poverty, hunger, and unemployment created a virtual army of vagrants who wandered the city's thoroughfares. Authorities recorded dozens of assaults and robberies in York Point and Portland's wharf district, typically attributing them to roving gangs of young men.[31] Though much of the violence occurred during holidays and significant events, such as elections, New Year's, and Guy Fawkes Day, it gradually became more directed and purposeful. Frustrated vagrants targeted élites and authorities; the 1840s witnessed assaults on newspaper editor Henry Chubb, several city alderman, ship captains, businessmen, constables, and even British soldiers.[32] These incidents clearly illustrated the deepening rift between classes in Saint John and Portland; indeed they mirrored those of New Brunswick's capital.

Major disturbances also broke out in the town of Fredericton, situated on the Saint John River approximately eighty miles north of Saint John. Fredericton served as the provincial capital, and during much of the nineteenth century British regulars remained garrisoned in the city. These two aspects – government and military – combined to shape Fredericton's history before Confederation.

St Anne's Point on the Saint John River, originally populated by Acadians and pre-Loyalist English, provided Fredericton's setting. When the Loyalists arrived after 1783 they displaced the Acadians, most of whom fled to the north shore or to the Madawaska area. Because of its central location, officials designated Fredericton as the seat of New Brunswick's government in 1785. An energetic citizenry carved a respectable capital out of the wilderness in the span of several years; by the 1840s government and educational edifices dominated the town's skyline: the Legislative Hall, the lieutenant-governor's residence, county courthouse, a jail constructed in 1843, and King's College, the oldest institution of higher learning in Canada.[33]

Shortly after the Loyalists arrived the military took root in Fredericton and continued to be an important influence until Britain withdrew its troops after 1867 from the newly formed Dominion. The military establishment dominated large sections of the town, especially along the shore frontage to the Saint John River. British detachments, periodically rotated, staffed an expansive network of barracks, arsenals, and training grounds.[34] Stationed in the capital during the period from the mid-1840s through 1848 was the Duke of Wellington's 33rd Regiment, under the command of Colonel Waunell.[35]

Fredericton also functioned as an important service hub for New Brunswick's interior during the early nineteenth century. The community housed several saw mills, tanneries, foundries, and grist mills. While these industries provided some employment, they lagged far behind Saint John in their relative significance for urban development.[36] Linkages to Saint John steadily improved; by 1816 a steamship regularly plied the waters of the Saint John River between the two cities.[37] While Fredericton lived in the shadow of the coastal behemoth, its proportionately larger number of government workers, professionals, and soldiers reflected its fundamental missions.[38]

Yet not unlike Saint John, the community danced to the tunes of a tightly interconnected governing coterie. Before incorporation, the various magistrates of the Court of Common Pleas administered justice to the Parish of Fredericton. The county sheriff shouldered the responsibility of chief law enforcer, as in Woodstock. Appointed constables served without pay for limited periods, largely as a civic duty. After incorporation, the elected mayor and appointed council assumed the burden for law and order; the mayor also functioned as chief magistrate. From 1848 until 1871, the mayor and his councillors administered justice directly.[39] The magistrates appointed to the York County General Sessions, as well as the mayors elected after the city's incorporation in 1848, overwhelmingly represented the upper ranks of Loyalists, merchants, artisans, and proprietary farmers. Moreover, virtually all of them belonged to a handful of Protestant denominations.[40]

The above factors partially explained Fredericton's relatively modest growth rate during the first half of the nineteenth century. Its population of 4458 in 1851 did reflect an over 200 per cent increase from 1824, but even that growth lagged behind the provincial average. Immigration accounted for most of the gain, especially after 1830. First Irish-Protestants and then Irish-

Catholics dominated the settlement rolls. By 1851, almost one-quarter of the community claimed Irish roots. Even more significantly, the Irish made up almost 80 per cent of all immigrants. The combination of natural increase and settlement provided the town with enough citizens to warrant incorporation in 1848.[41] By mid-century, Fredericton chaffed under the stresses caused by rapid transformation and redefinition; ideologically grounded as a Loyalist city, it contended with a growing and highly visible immigrant population.

Most fundamentally, Irish immigration affected the balance of religious denominations in New Brunswick's capital. A variety of Protestant churches, representing ubiquitous provincial denominations such as Episcopalian, Presbyterian, Methodist, and Baptist, served most of Fredericton's citizens until the early nineteenth century.[42] Immigration clearly disrupted the Protestant symmetry; while religious affiliation figures did not appear until the 1861 census, evidence points to a substantial growth of Roman Catholicism during the 1830s and 1840s. A small Catholic chapel built in 1824 served the entire region for almost two decades. Enough Catholics had settled by 1842 to warrant the establishment of a see, detached from the Charlottetown, Prince Edward Island, diocese, under the direction of Reverend William Dollard.[43] Construction soon began on a cathedral.[44] The Catholic Church's decision to locate New Brunswick's first see in Fredericton underscored the city's demographic transformation, as well as its role as provincial capital. Given the statistically insignificant Acadian population in the region, Irish immigrants accounted for the growth of Catholicism. During the 1840s the former Loyalist bastion, almost in a schizophrenic seizure, became New Brunswick's symbolic seat of Roman Catholicism. Census figures lent credence to the dramatic demographic transformation; Catholics far outnumbered Anglicans and constituted one-third of Fredericton's population in 1861. Virtually all of them claimed Irish roots.[45]

Thus, the 1840s brought the winds of ethnic and cultural change to New Brunswick's capital and garrison town. Tensions flared as the two groups, established and newcomers, clashed under the sullen cloud of economic malaise. The same cloud, shadowing similar socio-economic anxieties, spread far upriver to the hinterland community of Woodstock. For Fredericton and Saint John were not the only New Brunswick communities to experience riots between Orangemen and Irish-Catholics in 1847.

Woodstock, an agricultural and lumbering centre deep in New Brunswick's interior, provided one of the clearest examples of the rise of institutionalized nativism and attendant social violence. Approximately sixty miles from Fredericton and close to the United States border, Woodstock huddled against the banks of the Saint John River in the province's north-western frontier. Settled primarily by disbanded Loyalist soldiers after 1783, Carleton County's shiretown achieved strategic importance during the early nineteenth century owing to Anglo-American tensions.[46] The British stationed a small detachment of troops in Woodstock to protect the border, and they remained into the 1840s even after the signing of the Webster-Ashburton Treaty. With its Loyalist and garrison background, and an Acadian population some distance away in the Madawaska region and along the north shore, Woodstock enjoyed relative homogeneity before the 1830s.[47]

Yet an uneasy alliance between two vastly different styles of life intensified the town's frontier nature. While the earliest settlers demarcated and cleared farms in the rich soil of the Saint John River Valley, many of those who followed preferred lumbering in the hinterlands. Ultimately Woodstock adapted to accommodate both impulses. By the 1840s it catered equally to the needs of its permanent agrarian population and a seasonal lumbering community. Nevertheless farming remained Woodstock's focus in mid-century; three-quarters of the male population in 1851 counted themselves among the agricultural occupations.[48]

Woodstock, a generic appellation, in fact comprised three distinct communities. Starting from the south, the oldest settlement nestled at the junction of the river and the road to the American border town of Houlton. 'The Corner,' as locals referred to it, consisted of a cluster of houses and stores during the

1840s. About four miles upriver, where the Meduxnekeag River flowed into the Saint John, the traveller confronted 'The Creek.' The most recently settled community of the three, it also boasted the largest population and most commercial services. Two miles farther north lay Upper Woodstock, originally dubbed 'Hard-scrabble,' Carleton County's administrative centre. During the period of social tensions in the 1840s, two of the communities engaged in a bitter rivalry over which should be recognized as the true Woodstock. 'The Creek,' with its greater population, claimed that it should be the county's administrative headquarters; conversely, Upper Woodstock jealously guarded its court-house and jail in an effort to retain primacy.[49] This community rivalry symbolized the disparate nature of Woodstock Parish during the mid-nineteenth century.[50]

After its initial settlement by Loyalists, Woodstock attracted growing numbers of farmers and itinerant lumbermen. During the early decades of the nineteenth century, Protestant immigrants from the British Isles provided the bulk of these new-comers. But in the 1830s, reflecting provincial immigration patterns, Woodstock absorbed large numbers of Irish-Catholics. Its population grew by 25 per cent in the decade before mid-century; by 1851, 10 per cent of Carleton County claimed Irish birth. Many of these Irish, both Protestants and Catholics, immigrated in the 1830s; dramatic numbers also arrived in the wake of the potato famine of the late 1840s.[51] Thus, in a relatively short period evocative of Fredericton's experience, the Loyalist and Protestant bastion of Woodstock grudgingly coped with a dramatically different cultural and religious group.

These adjustments threw Carleton County's denominational balance into disarray. As in Fredericton Protestant denominations, including Anglican, Dissenter, Baptist, and Methodist, flourished among the population of Loyalists, English, and ex–New Englanders. While religious alignments helped to explain social divisions – for example, socially superior Loyalists favoured the Anglican church – a pervasive Protestant ideology provided multiple points of commonality between the denominations.[52] Similarities far outweighed distinctive ritual and dogma.

On the other hand, increasing numbers of Irish-Catholic immigrants introduced the Roman Catholic church as a powerful
cultural force. St Malachy's Church, established in 1836, received
its first permanent priest, Father James Veriker, six years later. By
mid-century St Gertrude's had joined St Malachy's in Woodstock,
under the pastorate of Father Thomas Connolly.[53]

Carleton County's changing ethnic composition exacerbated the
already turbulent social and economic conditions. Violent incidents involving hard-drinking itinerant lumbermen brought
supplemental troops from Fredericton in the late 1830s. Although
the militia quickly restored peace, the disturbances created a
legacy of animosity and suspicion between Woodstock's farmers
and timbermen. The possibility of border problems with the
United States, although minimal after the 1842 treaty, continued
to underscore Woodstock's role as a tenuous frontier post.[54]
Finally, uncertainty in the lumber trade during the 1840s cast an
economic pall over the region. Thus Woodstock and its environs
faced significant problems in mid-century. Magnified impressions
of harassing 'desperadoes' and the ever-present fear of renewed
outbreaks of violence filled the imaginations of many of its
citizens.[55]

Woodstock mirrored Fredericton and Saint John in its reliance
on magistrates, sheriffs, and constables for maintaining law and
order. The oldest and most established families, meaning predominantly those of Loyalist stock, served as the wellspring for
the community's justices of the peace. Throughout the two decades before mid-century a protracted struggle transpired between
the magistrates and members of the grand jury, a group that
presided over the quarter sessions. Grand-jury members needed
to fulfil the following requirements: a minimal county residency
of three months; a freehold of at least £10; and personal property
in excess of £100. Tensions between the two groups diminished
after 1851 as the community rapidly embraced more egalitarian
principles of self-government, meaning in this case elected local
officials. By 1856, Woodstock joined Fredericton and Saint John
as an incorporated town.[56] However, for the years leading up to
and including the riot, Woodstock's governing élite consisted

almost exclusively of men from established, typically Loyalist families, such as the Beardsleys, Ketchums, Dibblees, and
Connells.[57]

But the turmoil of the 1840s led many residents to question the
effectiveness of their duly appointed protectors. As the Irish-
Catholic population increased and became identified with the
turbulent lumbering community, Protestants began to seek alternative measures to ensure peace. To many, vigilantism emerged
as the most efficacious solution.[58] Although no conclusive evidence suggested that a single ethnic group predominated among
lumbermen, many Protestants believed that Irish-Catholic immigrants precipitated most of the county's violence. The milieu of
ethnic and cultural transformation set the foundation for social
violence that emerged fully constructed in the late 1840s.

Thus the three communities, while experiencing distinctive and
sometimes antithetical ideologies, political agendas, ethnic compositions, and rates of growth, all faced complex and poorly
understood transitions in the 1840s. Woodstock, long accustomed
to fundamental tensions between agricultural and lumbering
concerns, struggled to establish control over a hinterland while
its disparate villages grappled for administrative control. Fredericton, incorporated during the decade, also gained ascendancy
over a vast hinterland while reinforcing its role as provincial
capital and garrison town. Thanks to its location at the mouth of
the province's pre-eminent waterway, Saint John intermittently
experienced dramatic growth and sharp downturns created by
the fickle forces of the international timber trade.

While on some levels the hinterland community, capital, and
principal port seemed to exhibit few points in common, powerful
dynamics that they shared ultimately shaped and helped to
explain the tumultuous 1840s. All three flowered from deep
Loyalist roots; each experienced, with different manifestations, a
shock of economic confidence before mid-century; and perhaps
most importantly each, albeit in different proportions, grappled
with a rapidly changing admixture of peoples. Roman Catholic
settlers and transients from Ireland, steadily arriving during the
early decades of the century, flooded into the province as the

potato blight devastated the Emerald Isle's essential crop. The ubiquitous perception of the arrival of vast numbers of destitute Irish-Catholics triggered the riots of the 1840s. The Orangemen who arose to counter the 'invasion' and the Irish-Catholics engaged, for a time, in an almost ritualized and sometimes deadly dance of anger. Intricately woven into the fabric of these three communities in transition, they would take to the streets to defend their rights. They ultimately determined the political, social, and religious hegemony of each community.

# PART TWO: THE PROTAGONISTS

# 3

# The Irish-Catholics:
# Immigration and response

Ethnic homogeneity characterized New Brunswick in the late eighteenth and early nineteenth centuries. Loyalists and pre-Revolutionary War New Englanders made up most of the original population. Acadians hovered on the fringes of the colony, particularly along the northern and eastern shores. Immigrants arriving after 1785 came from the British Isles, other North American colonies, and the United States. But the nineteenth century would dramatically redesign New Brunswick's demographic face. The Protestant, Loyalist foundation would be shaken by the influx of a people with different racial, cultural, and religious backgrounds. Specifically, New Brunswickers would have to come to grips with the Irish-Catholics.[1]

After the first flurry of settlement by Loyalists, both the British and New Brunswick governments articulated plans to encourage immigration. The reasons were twofold: a healthy settlement pattern would help to establish New Brunswick as a viable province so that it could compete for colonial funds with the more established provinces of Nova Scotia and the Canadas. Second, the Home Office encouraged settlement as an insulation against a rapidly expanding United States. A series of military posts along the American border would provide a first line of defence against possible encroachment, and with the hinterland thoroughly settled by farmers, the reinforced frontier would be a stronger warning to Americans that New Brunswick indeed lay well within the British fold. Legislative measures gave substance to the impulse. A series of passenger acts after 1803, for example, regulated the numbers of persons allowed on transatlantic voyages according to ship tonnage. Ostensibly designed to curb abuses of shippers, the passenger acts favoured a high passenger-tonnage ratio, thereby lowering fares and facilitating increased immigration to British North America.[2]

The colony also used several tactics to encourage immigration. By 1819 the government installed a program to assist prospective settlers in finding land or employment. Within six years private and public agencies, such as the Fredericton Emigrant Aid Society and the New Brunswick Agricultural and Emigrant Society, actively sought suitable clients. Ethnic organizations proliferated in order to give emotional, financial, and cultural support to British immigrants. By the 1820s Saint John had branches of the St George's Society for English immigrants, St Andrew's for the Scots, and St Patrick's for the Irish.[3] The St Patrick's Society, appealing primarily to Protestants, championed militant Irish rights while it remained relatively aloof from partisan provincial politics.[4] Industrious colonists churned out emigrant aid manuals, each promising a taste of the good life to workers with strong hands and stout hearts.[5] New Brunswick's modest head tax also facilitated immigration. Created in the early 1830s and administered by agents in Saint John, St Andrews, the Miramichi, and Fredericton, the fees represented approximately one-half the price exacted at American ports.[6] Moreover, in 1840 respondents to a provincial survey indicated that emigration should be further encouraged to buttress dwindling pools of agricultural labourers and servants.[7] By the early nineteenth century New Brunswick had in place both official and unofficial policies designed to encourage British immigration.

The end of the Napoleonic Wars brought the first significant non-Loyalist immigration to New Brunswick, as it did to virtually all of British North America.[8] An estimated seven thousand British citizens landed in Saint John before 1820, including both Protestant- and Catholic-Irish. While previous studies assumed that virtually all Irish-Catholics arrived during the 1840s, Peter

Toner's creative, ongoing research has exposed the bankruptcy of this image. Nineteenth-century Ontario documents led Donald Akenson to basically the same conclusion. Irish-Catholics constituted a substantial immigrant group in pre-famine British North America.[9] After careful assessment of census records and other sources, Toner tentatively concluded not only that a number of Irish predated the Loyalists, but also that migration patterns to New Brunswick solidified during the early decades of the nineteenth century. Toner estimated that Catholics and Protestants emigrated in equal numbers from 1815 to 1824, and that throughout the remainder of the 1820s the Catholics probably outstripped their counterparts.[10] This view stands in glaring contrast to Kerby Miller's prodigious work, taken largely from American sources, in which he concluded that Irish-Catholics remained more firmly rooted to Ireland until the famine years of the 1840s. Miller's general characterization of the different class of immigrants remains useful for this study, however, because it parallels closely the New Brunswick experience. Irish-Protestants as a rule voluntarily migrated in search of opportunity; Irish-Catholics, especially during the 1840s, represented a more despondent class of evicted farmers and involuntary migrants.[11]

This trend continued for a few years until increases in fares and a general decline in shipping made the voyage prohibitive to prospective settlers. Because many immigrants found cheap transport in the empty holds of timber ships returning to North America, immigration patterns followed the fortunes of the staples economy in the first half of the nineteenth century.[12] For example, fares from Londonderry to Saint John in 1818 were 3½ guineas, or only one-third the fare to an American port.[13] By the late 1820s, riding the tide of a revitalized timber trade, immigration once again increased. From the first year of reliable immigration records in 1832 until the early 1840s, New Brunswick experienced fairly uniform immigration patterns. The numbers of immigrants dipped and peaked as trade fluctuated but stayed remarkably within the same range for over a decade. For example, aggregate immigration figures for 1832 and 1841 differed by only 12.[14]

Immigrants for these years originated from a relatively expansive list of European and North American ports. An 1842 report on immigrant relief offered an excellent illustration of the variety of embarkations. Vessels arriving in Saint John in that year, transporting a total of 7581 individuals, originated from a total of seventeen ports in Ireland, England, Scotland, Nova Scotia, and the United States. Cork sent nineteen ships, Sligo six and Londonderry eight. Eight ships arrived from Liverpool, an English port favoured by Irish immigrants. Compared to the ships that arrived in the famine year of 1847, 1842's tally attested to a heterogeneous immigrant pool; still, Irish ports accounted for over 70 per cent of the ships that arrived in New Brunswick.[15]

The fairly uniform immigration rate belied a profound shift in ethnic settlement patterns. The post–Napoleonic War period witnessed a substantial increase in the number of Irish immigrants to New Brunswick and other North American colonies. By the 1830s they clearly composed the bulk of settlers, a trend that would continue to mid-century; moreover, a New Brunswick official in 1831 estimated that Irish-Catholics made up one-quarter of the total immigrant population.[16] Only in 1853, after the famine immigration and New Brunswick's ethnic riots, would English immigrants once again outnumber their Irish counterparts.[17] Available evidence suggests that a modest majority of the Irish coming before the 1840s traced their roots to the Protestant northern counties.[18] Most claimed Scots or English ancestry, reflecting the British colonization of Ireland. Artisans and tenant farmers with limited savings, they sought a better life within the British colonial system. Most important, they shared cultural and ideological views with native-born New Brunswickers and other British immigrants they encountered. Because they adhered to Protestantism and supported the English constitutional and political domination of Ireland, they made a relatively smooth transition to their new lives in New Brunswick.[19]

Beginning in the 1830s, however, immigrant patterns within Ireland shifted and thereby profoundly altered the demographic face of New Brunswick. The more skilled, financially solvent Protestant-Irish from northern counties began to be replaced by more destitute Catholics from Ireland's poorer southern and western regions. The transformation occurred gradually; from 1838 to 1844 most of the Irish were not destitute, they merely took advantage of well-established immigration channels.[20] Over time a drop in shipping fares, coupled with a poor economic climate and a series of meagre harvests, convinced the poorer Catholics to abandon their homeland.[21] The percentage of Irish-Catholics who immigrated before 1840 escalated, so much so that probably by 1851 equivalent numbers of Irish-Catholics and Irish-Protestants resided in the province.[22] The once placid stream flooded as a tragic potato famine decimated Ireland's staple crop from 1845 to 1848. Facing starvation on small, overpopulated plots of land, thousands of peasants emigrated in the late 1840s, many of them from predominantly Catholic southern counties such as Cork.[23] But rather than resembling the calm, well-ordered migration of earlier decades, the famine exodus might best be characterized as a desperate evacuation. Moreover, the potato blight hit the western and southern Catholic counties with particular severity. The thousands of impoverished famine escapees who flooded ashore in British North America and the United States in 1845 were the vanguard of the first significant non-Anglo-Saxon immigration to the continent.[24]

Famine immigrants differed substantially from those who came before. Besides being almost entirely Celtic and Catholic, many suffered from contagious diseases. Most had little or no capital to start life anew in North America.[25] Thousands sacrificed all their worldly goods for the transatlantic fare; others made the voyage because their landlords paid the passage. The latter should not be interpreted as a noble gesture. An 1847 British proclamation that famine victims would be handled under the Poor Law, maintained by rates imposed on local property holders, prompted nervous landlords to rid themselves of a potential burden. Many landlords deemed paying fares to North America as a cheaper proposition than the poor rates, and peasants preferred emigration to eviction. Thousands of Irish-Catholics made their way to British North America and the United States in the late 1840s. And not surprisingly, financially strapped immigrants and landlords purchased the cheapest fares possible across the Atlantic. Thus New Brunswick's ports, being closer to Ireland than American cities or either Montreal or Quebec City, rapidly became a favoured destination for famine victims.[26] Most were desperately poor and diseased, and they received little assistance when they landed.

New Brunswick's demographic patterns changed dramatically in the 1840s to reflect shifting Irish immigration due to the famine. The first significant change in New Brunswick occurred in 1842 when the moderate immigration rate that began in the 1830s peaked at 7800. Yet the aggregate figure did not provide the key; the colony had absorbed nearly that many in 1834, 1837, and 1840. Eighteen forty-two was noteworthy because it signalled the directional shift in immigration, a trend immediately detected by native workers. One Saint John official complained that the arrival of penurious Irish placed a stress on the 'labouring population,' who found themselves 'already steeped in the deepest poverty and ... suffering extreme privation.'[27] Enough poor, indigent, and sick people arrived in 1842 to prompt Lieutenant-Governor Sir William Colebrooke to petition the Home Office to curtail Irish emigration. The next year's low figure of 873 proved that British officials found his argument compelling.[28]

But the temporary floodgates collapsed as the decade progressed, unable to withstand Ireland's socio-economic pressures. New Brunswick's immigration rate increased yearly by at least 150 per cent; the fifteen thousand who arrived during the peak year of 1847 indicated a seventeen-fold gain over 1843's figure. Immigration rates decreased dramatically after 1848, and by 1855, numbers would once again be on a par with 1843. Improvements in potato crops after 1848 accounted for the decline, though Ireland would be plagued with similar famines throughout the nineteenth century. Shipping rates to North America also increased in the 1850s, causing a decrease in landlord-sponsored emigration and a shift back to individuals who had enough capital to purchase their own tickets. Finally, regulations passed in British North America and the United States during the 1850s discriminated against poor and sickly immigrants as well as those without marketable skills.[29] In retrospect, New Brunswick's immigration figures rose dramatically and fell abruptly from 1843 to 1850 (see appendix B).

Immigration peaked from 1845 to 1847. Protestant emigrants from England, Scotland, and northern Ireland virtually disappeared, displaced by Catholics from Ireland's southern and western counties. In short, a decidedly Gaelic population disembarked the fever ships.[30] A brief analysis of emigration returns from 1846 succinctly illustrates this redirection. Irish accounted for over 99 per cent of the 9765 immigrants to New Brunswick that year. Of the adult males, 65 per cent listed 'agricultural labourer' as their original occupation; the remainder identified themselves as mechanics, servants, and tradesmen. These figures clearly reflected the trend towards agrarian immigrants from Ireland's Catholic south and west. Finally, 87 per cent landed at Saint John, underscoring the port's pre-eminent role as New Brunswick's immigration funnel during the nineteenth century.[31]

Eighteen forty-seven, the colony's banner year for accepting immigrants, echoed this pattern. Waves of despondent Irish-Catholics eclipsed the previous year's returns as they found their way to New Brunswick's shores. In 1846 for the first time starving Irish broke from the traditional spring and summer crossings and chanced autumn voyages. Coupled with the unprecedented numbers arriving during the summer months, these added crossings accounted for the dramatic increase. New Brunswick shared the immigrant burden with many other destinations; over one hundred thousand started out for British North America during the cruel winter and summer of 1847, while even more targeted the ports of the United States, Australia, and England. Thousands died in passage; many had embarked in Ireland with fever already upon them.[32] A chilling, but most assuredly not atypical example of the crossing emerged in the records of the ill-fated *Looshtank*, a passenger ship out of Liverpool bound for Quebec City. Two men probably contracted fever before boarding; eight days out scarlet fever ran among the children, killing many. Typhus spread. Seventeen days into the voyage, only the master and mate exhibited no symptoms of the various diseases that ran amok on the ship. By the time the vessel made landfall at the Miramichi, eleven of the twenty-four crew members had succumbed. In all, of the 462 who embarked at Liverpool, 146 died on board; an additional 96 died at the Miramichi's quarantine station at Middle Island.[33]

Others arrived safely only to succumb to diseases such as typhus, cholera, and smallpox in quarantine stations and hospitals.[34] Of those departing with New Brunswick as their intended destination, 823 died in passage and another 1292 in Saint John's quarantine station at Partridge Island and in city hospitals. Overall, 12 per cent did not survive the trip, leaving approximately fifteen thousand indigent famine victims in Saint John and other New Brunswick ports.[35] During the month of July alone, for example, twenty-eight ships arrived carrying over four thousand passengers, a rate of almost one a day. Of those, 186 died in passage or while quarantined at anchor in the harbour; another 112 died on Partridge Island before they could find transportation to the city. Thus an average of almost four a day perished on Partridge Island.[36]

Saint John, as did other British North American immigration ports, elected to quarantine and process immigrants on land physically removed from the city.[37] Not surprisingly, native Saint Johners considered them a health risk; most would no doubt have agreed with the observer who noted that the invasion shocked him like a 'thunderbolt.'[38] Set on a tiny parcel two miles into Saint John harbour, Partridge Island acted as a primitive buffer between passengers with communicable diseases and city residents. Administered by the Common Council, the quarantine unit consisted of two fever sheds with a capacity of approximately one hundred when the famine migration struck. A rudimentary hospital, under construction in 1847, remained unfinished because city labourers understandably refused to risk contracting disease by working on the island. The accommodations proved instantly and hopelessly inadequate; exhausted migrants slept on the floors, surrounded by their possessions.[39] During the crisis island tenants hastily constructed two additional sheds to accommodate the torrent of wretched human cargo.[40] The sick and dying crowded the Saint John Almshouse and Hospital, located one mile from the city in Simonds Parish; they filled the wards and gangways, prompting observers to dub the place a 'factory of disease.'[41]

Those who reached the mainland found precious few support facilities in the cities. Most possessed little or no money when they arrived, and those without friends or family connections fended for themselves in an alien culture. Saint John responded to the crisis by building an Emigrant Orphan Asylum in 1847; Fredericton opened an Emigrant Hospital in July of the same year. In the latter, doctors treated 130 immigrant patients within the first two months of operation. Twenty-one of those died within one day of admittance, most of them children.[42] Fredericton's city officials planned throughout 1847 to construct another building to accommodate the sick and indigent immigrants.[43] Despite these attempts, cities sought provincial aid as they realized their own woeful inadequacy in coping with the human onslaught.

During the summer of 1847, the height of immigration, Saint John's officials routinely instructed ships to quarantine their cargoes of sick humans for forty days. Casting blame upon the 'heartless system pursued by some of the Irish landlords,' and arguing that 'ninety-nine of every one hundred must be supported by the charity of this community,' the Common Council begged Lieutenant-Governor Colebrooke for financial support.[44] From 20 February to 30 September 1847, the city spent £2707 on immigrants, including £371 to operate Partridge Island.[45] A virtual barrage of appeals inundated Colebrooke's office, especially from Saint John and the Miramichi, the province's two largest reception stations.[46] Colebrooke basically ignored the petitions, thereby forcing the Common Council to resort in desperation to the tactic of offering free passage and water to those paupers who agreed to a return voyage.[47]

Attempting to cope with Partridge Island's overflow, city officials authorized the erection of temporary sheds on the grounds of a former artillery battery at the east end of St James Street.[48] The poorest flocked to these shelters and found that they offered only minimal protection against the rigorous climate. The more fortunate found themselves admitted to the Saint John Emigrant Hospital.[49] Moreover, the alien urban environment almost certainly baffled the immigrants, most of whom were agrarian peasants. A brief sojourn in Dublin or Liverpool at their journey's outset gave most of them their first taste of port life.[50] Collectively, Irish immigrants faced a most unpleasant reception in New Brunswick, a distraught and reluctant host. Having faced starvation, disease, and a rough passage, most now had to cope with poverty, minimal shelter, and alienation from a native population.

Though many immigrants found themselves in Saint John in the late 1840s, many had no intention of settling in New Brunswick. Participants in an established pattern, they represented a combination of those who had never intended the province as a port of entry to North America, as well as those who took advantage of the cheaper fares and ultimately planned to settle in the United States or the interior of British North America. The unusual autumn passages led to the former situation. For example, a frozen St Lawrence River in November forced a ship's captain to alter course from Quebec and unload 240 sickly passengers in Saint John instead. Saint John became, at least for the height of the famine immigration, a winter port for those heading towards Quebec City, Montreal, and Toronto. In addition, many Irish booked on an American passage found themselves unceremoniously jettisoned in Saint John as a result of the stiffer enforcement of landing codes. Nervous captains stopped in Saint John and forced their sickest and most destitute passengers to disembark for fear of their healthier charges being rejected in American ports.[51]

Many more Irish fell into the category of those who used Saint John as a temporary port. Attracted by the freedom from British institutions in the United States, or by the vast hinterland of the Canadas, the Irish took advantage of the cheaper fares to New Brunswick in order to gain a foothold on the continent. Work on the docks as a day labourer or stevedore would usually provide enough funds for a coastal passage to America in a short time. Thus Saint John became a way station for Irish 'birds of passage' during the 1840s; it maintained an appeal as a convenient and cheaper alternative for those who could not afford the fare to the United States or to the Canadas. During 1846, Saint John's emigration agent estimated that at least half of those arriving during the year had already moved on to the United States before the new year.[52] By the early 1850s, the same agent complained that so many had departed for destinations as far away as Australia that he feared a shortage of provincial labourers.[53]

Although many Irish used New Brunswick as a temporary station, approximately half of those arriving settled in the ports or interior of the colony. They did not clearly favour either an urban or rural environment.[54] During the 1840s, Irish-Catholic immigrants flocked to ghettos in the Saint John region: one at the north-eastern section of the city called York Point and another in the wharf district of Portland. While these two areas already contained some natives and more established Irish-Protestant immigrants, they became bastions of Irish-Catholicism in the Saint John region.[55] Outside the city, Irish-Catholics sought towns and larger agrarian communities. Indeed, city and provincial officials encouraged their outmigration from the ports, initially at least, as a sort of safety outlet for badly needed farm labourers and servants who would work for 'moderate wages' in the interior.[56] Their settlement patterns can be traced along the major river systems of the Saint John, the Miramichi, and later the St Croix. Large numbers of Irish immigrants migrated to the capital at Fredericton, where in 1851 45 per cent of the heads of households claimed Irish birth; moreover they settled in the agrarian community of Woodstock.[57] Along the Miramichi, they settled close to established communities on the tributaries and poorer land that had been passed over by original settlers. The Irish took jobs as wage labourers in lumber mills on the Miramichi; they set up tailor shops and clerked in urban Saint John and Fredericton. In rural Woodstock they pursued their old professions of farming and agrarian labour.[58] While Irish-Catholics eventually migrated into every corner of the province, the majority settled in the cities, towns, and larger agricultural communities (see table 1).

The phenomena described above made the transformation of Irish-Catholics to North Americans an exasperating experience.

TABLE 1
New Brunswick population: 1851, 1861

| | | New Bruns- wick | Saint John City | Port- land Parish | Freder- icton Parish | Carle- ton County |
|---|---|---|---|---|---|---|
| Total | 1851 | 193,800 | 22,745 | 8,429 | 4,458 | 11,108 |
| population | 1861 | 252,047 | 27,317 | 11,500 | 5,652 | 16,373 |
| | % change | +30 | +20 | +36 | +27 | +47 |
| Irish | 1851 | 28,776 | 7,531 | 3,163 | 1,084 | 1,101 |
| population | 1861 | 30,179 | 6,901 | 3,042 | 1,064 | 1,669 |
| | % change | +4.9 | −8.4 | −3.8 | −1.8 | +51.6 |
| % of Irish | 1851 | 14.9 | 33.1 | 37.5 | 24.3 | 9.9 |
| compared | 1861 | 12.0 | 25.3 | 26.5 | 18.8 | 10.2 |
| to total | % change | −2.9 | −7.8 | −11.0 | −5.5 | +10.3 |
| population | | | | | | |
| % of Irish | 1851 | 71 | 79 | 87 | 78 | 71 |
| compared | 1861 | 57 | 66 | 77 | 64 | 58 |
| to total | % change | −14 | −13 | −10 | −14 | −13 |
| immigrant | | | | | | |
| population | | | | | | |

SOURCES: 1851, 1861 New Brunswick censuses

Thrusting agrarian Celtic-Catholics into urban, Anglo-Saxon, Protestant strongholds led to a massive culture shock. The American dean of immigration studies, Oscar Handlin, called it an 'uprooted' mentality.[59] Faced with the purgatorial transition between vastly different ethnic and cultural groups, the Irish-Catholics clustered together for support.[60] To ward off alienation and to create a bulwark against their foreign neighbours, they clung tenaciously to their religion. The Irish-Catholic had for centuries looked to religion for emotional and spiritual support: 'His religion is *the faith* to him, and his acts are primarily, first and foremost, acts of religious devotion.'[61] Difficulties encountered in a transatlantic migration eclipsed this fervour. The Irish-Catholics in North America sought the church not only for spiritual comfort but also for a tangible reminder that the linkages to their homeland had not been completely severed.[62] If anything, the famine experience only served to intensify feelings of a love for religion and cultural and kinship networks.[63] As Handlin observed, 'The more thorough the separation from the other aspects of the old life, the greater was the hold of the religion that alone survived the transfer.'[64] The Catholic church, a familiar signpost to Irish immigrants, magnified its role in North America because it served as both a religious and a cultural repository.[65]

The Irish-Catholic experience in New Brunswick, however, differed substantially from that of the Canadas and the United States. American and Quebec Irish flooded to occupied areas and often joined established churches with French or even German roots, thereby laying the foundation for disputes over leadership and language. During the nineteenth century in most areas outside of Quebec, Irish-Catholics secured control of dioceses because of their superior numbers. They also cultivated enemies within their own religion.[66] In some regions, such as Upper Canada, both Catholic- and Protestant-Irish failed to develop vibrant mythologies as part of their 'survival equipment,' primarily because they experienced more geographic or socio-economic integration. Moreover, while the two groups feuded frequently, they shared important beliefs.[67] Throughout the same period New Brunswick's Catholics did not experience such profound divisiveness, although one historian noted that Saint John's Irish population tended to be split over issues such as ultramontanism and the repeal of the union of Britain and Ireland.[68] Virtually no formal linkages associated Acadians with the predominantly British-Protestant population. They clustered on the colony's northern and eastern shores and in the Madawaska region of the north-western interior. Protestants enjoyed pre-eminence in virtually all the central and southern counties and the urban areas.

When Irish-Catholics trickled into New Brunswick in the late eighteenth and early nineteenth centuries and settled in Protestant areas, they formed small chapels from scratch. When the trickle became a flood in the 1840s, the trend continued. Settling in regions practically devoid of Acadians, the Irish experienced no significant division within their churches. This relative lack of internal conflict would contribute to the rapid growth of institutionalized Catholicism in the province. In 1825, only a handful of Catholic chapels existed in the entire colony under the direction of six clergymen. Acadians accounted for most of these. But twenty years later, owing to Irish immigration, New Brunswick's Catholic population increased to the point that it warranted the establishment of a diocese at Fredericton. Reverend Dr William Dollard assumed control as the diocese's first bishop in 1845. Two years later Catholics boasted of over sixty churches and twenty-four priests. Workers set the foundation for a cathedral in 1853 at Saint John that fervent supporters hoped would soon become the capital of 'catholicity' in the province. The 1861 census registered the exponential growth: major cities and towns such as Saint John, Portland, Fredericton, and Woodstock all contained at least one significant Catholic church.[69] Irish-Catholic immigrants profoundly altered the religious landscape of New Brunswick. Unlike their Acadian co-religionists, they settled in the midst of Protestant strongholds. By mid-century, Catholicism bloomed in a Protestant garden.

The proliferation of Catholic institutions in New Brunswick mirrored the swelling tide of adherents. Acadians and their descendants provided the foundation of Catholicism; when the Irish became the largest immigrant group in the 1840s, the religion easily outstripped all Protestant denominations. By 1847, the height of famine immigration, Catholics accounted for nearly one-third of all inhabitants. This proportion would remain relatively stable throughout the 1850s.[70] Census data clearly show how profoundly Irish-Catholics altered the provincial landscape. In 1851 they accounted for 15 per cent of the population, and 71 per cent of all immigrants. Their numbers burgeoned in the more populated central and southern counties. Portland and Saint John, with populations well over one-third Irish, reflected the highest percentage of them compared to other immigrant groups, 87 per cent and 82 per cent respectively. Counties along the Saint John River, such as York, Carleton, Kings, Queens, and Sunbury, also indicated proportionately higher numbers of Irish. Finally, Charlotte and Northumberland counties, both with major ports, attracted a large number of Irish. Only Restigouche County, with a predominantly Acadian population, did not list the Irish as the largest immigrant group.[71]

The census of a decade later proved the entrenchment of Irish-Catholics. Outmigration and anti-Irish immigrant restrictions in the 1850s accounted for a 2 per cent drop in total Irish numbers, yet they still represented well over half of all immigrants. Moreover, the distribution by county remained essentially the same. The most striking revelation of the 1861 census came from its religious returns, the first in New Brunswick's history. In several counties with no, or negligible, Acadian populations, Catholics appeared in abundance. Over 40 per cent of Saint John County's residents, including Portland and the city of Saint John, claimed to be Catholic. Saint John's Sydney and Kings wards, the latter including York Point, reflected 60 per cent Catholic populations. York County had 20 per cent, while the old Loyalist bastion of Carleton County now had a 13 per cent Catholic following.[72]

These figures clearly show the tremendous changes wrought by Irish-Catholic immigrants through the mid-nineteenth century. They settled in the heartland of Protestant New Brunswick rather than in the Catholic strongholds of the Acadians to the north and east. Irish-Catholics lived among native New Brunswickers and Protestant immigrants, often in enclaves, and established their church as a religious and cultural bulwark against alienation. New Brunswick's Protestants could not ignore the Irish as they had the Acadians; propinquity forced them to come to grips with both a foreign culture and a threatening religion.

Though Roman Catholicism had been a fact to be reckoned with since the province's inception in 1784, because of the Acadians, the Loyalists and New Englanders worked from the outset to create a Protestant domain.[73] While Roman Catholics inherited a host of civil rights from Nova Scotia, New Brunswick's parent colony, Protestants soon began to dismantle some of the more liberal ones. Catholics voted without restrictions in the 1785 elections to form the first provincial government, yet six years later the legislature instituted requirements for electors to take state oaths. Although this change did not outlaw Catholic voters, the oath's wording severely curtailed their numbers. Compared to a 1789 Nova Scotia statute giving an unrestricted franchise to Catholics, the law designed by New Brunswick's representatives indisputably limited non-Protestants' freedoms.[74]

The New Brunswick legislature eased the voting restrictions in 1810 by requiring a simpler, less discriminatory oath of allegiance for Catholics.[75] The colony did not grant full emancipation until 1830, the year following Britain's celebrated Catholic Emancipation Act. New Brunswick used the English bill as a format, as did other colonies in British North America, but it did not remove all discriminatory measures. An oath of allegiance clause remained for Catholics sitting in the House of Assembly, and priests continued to be barred from legislative posts.[76] Many provincial officials considered it obligatory to pass a law similar to England's, yet the Roman Catholic emancipation bill met with stiff resistance. The opposition, spearheaded by John Saunders, the chief of the Legislative Council, argued that the Protestant majority adequately represented the Catholics.[77] This argument, no doubt inadvertently, appeared to be a variant of the old imperial-colonial debate on virtual representation.

Despite the statute of 1830, Catholics made slow political headway. A predominantly Acadian county elected New Brunswick's first Catholic legislator in 1846. Five years later, an Irish-born Catholic received appointment to the Legislative Council; 1856 brought the same results to the Executive Council.[78] In effect, Roman Catholics found themselves almost totally excluded from the corridors of power until well after mid-century.[79] Along with their Protestant counterparts, the Irish-Catholics found themselves virtually barred from the county militia in the 1830s and 1840s.[80] Moreover, attempts to incorporate the Roman Catholic bishop in 1846 met with virulent opposition. Protestant legislators in Fredericton and even several Catholic laypeople in Saint John argued that incorporating the bishop would place too much fiscal power in the hands of clerics. Though the bill passed, the dispute helped to foster resentment against the growing number of Catholics and their religious institutions.[81] Clearly New Brunswick's legislature displayed a history of dogged and official opposition to Roman Catholics from the colony's inception through the mid-nineteenth century.

Changes in provincial immigration policies served to buttress the legislative response to Catholicism. Since the early nineteenth century, New Brunswick's governmental and private sectors encouraged immigration from the British Isles. Even as the raw numbers of settlers who arrived in the colony's ports increased substantially, officials concentrated on keeping any of them from migrating to the United States or the Canadas. As late as 1843, Lieutenant-Governor Colebrooke actively courted expatriates living in America to return to New Brunswick.[82] Yet as hard times settled in during the 1840s, and as poorer Irish-Catholics began to dominate the bills of lading on returning timber ships, provincial policy shifted.[83] Emigration officials escalated their demands for selectivity; they sprang into action to codify immigration restrictions. Irish-Catholicism invoked destitution and quickly became synonymous with overburdened provincial and city tax structures. Although humanitarian concerns for the suffering famine victims no doubt provided the motivation for many officials, an overwhelming sense of fear and disgust pervaded the arguments to block unwanted immigration. Saint John's mayor and Common Council, fearful of an epidemic and with their eyes on maintaining social control over what they perceived to be the desperate masses, asked for provincial funds to supplement the anemic city coffers in September 1847. A month later they proposed a scheme to offer the return passage to Dublin, including provisions and water, to any Irish in the city. Colebrooke rejected the plan, primarily because of cost projections; yet it clearly demonstrated that New Brunswick officials, both local and provincial, attempted to cope with the immigration problem by discouraging Irish-Catholic settlement.[84]

While Colebrooke baulked at this blatantly anti-Catholic scheme, he had earlier taken a resolute stance indicating that his objections were not philosophical in nature. Following the several Orange riots of July 1847, he implored the Home Office not to send any more Irish immigrants without first diluting their numbers with at least equivalent amounts from the British Isles.

Because Irish-Catholics constituted the vast majority of immigrants over the course of several years, Colebrooke's proposal thinly veiled a condemnation of their impact on New Brunswick. The Home Secretary's response proved to be equally discriminatory; Lord Howick recommended a stiffer vagrancy law because British officials 'frequently found that the Irish immigrants this year are too confirmed in habits of vagrancy to apply to labor.'[85] The policy shift brought dramatic results. By 1848, the number of immigrants decreased by over 12,000 from the 1847 total; compared to the famine migrants, most people enjoyed relatively good health. Deaths en route and in quarantine barely reached 1 per cent of the total.[86] Although three years later, when a total of 1507 arrived, officials continued to characterize the immigrants as the 'humblest class' of Irish, clearly the disembarking passengers appeared less destitute and represented a substantially reduced burden on local resources.[87] Communicable diseases, however, continued to plague emigrant ships; for example, captains and physicians reported dozens of cholera cases in a series of 1854 voyages.[88] None the less, New Brunswick's problems with immigrants substantively declined after 1847 thanks to a precipitous drop in total numbers.

Collectively, Saint John's mayor and Common Council, the provincial emigration agent, Colebrooke, and Lord Howick articulated a new direction for New Brunswick's immigration policy. Arguably their responses might be justified on one plane, especially in light of forced landlord emigration and the pandemic suffering among famine victims in New Brunswick. Yet they also signalled a philosophical and institutional rejection of Irish-Catholic immigrants. By the late 1840s officials did not dispute the concept of immigration – just the type of immigrant. For example, New Brunswick's chief emigration agent, Moses Perley, presaged late-nineteenth-century arguments in his call for limiting immigration to only morally upstanding individuals, primarily those from overwhelmingly Protestant northern and western European countries.[89] Irish-Catholic immigration, unbeknownst to contemporaries, reached its zenith in the late 1840s. By mid-century Catholics made up one-third of New Brunswick's population. Many Protestants feared that Catholic numbers had approached critical heights; no longer a mere nuisance, they now constituted a threat.

Irish-Catholic immigration in the 1840s ushered in an age of nativism in New Brunswick. It evoked responses of fear and prejudice among Protestant New Brunswickers similar to those recorded in other British North American colonies and the United States during the same period.[90] John Higham pioneered a useful paradigm for interpreting nativism, and while he relied upon American movements and nationalistic interpretations to construct his model, it applies equally well for any nativist response. Higham defined nativism as the 'intense opposition to an internal minority on the ground of its foreign ... connections,' or a 'defensive type of nationalism.' Though Higham cautioned that the word 'nativism,' of nineteenth-century derivation, over time assumed pejorative connotations, his definition provides a durable intellectual construct for analysing people's reaction to immigrants.[91] If even parts of his guidelines are employed, New Brunswick clearly experienced a nativist response to Irish-Catholics during the 1840s. Protestants provided the ranks from which the nativist soldiers came, including those of Loyalist, New England, Scots, English, and Irish extraction. Opponents waged the anti-Irish-Catholic campaign on several fronts in New Brunswick, as they did elsewhere. Yet taken together these skirmishes formed a withering offensive – one that left few corners of the colony's political, economic, or social sectors unscathed in the mid-nineteenth century.

The notion that Irish-Catholics either purposely or inadvertently invaded a Protestant, Anglo-Saxon domain became the essential underpinning of New Brunswick's nativist response.[92] Protestants feared that Catholics besieged the fundamental British institutions of liberty and justice. Because all Catholics owed sole allegiance to Rome's pontiff, the argument went, they were inherently anathema to the British Crown and Parliament. This concept, which one historian has labelled 'the neurosis' of Anglo-Saxon Protestants, dated back to the English Reformation under Henry VIII. Essentially at the core of British Protestantism, it transferred intact to the farthest reaches of the colonial empire.[93]

Evidence suggests a strong concern in mid-nineteenth-century New Brunswick that Catholics threatened British institutions. As early as 1842, editorials affixed the appellation 'lowly class of people' to Irish-Catholics, accusing them of acting at variance with every salutary provision of English law and religion. Fervent editors entreated Protestants to band together to ward off the assault in order to restore the once 'happy colony' to its former stature. New Brunswick needed to purge the Irish-Catholic malignancy.[94] This perception of invasion manifested itself in several ways. According to anti-Catholic propaganda, virtually every portion of New Brunswick's existing social fabric was in jeopardy as a result of the attack.

An elaborate conspiracy theory, which reasoned that the Catholic migration to the colony was but a single campaign of a battle plan masterminded at the Vatican, represented the most pervasive of these manifestations. The fear of conspiracy or of a larger purpose to Catholic immigration furnished the essential glue to anti-Catholic literature in North America.[95] Protestants usually levelled their counterattack at the most visible of all Catholic institutions – the church. The Roman Catholic religion had for centuries represented a tangible foil for British-Protestants, a passionate reminder of the spirit of Reformation.[96] Yet the dogma of anti-Catholicism evolved over time. Protestants progressively engaged less in philosophical debates over religious theory, and concentrated more of their energies on targets such as the institutionalized Catholic church and hierarchy.[97] In nineteenth-century Britain and North America, Protestants warily eyed the immigrant 'papists.' They believed that all Catholics received political and cultural signals from Rome, and obediently carried out the Pope's commands. Thus papism insidiously threatened both Britain and its colonial network. According to the theory, any Catholic could not be loyal either to the Crown or British law, for the Crown was synonymous with Protestant ascendancy, and law followed the Crown.

Evidence of the fear of a papal conspiracy surfaced in New Brunswick in the early nineteenth century. Northumberland

County magistrates swore oaths in 1817 that included a clause against papists. The oath's wording effectively prohibited Catholics from becoming justices of the peace.[98] During the debate over the passage of the Roman Catholic emancipation bill in 1830, opponents invoked the theme that all Catholics owed allegiance to Rome.[99] Even after the realization of emancipation, critics propagandized that 'Mickey' voters were the minions of the Pope. Moreover, any Catholic elected to office would be hopelessly 'priest-ridden,' and therefore unable to govern judiciously.[100]

By mid-century anti-papal rhetoric in New Brunswick was ubiquitous. The dismantling of anti-Catholic legislation in Britain and the empire, as well as news of revolutions fomenting in several Catholic countries in Europe, gave the colony's fervent Protestants more ammunition. In apocalyptic language, one newspaper succinctly reflected the anti-papal crusade's intensity: 'A great perhaps a final, conflict is at hand between Protestant truth and Popery leagued with Infidelity.'[101] Many feared that the papists had targeted New Brunswick for Catholic ascendancy. 'The Spirit of Popery,' which was 'aggressive, tyrannical and persecuting,' had firmly planted its banner on Loyalist soil as a result of the famine immigration.[102] The fountainhead of this plot was the Pope, who 'rules the priests with unquestioned despotism, the priests the people, and the people under the control of their ghostly fathers, stand ready tools to do their bidding even to the shedding of the blood of their innocent fellow man.'[103] According to anti-papal dogma, the Pope's agents surreptitiously undermined the colony's bedrock of British institutions. The Catholic church, using 'pomp and external forms' that appealed to the 'uncivilized mind[s]' of its adherents, actively sought recruits among the non-British population such as Amerindians.[104] The Catholic agents, according to fearful Protestants, capitalized on sacramental provisions of the church and were thus free to use even the most scurrilous methodologies to achieve their goals. According to nativists Catholics lied, cheated, and even murdered without compunction, secure in the knowledge that they would receive temporal forgiveness from corrupt

priests.[105] Ultimately, the conspiratorial theme became the dominant characteristic of nativist dogma in mid-nineteenth-century
New Brunswick. Fear of popery, the visible spread of Catholic
churches, and a general paranoia that the famine immigration
signalled Catholic ascendancy all contributed to the nativist's
arsenal.

Another touchstone for anti-Catholic forces involved the more
tangible concern of economic competition between natives and
Irish immigrants.[106] As discussed above, the 1840s brought a
series of depressions to New Brunswick's critical timber industry.
Irish famine immigrants, arriving during the worst years of
economic distress, willingly worked for wages far below the
average native workers'. Thus, increased immigration acted as a
depressant for general wage scales. Native-born New Brunswickers, used to a higher standard of living and facing long-term
financial commitments, would not be able to compete with Irish-
Catholic labourers who often cared about little more than earning
the requisite passage fare to America.

Native-born New Brunswickers established a pattern of resist-
ing foreign competition long before the 'hungry forties,' thus
facilitating the rejection of Irish immigrant labour.[107] As early as
1810, Americans working in Saint John had refused to join
combinations and drove wages down as eager employers paid
their lower rates.[108] This began a history of resentment towards
American labourers. As combinations and unions gathered
strength, native-born workers aggressively sought to protect their
jobs. A flurry of massive labour meetings from 1839 to 1841
generated impassioned resolutions against the employment of
any foreigners. The Mechanics Institute and even the Saint John
Common Council added to the chorus of those clamouring to
protect the rights of New Brunswickers.[109]

Thus patterns of economic nativism, established decades before
the mid-1840s, guided workers when distressingly large numbers
of Irish-Catholics poured into the colony's depressed cities and
towns. Unskilled native labourers, fearing for their jobs, greeted
the penniless immigrants as 'social pariahs.'[110] The dockworkers
in Saint John and Portland, the day labourers in Fredericton, and

the lumbermen of Carleton County and the Miramichi, all were prone to antipathy towards the hungry Irish immigrants. The destitute Catholics often took the most demanding and lowest paying of unskilled jobs that in a thriving economic climate would be vacant. But in the depressed 1840s, native-born New Brunswickers scrambled to compete for these jobs with immigrants who would gladly work for less.[111] This competition played an important role in the growth of nativism. Protestants called for economic segregation; merchants and employers should do business with members of their own religion, they argued. Ultimately, they hoped that ostracism would curtail Irish-Catholic immigration.[112] Thus, New Brunswick nativists exploited a traditional fear among workers and shaped it into a devastating salvo for the campaign against Catholics.

Another vital weapon in the nativist's arsenal capitalized upon the idea that Celtic-Irish were inherently a violent and disorderly people. This sentiment found its roots in Ireland's historical resistance to English domination. Disruptive agrarian societies such as the Ribbonmen of the eighteenth century helped to reinforce the violent stereotype.[113] According to nativist rhetoric the average Irishman was boisterous, hard-drinking, ignorant, and belligerent.[114] Quick with his fists, he would rather fight than reason with his foes. Poorer Catholics who flooded to North America in the nineteenth century often took jobs that carried a mythology of the same disorderly traits. When Irishmen toiled as stevedores, lumbermen, ditch diggers, and railroad navvies, the stereotypes of Celtic belligerence melded with occupational prejudices.[115] This marriage served as an important propaganda tool for North American nativists.

Irishmen undeniably contributed to their reputation for using violence to realize political and economic goals.[116] Frustrations born of English subjugation kindled this dynamic. Disruptions involving Irish-Catholics also erupted in North America, usually in areas of heaviest settlement. Philadelphia, Boston, Bytown [later Ottawa], Montreal, and Toronto all experienced major confrontations involving Celtic immigrants. To native-born North Americans, blind to their own crucial roles in these affrays, the

Irish appeared prone to 'belligerent self-assertion.' Contemporary observers believed that the Irish crossed the Atlantic with their uncivilized 'cultural baggage' in tow. North Americans cursed mightily the historical disruptiveness of the Irish, both at home and abroad.[117]

Nativists in New Brunswick used this theme to foment anti-Catholic sentiment. When riots erupted in the 1840s between Protestants and Catholics, nativists instantly attributed them to ancient patterns of Celtic violence. They bandied familiar stereotypes of belligerent and drunken Irishmen. Newspaper editorials called for a dispersion of immigrants among law-abiding natives in order to minimize the opportunities for social disorder: 'No one can deny that the lower orders of the Roman Catholic Irish, are a quarrelsome, headstrong, turbulent, fierce, vindictive people.'[118] Perennial feuding between Protestants and Catholics, especially in the large immigrant enclaves at Saint John, Portland, Fredericton, and Woodstock, lent credence to the mythology of Celtic violence. Moreover, rising crime rates in crowded urban areas such as Portland's wharf district and the York Point section of Saint John convinced even the most dispassionate and charitable observers that the 'troublesome ... lower orders' must be dealt with severely.[119]

Tragically, nativists painted all Irish-Catholic immigrants with the same brush. Though even the most scurrilous propagandists recognized that all immigrants were not participating in this orgy of crime, they nevertheless called for the erection of barriers to Irish-Catholic settlers. Each one, they argued, was a potential criminal: 'We are opposed – strongly opposed, to an influx of Roman Catholic emigrants; even though they were healthy and willing to settle. Let us not be understood as writing against *all* of the Roman Catholic Irish. We believe there are many quiet and orderly men among them; but unfortunately men of another class preponderate; and whenever they congregate together, so as to form anything like a commercial force, the peace of the community and the safety of life and property, is at once destroyed.'[120] Solutions to the problem included curtailing or banning Irish-Catholic immigration, barring them from voting and holding office, and prohibiting them from serving on local constabularies and juries. For having a Catholic function in any public office, the nativist argued, would be tantamount to leaving the 'wolves charged with the protection of the lambs!'[121]

New Brunswick nativists who exploited themes of Celtic violence were able to make use of ammunition not available to their American counterparts. The colony's Acadian community, also fervently Catholic, provided a natural foil for cultural comparisons with the Irish. According to nativist rhetoric Acadians remained demonstratively quiet and peaceful, an inoffensive and uninspired people with a history of relatively passive subjugation to British colonization. Conversely, the disruptive newcomers, Irish-Catholics, needed to be purged in the interest of maintaining a peaceable society. If only the Irish acted as docile and law-abiding as their Acadian co-religionists, Protestants bemoaned, then they too would be welcomed with open arms.[122]

Evidence proved the nativists incorrect on both counts. Neither as passive nor as unimaginative as believed, most Acadians lived in the north-western interior and along New Brunswick's northern and eastern shores; they had little contact with Protestant Loyalists and immigrants. Thanks to segregation, the 'peace' of the nineteenth century materialized as a historical sleight of hand. The Acadians, to cite one example, proved themselves fully capable of using collective and disruptive tactics to pursue their goals at the Caraquet riots of 1875.[123] Conversely, the Irish-Catholics settled *among* the Protestants in established communities such as Saint John, Fredericton, and Woodstock. They vigorously competed for limited jobs and arable tracts of land. The violence that erupted between Irish-Catholics and Protestants in the 1840s resulted from propinquity, not cultural deficiencies.

Yet another tack taken by New Brunswick nativists lay rooted in a fundamental and deplorable tradition of the British colonial experience – racism. The belief in the superiority of the Anglo-Saxons and their institutions underscored a theme traceable throughout centuries of British colonial expansion.[124] During Victorian times the British saddled the Catholic Irish with a 'double dose of original sin.' Irish-Celts fell below the Anglo-Saxons on the evolutionary scale; they were both culturally and spiritually inferior.[125] As zealous Scots and English-Protestants colonized Ireland, they relegated the Catholics to a lowly status as agrarian peasants, servants, and menial labourers. When the Irish flocked to English mill towns to provide muscle for the industrial revolution, racism proliferated.[126]

North Americans shared a similar disdain for inferior peoples and cherished the Victorian notion of Anglo-Saxon superiority. Indeed, racism played a key role in the American nativists' rejection of foreigners.[127] British North Americans also displayed racial hostility to outsiders, particularly when the dispossessed Irish streamed across the Atlantic in the 1840s.[128] In New Brunswick racism abounded; people invoked its principles with a relish comparable to rhetoric in America and other British colonies. Ethnicity and class mingled and then appeared fused in the writings of nativists. They railed against the ignorant 'Mickie' hordes who formed a substandard 'class of people.' The Irish-Catholics' status and behaviour in New Brunswick illustrated their inherent inferiority. The Anglo-Saxons must retain legislative and judicial control, argued the nativists, in order to ensure the colony's peaceful survival.[129]

Native propagandists exploited the racial theme with devastating effect. 'Ignorant' and 'superstitious' Irish-Catholics must be banished from the colony, some reasoned, for the task of converting them to acceptable social skills would ultimately meet with defeat. One sarcastically observed that you might as well 'attempt to change the colour of the Leopard's spots, or to "wash the Ethiope white," as to attempt to tame and civilize the wild, turbulent, irritable, savage, treacherous, and hardened natives of the Cities and Mountains of Connaught and Munster.'[130] Throughout the late 1840s and early 1850s nativist newspapermen hammered at the themes of racial inferiority and called for a province-wide ban on all Irish-Catholic settlers. Editors of the *Loyalist* in Fredericton, the *Carleton Sentinel* in Woodstock, and the *Weekly Chronicle* and *Christian Visitor* in Saint John regularly exposed their readers to racist editorials, Irish jokes, and vignettes that pointed out the supposed defects of Celtic immigrants.[131] During the 1850s the *Carleton Sentinel* regularly ran a

'Protestant Corner,' wherein alarmist letters and editorials about Roman Catholicism, popery, Satanism, and Romanism flourished. 'The Story of a Mad Priest,' published in the paper's literary section, illustrated this genre of vituperative articles.[132] Another joke, entitled 'How he did it,' typified the period's racist humour: 'A Roman Catholic curate to free himself from the great labor of confessions in Lent, gave notice to his parishioners that on Monday he should confess liars; on Tuesday, the misers; on Wednesday, the slanderers; on Thursday, the thieves; on Friday, the libertines; and on Saturday, the bad women. His scheme succeeded; none attended.'[133] Scurrilous embellishments flowed unchecked from the pens of nativist editors. Roman Catholics became 'the Offscum of Ireland,' while Timothy Warren Anglin, the Irish newspaperman who arrived in Saint John in the late 1840s, received curt dismissal as a 'Klonikilty Bog-Trotter.'[134] Thus, racist propaganda joined the other nativist weapons in the battle against Irish-Catholic encroachment.

The various tactics used by New Brunswick's nativists, channelled as they were into an intensive campaign, erected a formidable barrier to the assimilation of Irish-Catholics into colonial society. Natives and Protestant immigrants chose from a seemingly inexhaustible menu of illustrations to rationalize their fears of the Irish-Catholic. They could point with alarm to the 'invasion' of disloyal Irish, thereby concluding that British institutions suffered assault. Nativists could speak of the papal conspiracy; as Catholic churches and chapels multiplied, the papal flag appeared to be firmly planted in British soil. On a more personal level, they could complain about the economy and blame the famine immigrants for depressing wages. By mustering statistics that illustrated an increase in crime and rioting, they could telescope the rhetoric so that the turbulent Irish-Catholics appeared the fountainhead of all social disorder. And finally, by exploiting concepts of racial superiority, the nativists could fuse images of the Irish-Celts with all uncivilized 'classes' that threatened British ascendancy. Used alone or in combination, these ideas yielded grist for the mills of New Brunswick's nativists.

During the early 1840s the province's nativist campaign was

rather amorphous, but as the decade progressed, the rising tide of famine victims provided nativists with a more tangible foil. Moreover, the sheer size of the Irish-Catholic immigration demanded a concerted Protestant defence. Trumpets sounded a clarion call to muster an efficient organization that could unify disparate Protestants, both native-born and immigrants, and channel their energies into an effective counter-offensive:

The necessity ... for Protestant organization in this Province, arose not more from the many murderous attacks committed upon quiet and unoffending Protestants, by Catholic ruffians, than from the dreary prospect which the future presented. The facts were these: – several thousands of immigrants were annually landing upon our shores: they were nearly all Catholic, nearly all ignorant and bigoted, nearly all paupers, many of them depraved ... What have we to expect but murder, rapine, and anarchy? Let us ask, then – should not Protestants be united? Should they not organize?[135]

The Loyal Orange Order, an organization with a history of responding to similar entreaties in Ireland and Britain, answered the summons to battle.

# 4

# The Orange Order:
# Institutionalized nativism

The Orange Order, an ultra-Protestant organization with a history of fervent loyalty to the British Crown and opposition to the spread of Roman Catholicism, assumed the role as vanguard of institutionalized nativism in mid-nineteenth-century New Brunswick. Established long before the tumultuous 1840s, when nativism crystallized, the fraternity blended historic ideologies to indigenous needs. Yet far from being a bastard child, New Brunswick's Orange Order transplanted and cultivated those very tenets that members found useful in the mother organization. In the panic of famine migration it became the province's most vigilant and effective vehicle for warding off Irish-Catholic settlement.

Given its violent birth in Loughgall, Ireland, in 1795, the Loyal Orange Order embodied the spirit of defensive Protestantism. Its roots lay in a feuding tradition between Protestant and Catholic weavers and agrarian peasants who often competed for limited employment. Taking its cue from older Protestant groups such as the 'Peep O'Day Boys,' who engaged in bloody skirmishes with counterparts such as the Catholic 'Defenders,' the Orange Order quickly developed an intricate network to champion the Protestant cause. For philosophical and ritualistic purposes, the Order harked back to the 1690 defeat of Catholic King James II at the Battle of the Boyne by the Prince of Orange, King William III. The victory signalled Protestant ascendancy in Ireland and left a legacy of bitter disputes over whether control should reside in the hands of a Protestant minority centred in Ulster or the Catholic majority to the south and west.[1]

The Orange Order pledged to maintain Protestant ascendancy in the British Isles, including Ireland, by using William III's 'defeat' of Catholicism as its symbolic base. By borrowing ritualistic traditions from fraternities such as the Masons, the Orange Order developed a plethora of secret signs, initiation rites, oaths, hierarchical ranks, and festivals. The most important of the latter, the annual celebration of King James's defeat at the River Boyne on 12 July, was to have profound implications for Orangemen and Catholics living in close proximity to each other. In the initiation oath, Orangemen promised to observe 12 July every year if possible. Processions evolved as the most popular means of celebration; they also virtually assured yearly confrontations with Roman Catholics.[2]

Although the Orange Order originally acted as a bulwark against Catholic encroachment in the north of Ireland, by the turn of the century it had extended its appeal to all corners of the British Empire. Loyalty to the British Crown became the new watchword following the United Irishmen's Rebellion in 1798 and the union of Ireland and England two years later. During its first years, the Orange Order developed into an exclusively Protestant and male organization that extolled the virtues of British institutions. For the entire nineteenth century, wherever the Orange Order evolved, fervent members would uniformly cry 'no surrender' to either Catholicism or disloyalty.[3]

The Orange Order's violent beginnings, marked by bloody clashes and secretive raids on similar Catholic groups, explained its inherent paramilitary nature. But after 1800 Orange leaders, sensitive to a deafening chorus of criticism among even the most ardent of Protestants in Ireland and England, attempted to purge the organization of its more belligerent philosophies and members. Most Britishers viewed violence as an unpalatable tactic, even if wielded for the most virtuous of goals. Orange leaders began to look for members outside of the traditional ranks of farmers, labourers, and servants; they recruited artisans and gentry to give the organization an aura of 'respectability.' This campaign bore fruit in the early nineteenth century as some landlords and even nobility grasped the order's tenets. Recruitment among British regulars stationed in Ireland, however, would have the most profound implications for the spread of Orangeism throughout the empire. Highly mobile and certainly loyal, troops who routinely served at many posts during their careers provided an excellent carrier for the organization's seeds.[4] Thus, the attempts to broaden the institution's appeal ultimately ensured the transferral of the Orange Order to the British colonies.

Despite efforts to de-emphasize the paramilitary nature of Orangeism, confrontations with Catholics continued to plague the organization. July twelfth riots broke out frequently in the early nineteenth century as Orangemen exuberantly marched through Irish-Catholic neighbourhoods. Both sides clashed willingly; even the most tenuous of excuses or the mildest of insults provided enough kindling to ignite a bloody confrontation. Major riots in 1823 led an alarmed House of Commons to legislate against unlawful oaths in Ireland. Two years later, in an attempt to eradicate religious conflict, Prime Minister Robert Peel ordered the dissolution of all Orange lodges.[5] Peel's dissolution edict, which included no legal machinery for implementation, lapsed in 1828. Violence soon reappeared. Orangemen, critical of the government for undermining Protestant hegemony in the 1832 Reform Bill, renewed their annual processions. Collective violence with Catholics broke out anew, prompting the government to contemplate stronger anti-Orange measures. An emotional debate in the House of Commons in 1836 resulted in a recommendation that Orangemen voluntarily disband. Under Parliament's guidelines, King William IV posted an edict to 'discourage' all British Orange institutions. In addition, he extracted a promise from the Orange Grand Master, his brother the Duke of Cumberland, to order the organization's dissolution.[6]

These repressive measures met with partial success, although Orangeism persisted because Parliament failed to legislate dissolution and relied instead on voluntary compliance. The emphasis on Protestantism and loyalty continued to draw garrison troops into the folds of Orangeism, despite a clear order to quit the organization from the commander-in-chief of British forces in 1835.[7] Coupled with the rising tide of Irish-Protestant emigration in the early nineteenth century, the troops helped to transplant Orangeism throughout the empire.[8] The British North American colonies, which received thousands of British troops to maintain a defensive network of garrisons against possible American invasion, also absorbed many of the Protestants who fled Ireland in search of improved living conditions and opportunities. Together these groups formed the foundation of the Loyal Orange Order in Canada.

Members held the earliest known British North American Orange meetings in Halifax in 1799 and in Montreal around the turn of the century. From these associations, peopled entirely by British regulars, grew a network of lodges that found fertile ground among the Loyalists and Irish-Protestant immigrants in the Canadas and New Brunswick. Within a few years Orangeism had gained a tenacious foothold in North America, primarily along the north shore of Lake Ontario and the Fundy coast of New Brunswick. Throughout the nineteenth century, the Orange Order would enjoy its greatest successes in these same two areas.[9]

Upper Canadians wrested control of the British North American Orange Order early in the century. Emboldened Orangemen counted sufficient members to hold 12 July processions in Perth, York, Kingston, and the Ottawa Valley during the 1820s. Riots between Catholic immigrants and Orangemen date from this same period, as evidenced by the Perth disturbances in 1824. In 1830 Canada's Orangemen successfully petitioned their Irish superiors for permission to issue their own warrants for establishing new lodges, thus giving birth to the Grand Lodge of British North America. Under the spirited direction of Ogle R. Gowan, a northern Irish immigrant, it quickly obtained warrant-granting rights for all the American colonies except New Brunswick.[10]

While this North American counterpart to the Irish Orange

Order displayed many similarities and borrowed much of the original regalia and ideology, it evolved into a distinctively Canadian organization. The 'cultural baggage' brought by British troops and Irish-Protestant immigrants, once deposited in the colonies, was picked up and used by Loyalists in a fashion that little resembled its original purpose. By concentrating their energies on the tenets of Protestantism and loyalty to the Crown, Canadian Orangemen embodied a defensive, garrison mentality. They fashioned a formidable bulwark, especially in Upper Canada and New Brunswick, against both the spread of French Catholicism and Irish-Catholic immigration. They sought to maintain Protestant domination in North America and to keep the colonies firmly rooted to the British Empire.[11]

Three patterns underscored the British North American Orange Order's unique development, the most fundamental of which involved membership. A more elaborate mosaic of peoples than was found in either Ireland or England inhabited the colonies, therefore the pool of prospective members represented a wide range of ethnic groups. Ultimately, of course, all were either newcomers or the descendants of immigrants. Congregationalist Loyalists from the rebellious southern colonies, Scots-Presbyterians, English-Methodists, and Irish-Anglicans all flocked through the portals of the burgeoning Orange Order. The call of 'no surrender' played a siren song to these men. Many joined because of their desire to keep the colonial link to the Crown, and because they feared French and Irish-Catholic ascendancy.[12] Since the membership differed dramatically from either Irish or English lodges, colonial Orangeism evoked singular goals and strategies.

Another distinctive pattern that emerged in North American Orangeism involved colonial politics. Rather than borrowing only Irish and English political concerns, the Canadian Orangemen charted a course that addressed local issues and attempted to solve indigenous problems. Thus an Orange Order developed, especially in Upper Canada, that reacted primarily to provincial stimuli. Orangemen across British North America preferred Tory platforms. They worked feverishly throughout the nineteenth century to keep the colonies British in the face of England's withdrawal. Orangemen supported the government in the abortive rebellions of 1837, and they zealously opposed the Rebellion Losses Act because they believed it favoured Catholics. They campaigned against the separate-schools issue and the Jesuit Estates Act, and played an active role in defusing the Fenian threats and crushing the Northwest Rebellions. British North American Orangemen, while motivated by the ubiquitous Orange tenets of loyalty and anti-Catholicism, steered a distinctively Canadian political course.[13]

Finally, colonial Orangeism differed dramatically from the parent organization in its philosophical outlook and its publicized reasons for existence. Canadian Orange lodges certainly retained the rituals and regalia of their Irish counterparts. Secret codes, initiation oaths, and the hierarchical structure in which members passed through a series of degrees all made the voyage across the Atlantic intact. Yet many of the essential underpinnings of Irish Orangeism were not valid or applicable in British North America. The task of defending Protestants against militant Catholic agrarian groups, significant for Irish Orangemen, appeared meaningless to Canadian members who faced no such threat. Without the motivation of defensive belligerence, Canadian Orangemen turned to social justifications for their lodges' existence. They established a Protestant barrier against the dissemination of Catholic culture. Many lodges declared themselves 'benefit' fraternities wherein members provided a financial network for mutual aid and established a primitive insurance system to cover burial costs and even provide lump-sum payments to widows. Most expected full attendance at the funerals of brethren. As the nineteenth century progressed, Orange lodges endowed charitable institutions such as orphan homes. In addition, some lodges actively supported temperance, while others created self-help groups along the lines of the Mechanics Institutes. Annual dinners were apt to be followed by guest lectures delivered by local politicians, clergymen, and entrepreneurs.[14] Clearly lodges had a variety of emphases, whether rural, urban, agrarian, or artisanal, whether in hinterland communities in Carleton or York counties or in more cosmopolitan centres such as Saint John and Portland. All primary Orange lodges, however, shared the tenets of anti-Catholicism and loyalty to Britain. The foundations may have been identical, but the superstructures took profoundly different shapes. Therefore, a distinctive network evolved in British North American Orange lodges, one that reflected local priorities rather than Ireland's social, political, and economic afflictions.[15]

While Canadian Orangeism created a style of its own, it kept the two most important Irish values intact. For one, loyalty to the British cause remained. Orangemen pursued this with such fervour that they ignored edicts from the King and Parliament, as in 1825 and 1836, whenever they believed them potentially harmful to British institutions. Perhaps the strongest glue bonding all Orangemen, however, was anti-Catholicism. By definition Orange lodges could admit only Protestants; by sacred pledge, Orangemen promised never to embrace Catholicism or marry a Catholic. These two concepts provided the philosophical bedrock for all members. As one of its official rulebooks succinctly stated: 'The Orange Society, lays no claim to exclusive loyalty or exclusive Protestantism, but it admits no man within its pale whose principles are not loyal, and whose creed is not Protestant.'[16]

These tenets would provide the framework for Orangeism throughout British North America, yet provincial and local lodges would vary tremendously in membership and purpose. Of all the Orange associations, New Brunswick's exhibited the most independence. The province continued to issue its own warrants for primary lodges throughout the nineteenth century, despite pressure from Ogle Gowan to join the Canadian group.[17] This independent spirit infused New Brunswick's Orangeism; it helped to create a unique organization that devoted most of its energy to local issues and provincial problems.

New Brunswick's organized Orange lodges clearly traced a pattern of British-military and Irish-immigrant conveyance. The earliest known lodge, formed among soldiers of the 74th Regiment in Saint John, met regularly by 1818. The first official warranted lodge, instituted in 1824, grew among British troops in the same city.[18] After several abortive efforts to establish civilian lodges in the mid-1820s, Orangeism rooted among Saint John's Irish-Protestant population in 1831. Seven men, meeting at the home of James McNichol, 'the Father of Orangeism in Eastern Canada,' formed Verner Loyal Orange Lodge no. 1.[19] Verner served as the fountainhead of all other lodges in New Brunswick for the next seven years. Sluggish growth ensued, most of it confined to the region. Saint John and Portland housed seven of the province's first eight lodges. By 1838 New Brunswick claimed fifteen lodges: ten in Saint John County, three in Kings and two in Queens.[20] Thus, early Orange development in New Brunswick concentrated in the port and garrison city of Saint John as well as in the lower Saint John River Valley.

The Orange Order entered a new phase in 1837 when all the lodges organized under the auspices of a New Brunswick Provincial Grand Lodge directed by Grand Master James McNichol. Yet rather than facilitating growth the provincial organization became mired in internecine struggles and almost collapsed. In an attempt to circumvent local issues, New Brunswick's Orangemen sought outside help, and in July 1844 Gowan's British North American organization assumed jurisdiction over the entire New Brunswick network. The provincial order retained the right, however, to issue its own warrants.[21] The amalgamation 'legitimized' local lodges and, coupled with an emotional campaign against petitioners to the legislature who wanted to suppress Orangeism in 1843, it boosted membership.[22] Over 150 Orangemen gathered in Saint John on 12 July 1844 to usher in the new era. With voices 'too numerous to be molested,' New Brunswick's brethren resolved to ensure Protestant ascendancy and to strive for a continued integration with the British Empire.[23] Their task, couched in noble rhetoric, would prove formidable.

The rising tide of Irish-Catholic immigration in the 1840s provided provincial Orangemen with a tangible enemy and, coupled with the new legitimacy, spurred growth. Twenty-seven lodges dotted the countryside by the close of 1844; of these, ten were less than a year old. The young lodges signalled both a filtering into counties already represented, such as St Martins Parish in

Saint John County, and an extension into different counties. One of the most important new lodges, Graham no. 20, appeared in Fredericton in 1844. It enjoyed explosive growth under the direction of its founder and first Worshipful Master, Thomas Hill. Hill also edited and published the *Loyalist*, which became a semi-official Orange organ in the mid-nineteenth century.[24] Within two years, Orangeism swept up the northern Saint John River Valley into Carleton County. First Woodstock Lodge no. 38 convened with 110 original members under the leadership of Charles Connell. Later in 1846 nearby Bairdsville received a lodge of its own.[25] These two organizations provided the core for one of New Brunswick's greatest Orange success stories of the nineteenth century. Loyalist Carleton County would emerge as an Orange stronghold and its residents would support Orange causes with an enthusiasm rarely matched in other counties.

Lodges shared key traits. Along with the already discussed oaths and regulations that virtually forbade all associations with Roman Catholics, all members promised to observe 12 July.[26] During the 1840s these annual gatherings changed from local dinner parties in lodge halls to more visible displays, such as parades, in the larger Orange centres of Saint John, Fredericton, Gagetown, and Woodstock. Most lodges met regularly, usually once a month. Many of the more affluent lodges erected meeting halls as the century progressed; others rented rooms or buildings at convenient locations. Attendance at primary lodge meetings varied wildly. As a rule, the number present would often be well below the official membership tally. For example, Eldon Lodge no. 2 in Saint John averaged between seven and eleven in attendance at meetings in 1841 when its roll book accounted for 103 dues-paying members.[27] Strict regulations shaped the meetings, while ceremonies followed prescribed formats. Prospective members needed the recommendation of at least two Orange sponsors; they then faced a vote of approval by attending members. Successful candidates gained entry at the most basic level – Orange – after an elaborate initiation ceremony unveiled the 'mysteries' of the order. Larger lodges often held separate meetings restricted to members who achieved superior degrees, such as Purple, Blue, and Royal Arch Purple.[28] Brethren risked fines or expulsion for infractions of the Orange oath or lodge rules. Some of the more common offences included maligning a brother, profanity, fraternizing with a Roman Catholic, intemperance, and a general disregard for authority.[29] Leaders also exercised control by maintaining close correspondence with local lodges. An extensively employed blackballing system, for example, effectively blocked recalcitrant members from joining neighbouring lodges in the Saint John region in mid-century.[30] At the same time, feuds were not uncommon between primary lodges as they struggled to cull members from the same pool of Protestant residents, as was often the case in Saint John and Portland.[31]

In addition to primary lodges, county and district lodges mushroomed in the regions with the highest proportion of Orangemen. Saint John and Queens counties housed several by the late 1840s. Eligibility for membership in these superior organizations depended upon an individual's rank. Five degrees encompassed the Orange hierarchy: Orange, Purple, Blue, Royal Arch Purple, and Royal Scarlet.[32] Local members who achieved the first three ranks became eligible to attend district lodge meetings. Those who added the Royal Arch Purple degree advanced to the county level, and brethren who completed all degrees participated in the prestigious provincial lodge.[33] The extension from primary to superior lodges, with its concomitant emphasis on advancement, theoretically motivated individual members. The pyramid structure also provided cohesion for disparate primary lodges. Ultimately, the hierarchical system strengthened and entrenched Orangeism in New Brunswick.

The latter half of the 1840s, the period of intensive social violence between Irish-Catholics and Orangemen, witnessed Orangeism's most dramatic growth spurt in the nineteenth century (see appendix B). From a total of 27 in early 1845 to 123 in mid-century, Orange lodges increased by 455 per cent.[34] The high incidence of ethnic and religious rioting, blamed for the most part on Irish famine immigrants, explained the magnetic pull, or 'expediency,' of Orangeism to native Protestants.[35] All the communities touched by riots experienced this phenomenon. For example,

Portland's Wellington Lodge initiated ten members in the meeting following the 12 July 1849 riot, by far the largest number since the organization's inception five years earlier.[36] Fredericton's riot in 1847 served to reinforce the city's Graham Lodge, and the following year several Orangemen involved in the disturbance successfully petitioned for a new lodge in nearby St Mary's Parish.[37] Moreover, Carleton County's Orange population increased an estimated tenfold following the 1847 Woodstock riot. According to one observer, few Protestants remained in the county who did not either belong to an Orange lodge or sympathize with the goals of Orangeism.[38] By 1849, the province and its nascent Nova Scotia affiliate claimed approximately ten thousand members. Since the Nova Scotian appendages dated their charters from 1847, a mere two years, the overwhelming majority represented New Brunswick's Orangemen.[39] Primary lodges at mid-century remained most heavily concentrated in traditional Orange counties such as Saint John, Kings, Queens, York, and Carleton, but they also reflected new growth in Sunbury and Victoria.[40] Not surprisingly, New Brunswick's Orange Order characterized the late 1840s as exceedingly propitious years.

Traditional membership pools did not account for the explosive growth of Orangeism. Irish-Protestant immigration dropped dramatically during the 1840s, becoming negligible by mid-century. Assuredly, the sons of Irish-Protestant immigrants displayed great interest in the organization. Yet establishing generational impact remains problematic. As one of the deans of immigration studies wisely observed, 'One of the hardest things for social historians to trace is what happens to the certain attitudes of members of an ethnic group in their second, third, and subsequent generations.'[41] Regardless, the numbers of Irish-Protestants with a cogent memory and perhaps direct experience of ethnic tensions in the Old World diminished as the nineteenth century unfolded. Moreover, Britain reduced its garrison troops because of budgetary constraints. What, then, explained Orangeism's meteoric rise? And how did the Orange Order broaden its appeal to ensure entrenchment in a colony dominated by non-Irish-Protestants? The organization's tenets and professed goals provided keys for unlocking the answers to these questions. Officially, New Brunswick's Orangemen adhered to fundamental concepts shared by brethren everywhere.[42] But individual motivations for joining the Orange Order are impossible to ascertain, except in rare cases where personal memoirs exist, so the aspirations of Orangemen must be construed from the organization's rhetoric, collective activity, and membership patterns.

Simply put, to tell the story of the Orange Order in mid-nineteenth-century New Brunswick is to trace the growth of an indigenous social movement.[43] Orangemen borrowed their rituals and symbols from Ireland, and paid homage to their historical roots. Yet these facts alone could not account for Orangeism's phenomenal success in the colony. A willing pool of Protestants provided the manpower necessary for growth; the descendants of Loyalists and New Englanders, as well as Scots and English immigrants, flocked to the organization. No stretch of the imagination could make New Brunswick's Orange society a mere reflection of Irish-Protestant 'cultural baggage.' The Orangemen's welcoming address to newly appointed Lieutenant-Governor Sir Edmund Walker Head in 1849 sharply illuminated their indigenous priorities, shaped by the colony's unique membership and aspirations: 'Our chief objects are the union of Protestants of the several denominations, to counteract the encroachments of all men, sects or parties, who may at any time attempt the subversion of the Constitution, or the severance of these Colonies from the British Empire; to bind Protestants to the strict observance of the laws, and to strengthen the bands of the local authorities, by the knowledge that there is ever a band of loyal men ready in case of emergency, to obey their commands, and assist them in the maintenance of order.'[44] Clearly, New Brunswick's Orangemen stood ready to combat any foe of Protestantism or colonist of questionable loyalty.[45]

Who was the enemy, and whence came the invasion? Catholics, pouring out of famine Ireland in the 1840s, became the Orangemen's ideological foil and often willing opponent. Nativist dogma infused the organization. It gathered zealous and frightened Protestants within its lodges, including native-born and immigrants who perceived their religion and culture to be under attack. The Orange Order gave them fellowship, it provided an institutional platform from which to launch their assaults, and perhaps most important, it moulded them into a cohesive unit under a monolithic command system. Orangemen and Irish-Catholics would clash in the 1840s, not in isolated guerrilla actions, but in riots involving hundreds of participants.[46] In fact, the Orange Order's actions and propaganda reflected and magnified every major element of nativism in New Brunswick.

Orangeism's primary function in the mid-nineteenth century was twofold: to ensure Protestant ascendancy and to maintain the British connection. All rhetoric and collective activities focused on these tasks. The perception that New Brunswick faced a deleterious invasion of Irish-Catholics served as the wellspring of nativism. If allowed to flow unchecked, Orangemen argued, the newcomers would fundamentally alter the ethnic, religious, and economic supremacy of Protestants. 'Foreign' immigration would inevitably 'undermine civil and religious liberty'; only strict Protestant vigilance, and ultimate mastery, could ensure the colony's peaceful survival.[47]

In this battle against the Irish-Catholics to maintain a Protestant and loyal bulwark, Orangemen employed classic nativist tactics. Perhaps the most virulent originated from the perception that poor Irish-Catholics would use crime and riot to sabotage the peace and 'good government' of New Brunswick. While still members of a relatively small fraternity in the early 1840s, Orangemen clustered together for defensive support on lodge meeting days and during the annual Twelfth of July celebrations. As Irish-Catholic immigration expanded during the decade, alarmed Orangemen habitually armed themselves in public for 'self-defence.' Belief in the uncivilized and violent nature of the Celt furnished sufficient justification to warrant protective armament.[48] As Orangemen embraced weapons, and acted increasingly belligerent in public, they faced similar displays in the swelling Catholic communities. Blinded perhaps by their zealousness, Orangemen failed to realize that their posture encouraged reciprocal behaviour. When similarly fervent Catholics demonstrated with weapons, purportedly for *their* own 'self-defence,' the Orange Order used it as 'proof' of Celtic incivility.[49]

As the 1840s progressed, and especially in the aftermaths of the massive Protestant-Catholic confrontations in 1845 and 1847, the Orange Order embarked on a comprehensive vigilante campaign against Irish-Catholics. Orangemen began to trace their historical roots to the advent of famine immigration. While chronologically faulty, the analysis accurately pinpointed an essential dynamic: Orangeism stagnated until a sizeable 'enemy' appeared. 'Orangeism had its origin in the *necessity* of the case; it has spread in this Province, also from *necessity*, for had not the country been infested with gangs of lawless ruffians, whose numerous riots, and murderous deeds compelled Protestants to organize for mutual defence, Orangeism would have been scarcely known. And whenever the *cause* shall disappear, Orangeism may retrograde.'[50] With the goal of purging New Brunswick of Irish-Catholics, Orangemen launched a propaganda barrage in official correspondence, public and legislative speeches, editorials and letters in newspapers, and testimonials in the judicial system. The trumpet beckoned all loyal Protestants to the crusade – Orangemen would lead the charge.[51]

Vigilante fervour intensified following every confrontation with Irish-Catholics. When the constabulary and magistracy failed to dampen Catholic violence, according to Orange propaganda, all Protestants could claim the right to arm themselves. But more significantly, the Orange Order assumed a self-imposed responsibility to assist authorities with the 'maintenance of order.'[52] Ironically, as ethno-religious riots escalated in the 1840s, Orangemen overlooked their own armed complicity. They insisted that each incident provided further proof that the law was a 'dead letter,' and that Orangemen stood alone as the true defenders of the 'rights' of New Brunswick's Protestants. In the course of every major riot Orangemen walked the streets heavily armed 'to protect' the townspeople.[53] When peace returned after a bitter confrontation, such as the calm following the 1847 Woodstock Riot, Orangemen exuberantly deemed their vigilante tactics a success. For example, Charles Connell, a Woodstock justice of the peace and lumber merchant, argued along with his colleagues that the Orange Order brought order to tormented communities, especially Woodstock and Fredericton. As the *Carleton Sentinel* observed, 'Since the lawful authorities will not protect us, we must combine and protect ourselves.' 'Quiet' reigned, the paper asserted, in those areas where the Orange Order had achieved supremacy.[54]

Rioting significantly reinforced the illusions of the righteousness and effectiveness of armed Orange patrols. Lodges enjoyed tremendous growth immediately following major confrontations. Loyalists and their descendants, as well as Scots and English immigrants, recognized the organization as the most effective bulwark against Irish-Catholic incursions.[55] This phenomenon explained the fraternity's growing legitimacy as the decade progressed. In many areas, it also acted as a bonding agent between the Orange Order and elected or appointed authorities at all levels. While abundant evidence pointed to a tradition of interconnection, the Orange lodges increasingly culled their members from provincial militia units. Moreover, Orangemen held positions of authority such as magistrates, constables, civil servants, barristers, and provincial legislators.[56] Thus, mid-century found a marriage between the tenets of Orangeism and a Protestant belief in self-defence; the offspring, tragically, was ethno-religious confrontation.

Although the Orange Order's vigilante reaction to famine immigration appeared to be successful, its 'necessity' was strictly illusory. Aggressive Orangeism in the 1840s partially created the milieu for social violence. Rather than being the solution to riots with Irish-Catholics, the Orange Order either inadvertently or deliberately encouraged them. Any victories claimed by Orangemen, such as the restoration of peace following the Woodstock riot, reflected not the righteousness of Orange principles but the ascendancy of militant Protestantism. Protestants enjoyed a two-thirds majority over Catholics in mid-century; if Orange nativists successfully repelled Irish counter-demonstrations, they did so because they could tap a larger pool of sympathetic co-religionists. New Brunswick would continue to be instrumentally shaped by Protestant and Loyalist principles, much as it had been at its inception in the 1780s.

Orange propagandists also combated Irish-Catholic immigration by encouraging Protestant fears of papal dominance over each parishioner's political, social, and religious life. A vituperative anti-Catholic strain lay at the heart of the institutionalized Orange Order as created in Ireland. New Brunswick's Orangemen unswervingly accepted the organization's axioms. All members promised to eschew contact with Catholics; restrictive clauses permeated the initiation oath.[57] Though individual initiates might join the organization for a variety of reasons, all shared a common loyalty and religion. Exclusivity bound together Orangemen of different Protestant denominations.

New Brunswick's Orangemen perceived the Irish-Catholic immigration as an offensive front in a worldwide invasion. They characterized Catholics as the 'enemy of human kind.' Though but a skirmish in a global battle, the provincial confrontation achieved glorious stature as a 'struggle of life and death.' New Brunswick's Orangemen, echoing rhetoric from nativists in the United States and other British colonies, apocalyptically warned that 'the greatest contest in the world is between Romanism and Protestantism.'[58] Since the English Reformation the Protestant religion provided the crucible of freedom and civil liberty. To the colony's Protestants the 'wise, moral and temperate' Orange society fortuitously materialized as a natural ally in the struggle against Catholicism: 'The time has arrived when it behooves every British subject, and every lover of Liberty, to be up and doing, and to decide whether Protestantism itself shall stand, or whether we shall let go the firm anchor of our faith, and drift, without chart or compass, into the shoreless ocean of Impiety, of Infidelity, and of Popery.'[59]

To support their rhetorical campaign, New Brunswick's Orangemen pointed with alarm to recent gains made by Catholics in the British Isles. Condemnation poured forth to the House of Commons for slackening controls over non-Protestants. The Roman Catholic Emancipation Bill of 1829, followed by the Reform Bill of 1832, symbolized an erosion of Protestant hegemony. A mid-century attempt to buttress the foundering Roman Catholic church in England, coming hard on the heels of revolutions in several predominantly Catholic European countries, fuelled Protestant paranoia in the colony. Orangemen appealed to Queen Victoria to reverse the liberal trend. Their diatribe against the 'insidious effort to undermine' Protestantism generated a lacklustre response; apparently those to whom Orangemen swore fealty did not share the Armageddon philosophy.[60]

New Brunswick's Orangemen also drew heavily on local conditions to support their anti-Catholic crusade. They maintained that the legislature 'pandered' to Roman Catholics by parroting England's emancipation bill in 1830, thus removing restrictions on Catholics for voting and serving in the legislature. Though only a handful of Catholics functioned in any official capacity by mid-century, either locally or provincially, each small gain represented a step towards 'tyranny, oppression, and outrage.'[61] More recently, the infestation of Irish-Catholic immigrants fanned the flames of Orange zealotry. Orangemen feared the firm implantation of the papal flag on Loyalist soil. Through the priests, the key papal agents, the ignorant masses of Irish and French could easily be duped into supporting Catholic ascendancy in New Brunswick. Nervous about the potential effects of Catholic bloc voting, Orangemen implored Protestants to reject Catholic candidates. In one Orange circular, the author called to fellow Orangemen to combat the 'soul-crushing shackles of Rome.' Rome's political control over the Catholic flock was virtually unshakable, 'unless God in his mercy should clear the mental optics of their descendants and enable them to see the light of a purer faith.'[62] Given their superior numbers and effective organizational skills, Protestants would thus be assured political control.[63]

Political implications aside, Orangemen feared the institutionalized grip that the Catholic church might have over its parishioners. The Roman Catholic flock, they argued, was a literal rather than metaphorical appellation; with as much independent spirit as a lamb a Catholic obsequiously obeyed even the most outrageous commands of the church hierarchy.[64] Indeed, belief in the total control the church had over its followers prompted

some Orangemen to articulate seemingly compassionate sentiments for their adversary: 'We intensely loathe and hate the
system [Roman Catholicism], as a system of darkness and guilt,
but we pity the men connected with it.'[65] Clearly, Orangemen
encouraged anti-Catholicism. Both the religious and political
potentialities of the church terrified them.

Yet another significant nativist barb permeated their responses
– racism. Orangeism operated under the implicit assumption that
all Catholics, and especially Irish immigrants, were inherently
ignorant and uncivilized.[66] Thinly veiled and extensively employed, racist dogma underscored the Orange response to Catholicism. But indiscriminate attacks on all Catholics proved too
formidable a task for provincial Orangemen in mid-century.
Therefore, they drew distinctions between New Brunswick's two
significant Catholic populations – the Acadians and the Irish. The
tactic served two purposes: it freed Orangemen to concentrate
their rhetorical attacks on Irish immigrants, because the Acadians
remained 'peacefully' ensconced far to the north and east and
therefore represented no immediate threat. Moreover, the ethnic
distinction created an artificial barrier between the older Acadian
population and the incoming Irish. By publicly favouring one
group, Orangemen hoped to drive a wedge between Catholics
and turn the Acadians and Irish into competing interests.[67]

Orange propagandists wielded the racist tool with enthusiasm,
variously characterizing Irish-Catholics as the 'ignorant masses'
and 'untameable barbarians.' Famine immigrants became the
'lower orders,' their civility suspect because they appeared 'unrestrained by any code of morals.' Protestants heeded the message.
The suspicion and hatred of Irish-Catholics because of their Celtic
origins opened new avenues for Orange membership; it permitted even those who did not share the Orangemen's rabid loyalty
or fervent anti-Catholicism to support the organization. The
desire to keep substandard Irish-Celtic peoples out of a racially
superior British colony furnished sufficient motivation for many
New Brunswickers to join the Orange Order.[68]

Finally, New Brunswick's Orangemen adopted the nativist's
rejection of Irish-Catholic immigration because of economic fac-

tors. The famine victims of the 1840s triggered responses on two levels. First, port cities such as Saint John shouldered the burden of sheltering and feeding the most destitute arrivals. During an era of depressed timber trading, this placed a tremendous strain on local treasuries. Moreover, the poorer Irish tackled even the most menial of jobs for a minimum wage. Since many desired only to earn enough for passage to the United States, they exhibited virtually no commitment to the maintenance of traditional labour standards. As the Irish flooded to the colony in the depressed 1840s, native workers found themselves competing for fewer jobs. Wage scales plummeted as employers took advantage of the Irish proclivity to toil for less. Thus, Irish immigration exacerbated New Brunswick's depressed economic climate.[69]

The Orange Order capitalized on the colony's economic distress. Lodges spearheaded a movement in the mid-1840s to segregate employment, while individual members appealed to Protestant employers to hire only non-Catholic labourers. This would force Irish immigrants to work for Catholic businesses, of which there were comparatively few, or to seek employment outside the province.[70] Evidence indicated that the segregation policy enjoyed modest success. During 1847, Protestant businessmen ostracized their Catholic neighbours in Carleton County as a 'remedy' to their ethno-religious disputes. Whenever possible, merchants dealt only with customers who shared their faith. In Fredericton, documents also pointed to a discriminatory economy. Teamsters hauled goods for their own kind; the Protestants, secure in their greater numbers, easily moved their freight while Catholics were forced to seek out 'Mickey' cartmen.[71] The economic assault against the Irish, while only one weapon in the Orange arsenal, reflected the nativists' determination to drive the immigrants out of New Brunswick.

During the mid-nineteenth century, New Brunswick's Orange Order embodied institutionalized nativism. Yet had the organization been staffed entirely by Irish-Protestant immigrants, the concept of nativism would ill apply. An analysis of a variety of sources, including official Orange documents, clearly proves that this was not the case. By mid-century, the Orange Order overwhelmingly represented an older stock of New Brunswickers such as the descendants of Loyalists and New Englanders. Immigrants from Ireland, England, Scotland, and other British colonies also appeared in its ranks. Members represented all major Protestant denominations, with the majority being Anglicans, Presbyterians, Methodists, and Baptists.[72] By all indications the Orange Order qualified as a nativist body. Motivated by locally defined problems and prejudices, it represented and served the needs of natives and immigrants alike. New Brunswick Orangeism flourished not as a simple adjunct of the Irish parent organization. It reflected neither a strict membership transfer of Irish-Protestants nor a displacement of traditional Irish squabbles to North America.

Orangeism thrived in the 1840s precisely because it appealed to the native-born population. With Irish-Protestant immigration slowing to a trickle, the Orange Order had no alternative but to seek reinforcements from other quarters. The deviation in membership patterns first became apparent in the late 1830s.[73] Native-born New Brunswickers helped to create the Provincial Grand Orange Lodge in 1844. Influential charter members included William H. Needham, a barrister and magistrate, H. Boyd Kinnear, a lawyer, and Thomas W. Peters, Jr, a city official. During their careers all three of these Saint Johners assumed leadership positions within the Orange Order.[74] As the organization grew in the 1840s, it traced a route up the Saint John River Valley. New Brunswick's Loyalist heartland tendered fertile soil for Orange principles. Lodges proliferated and membership soared in counties with large Loyalist populations such as Carleton, York, Kings, and Queens.[75] First and second generations of immigrants also found the order appealing. For example, the son of an English-Methodist, Robert Chamberlain, became one of Queens County's first prominent Orangemen. And in Carleton County, the list of Woodstock's Orange founders included a Scots-Russian.[76]

During the era of concentrated social violence – in 1845–9 – native-born New Brunswickers flocked to the Orange Order in droves. Attracted by the organization's rhetorical campaign to protect Protestantism and the British connection, they eagerly joined the efforts to dampen the effects of Irish-Catholic immigration. Following the bloody 1847 riot in Woodstock, for example, Carleton County's Orange membership increased tenfold. Within one year of the confrontation, critics and supporters alike estimated that 90 per cent of the population had either joined a lodge or openly approved of Orangeism.[77] The same phenomenon applied to Saint John, although the numbers failed to achieve such dramatic proportions. Following the major clashes of 1845, 1847, and 1849, Protestants swarmed to established Orange lodges and even petitioned for new warrants.[78]

In Fredericton, loyal New Brunswickers joined so swiftly after the 1847 riot that many had no knowledge of either the history or the symbolism of the Orange Order. They cared only that the organization stood as a Protestant and loyal fortress against Irish-Catholic invasion. Fredericton's custom-house officer and constable, Benjamin Wheeler, superbly illustrated this point. A proud man of Loyalist stock, he joined the local lodge on New Year's in 1847 and participated in the 12 July riot. In subsequent trial testimony, he admitted his ignorance of Orange history and swore he knew nothing of the significance of the Battle of the Boyne.[79] Similarly, J.A. Perley, native-born proprietor and special constable, took the oath in the riot's wake after concluding that duly constituted civil authorities no longer exhibited the capability to maintain civil control. He knew nothing of the Orange Order except that it functioned as a Protestant vigilante group, one that could cope effectively with the seemingly lawless Irish-Catholics.[80]

Evidence of the Orange Order's appeal to New Brunswickers, both native-born and immigrants, emerges when the names of members who belonged during the 1830s to 1850s are traced to the manuscript censuses. A variety of documentary sources ultimately yielded the names of almost 1150 Orangemen; they included official membership rolls, minutes books, correspondence, and petitions for incorporation.[81] In addition hundreds of Orangemen were identified in court records, newspaper accounts, letters, diaries, and official New Brunswick and Colonial Office records.[82] Whenever possible, the names of identified Orangemen were traced in the New Brunswick censuses of 1851, 1861, and, in a few cases, 1871. Available information germane to this analysis included the member's residence, birthplace, immigration date if foreign-born, year of birth, occupation, primary lodge affiliation, and initiation date. Many of the individual portraits could only be partially constructed, owing to the inconsistent nature of nineteenth-century Orange records.[83] While the file of Orangemen is quite large, considering the official estimates of ten thousand members in New Brunswick and Nova Scotia around mid-century, it does not reflect a systematic survey of complete documentary sources. Most notably, only Orangemen from the counties closely associated with this study were included.[84] Nevertheless, it provides a useful lens for sharpening the picture of Orange membership in this period.

For example, an important image of the Orangemen's birthplaces emerged from the file that essentially corroborates the arguments presented above. Virtually all the valid members in the decades around mid-century fell into two large groups: over 62 per cent were born in North America – 59.3 per cent in New Brunswick. Not surprisingly, the Irish-born constituted the other significant group, accounting for 29.1 per cent of the data file. Other Europeans made up the remaining 8.5 per cent; with only one exception, all claimed either English or Scots birth. Owing to the abundant Orange sources of several primary lodges, Saint John and York counties were disproportionately represented in the analysis, with 33.9 per cent and 37.8 per cent of the pool respectively. Still, membership variations between the counties crystallized when variables such as the age of members, initiation dates, and birthplaces were factored into the analysis. Within Saint John County, New Brunswick's busiest port region and primary embarkation point for immigrants, Irish-born members constituted just over half the identified membership compared to roughly one-third native-born. The relative proportions shifted dramatically outside Saint John's environs. The native-born component of members in Carleton, Kings, and Queens counties reached the sixtieth percentile, while York County, partially as a result of

TABLE 2
Birthplace of Orange lodge members according to residence

| | New Brunswick–born | | Other North American–born | | Irish-born | | Other European-born | | Total N |
|---|---|---|---|---|---|---|---|---|---|
| | N | % | N | % | N | % | N | % | |
| Combined counties | 320 | 59.3 | 17 | 3.1 | 157 | 29.1 | 46 | 8.5 | 540 |
| Saint John County | 63 | 34.4 | 4 | 2.2 | 94 | 51.4 | 22 | 12.0 | 183 |
| Kings, Queens, Sunbury counties | 39 | 68.4 | 3 | 5.3 | 12 | 21.1 | 3 | 5.3 | 57 |
| York County | 161 | 78.9 | 2 | 1.0 | 30 | 14.7 | 11 | 5.4 | 204 |
| Carleton County | 57 | 59.4 | 8 | 8.3 | 21 | 21.9 | 10 | 10.4 | 96 |

% = valid percentages

the abundance of documentary information gleaned from Fredericton and several rural hamlets, indicated a native-born membership approximating 80 per cent as well as the pool's proportionately lowest Irish-born component of under 15 per cent. This signifies that communities with the largest immigrant populations relative to the total populations, such as Saint John, reflected the greatest Irish-Protestant membership in the Orange Order (see table 2).

When birthplace is used as the governing variable, a portrait emerges of the Orange Order that suggests revision of the argument that Irish-Protestants accounted for the bulk of British North American membership during the first half of the nineteenth century. While the vast majority of members were either native- or Irish-born, the evidence uncovered other minor categories such as European-born, which included English, Scots, and

TABLE 3
Birthdate and initiation date of Orange lodge members according to birthplace

|  | New Brunswick–born | Other North American–born | Irish-born | Other European-born |
|---|---|---|---|---|
| Birthdate (mean) | 1819.0 | 1805.5 | 1812.8 | 1810.3 |
| Initiation date (mean) | 1850.7 | 1851.0 | 1845.7 | 1844.3 |

German, and North American–born, comprising members from other British North American colonies and the United States. Overall the native and North American groups averaged younger birthdates and joined the organization later than did their Irish-born counterparts (see table 3). The six- and five-year spreads, respectively, indicate that the organization increasingly reflected a native-born membership. This may be attributed to the fact that Irish-Catholic immigrants dramatically outnumbered their Protestant counterparts during the famine holocaust of the late 1840s.

A brief analysis of the foreign-born members' immigration dates reinforces this general argument. The average immigration date of the Irish-born was 1832, while the other combined European groups averaged three years earlier. Given the fact that a majority of the foreign-born members arrived in New Brunswick in the early 1830s, and that a majority of the members joined the organization in the late 1840s, the evidence strongly suggests that the initiates, independent of their ethnic roots, decided to join the organization after living in the province for well over a decade, on the average (see table 4). While the lag time between immigration and initiation can partially be attributed to young Irish-born immigrants who joined the organization when they came of age in New Brunswick, it is clear that most of the Irish-born mem-

TABLE 4
Foreign-born Orangemen: Immigration date and initiation date

| | Immigration date | | Initiation date | |
|---|---|---|---|---|
| | mean | median | mean | median |
| Irish-born | 1832.0 | 1833 | 1845.7 | 1846 |
| Other European–born | 1829.0 | 1830.5 | 1844.3 | 1844 |

bers did not come to the colony with Orange certificate in hand. Therefore, indigenous stimuli and other personal characteristics must be carefully considered in addition to the more obvious ethnic traditions of Orange members. Indeed, other factors such as residence, age, and occupation were as instrumental as lineage in determining the membership of an organization that was subordinating its Irish-Protestant roots to the social and political realities of the colony by mid-century.

Occupation provided the only useful variable for gaining insight into the social standing or general class orientation of Orange members during this period. Dozens of occupational categories encompassed the entire membership, but for the purpose of this analysis, the occupational groups were condensed into five basic categories: farmers; labourers and unskilled; artisans and skilled; merchants and proprietors; and professionals.[85] Of the valid cases, farmers made up 44 per cent of the pool, followed by artisans and skilled at nearly 25 per cent. The categories of labourers/unskilled, merchants/proprietors, and professionals fell within a few percentage points of one another (see table 5).

When the total figures were broken down into counties, a sharper image of the occupational tendencies of Orangemen emerged. York and Carleton counties accounted for the bulk of the farmers, with 63 and 24 per cent of the total respectively, while the coastal county of Saint John housed the majority of both the labourers/unskilled and artisans/skilled categories, with 61 and 63 per cent respectively. The professional category, com-

TABLE 5
New Brunswick Orange lodge members: Occupational groups

|  | Farmer | Labourer/ unskilled | Artisan/ skilled | Merchant/ proprietor | Professional |
|---|---|---|---|---|---|
| Valid number | 247 | 77 | 130 | 48 | 57 |
| Valid precentage | 44.2 | 13.8 | 23.3 | 8.6 | 10.2 |

$N = 559$

prising clergymen, physicians, publishers, barristers, bankers, and government officials, including members of the House of Assembly, was more evenly distributed between the three counties of Saint John, York, and Carleton. This implies that despite the obvious economic orientation of individual counties, such as those in the agricultural hinterland, the Orange Order attracted a cross-section of members from the upper social ranks in each community (see table 6).

Certainly the economic orientation of each county dramatically shaped the organization's local membership, yet as clearly the Orange Order tended to cut across occupational lines in attracting members. This demonstrates that the magnetic attractions of anti-Catholicism and loyalty to the British Crown were often stronger than the countervailing forces that moulded the fraternity according to the class or social standing of its individual members. Thus, the image of a prosperous physician or provincial official sitting down to dine with a hard-scrabble stevedore on an Orange holiday, despite its apparent implausibility, was not an inaccurate one in mid-nineteenth-century New Brunswick.

When the correlation between the identifiable occupations of Orangemen and their birthplaces was explored, several interesting patterns emerged that further illustrated the organization's varied dimensions. For example, the farmers and professionals, whose occupations were vastly dissimilar, had strikingly similar profiles. The overwhelming majority of each group was North American–born, with 77 and 69 per cent respectively, while the

TABLE 6
Occupational categories of Orange lodge members according to residence

|  |  | Farmer | Labourer/ unskilled | Artisan/ skilled | Merchant/ proprietor | Profes-sional | Total |
|---|---|---|---|---|---|---|---|
| Saint | N | 6 | 47 | 82 | 28 | 18 | 181 |
| John | % (c) | 3.3 | 26.0 | 45.3 | 15.5 | 9.9 | |
| County | % (o) | 2.4 | 61.0 | 63.1 | 58.3 | 32.1 | |
| Kings, | | | | | | | |
| Queens, | N | 27 | 4 | 6 | 2 | 8 | 47 |
| Sunbury | % (c) | 57.5 | 8.5 | 12.8 | 4.3 | 17.0 | |
| counties | % (o) | 10.9 | 5.2 | 4.6 | 4.2 | 14.3 | |
| | N | 155 | 22 | 29 | 14 | 7 | 227 |
| York | % (c) | 68.3 | 9.7 | 12.8 | 6.2 | 3.1 | |
| County | % (o) | 62.8 | 28.6 | 22.3 | 29.2 | 12.5 | |
| | N | 59 | 4 | 13 | 4 | 23 | 103 |
| Carleton | % (c) | 57.3 | 3.9 | 12.6 | 3.9 | 22.3 | |
| County | % (o) | 23.9 | 5.2 | 10.0 | 8.3 | 41.1 | |
| Total | N | 247 | 77 | ⸲ 130 | 48 | 56 | |

*%(c) = percentage of county figures (along row)
 %(o) = percentage of occupational figures (down column)

Irish-born component of each occupation made up less than 20 per cent. Comparatively, the balance between North American–born and Irish-born was more closely aligned in the remaining non-professional groups. Undeniably the preponderance of native-born members in the farming communities helps to explain these comparisons; moreover, the data support well-documented nineteenth-century patterns wherein the professional occupations tended to be dominated by native-born North Americans.[86] However, the relatively uniform division within the other three categories, at least statistically, suggests that the Orange Order attracted members from all occupational groups, somewhat independently of the individuals' birthplaces (see table 7).

Another dimension of the Orange profile can be drawn by

TABLE 7
Occupational groups of Orange lodge members according to birthplace

| | New Brunswick–born | | Other North American–born | | Irish-born | | Other European-born | | Total N |
|---|---|---|---|---|---|---|---|---|---|
| | N | % | N | % | N | % | N | % | |
| Farmer | 166 | 74.8 | 5 | 2.3 | 39 | 17.6 | 12 | 5.4 | 222 |
| Labourer/ unskilled | 26 | 40.0 | 3 | 4.6 | 31 | 47.7 | 5 | 7.7 | 65 |
| Artisan/ skilled | 56 | 47.1 | 4 | 3.4 | 45 | 37.8 | 14 | 11.8 | 119 |
| Merchant/ proprietor | 17 | 37.8 | 2 | 4.4 | 20 | 44.4 | 6 | 13.3 | 45 |
| Professional | 28 | 66.7 | 1 | 2.4 | 7 | 16.7 | 6 | 14.3 | 42 |

% = valid percentage

using the occupations as a fixed variable and checking to find if there were significant variations between the groups as to the members' ages and initiation dates. The resulting picture exposed two compelling points: first, the average age of members did not differ significantly according to occupation, with the exception of the merchant and professional categories, both of which were relatively small compared to the larger survey. This means that the older members were well-established, propertied, and monied; they held positions of responsibility in their communities; they haunted the corridors of power in Fredericton; and they owned the merchant establishments of Saint John. Second, when the initiation dates are scrutinized the farmers constituted the most recent initiates with an average of 1851, while the artisan/skilled, merchant/proprietor, and professional groups all averaged within one year. The most frequent date of initiation for the groups was remarkably close – indeed three of the cate-

TABLE 8
Birthdate and initiation date of Orange lodge members according to occupational
groups (mean/mode)

|  |  | Farmer | Labourer/ unskilled | Artisan/ skilled | Merchant/ proprietor | Profes- sional |
|---|---|---|---|---|---|---|
| Birthdate |  |  |  |  |  |  |
|  | N | 242 | 69 | 119 | 45 | 37 |
|  | Mean | 1819 | 1818 | 1817 | 1811 | 1807 |
|  | Mode | 1830 | 1811 | 1821 | 1811 | 1801 |
| Initiation date |  |  |  |  |  |  |
|  | N | 136 | 36 | 42 | 15 | 10 |
|  | Mean | 1851 | 1849 | 1845.5 | 1844 | 1845 |
|  | Mode | 1848 | 1848 | 1848 | 1838 | 1842 |

gories shared 1848 (see table 8). In sum, the lack of dramatic variations, at least from this survey, reinforces the argument that the Orange Order was appealing to all occupational groups throughout the period. The fact that younger members and most recent initiates tended to be farmers essentially reflected the growth of the institution in the northern reaches of the Saint John River Valley, as well as the rich evidence gleaned from some of the primary lodges in the agricultural parishes of York County. Thus, even when the ages of members and initiation dates are considered, the Orange Order transcended the occupational and social divides of mid-nineteenth-century New Brunswick.

Another fruitful angle for gaining a composite image of Orangemen is to use the primary lodge as the governing variable. The list yielded at least one active member in each of eighty-five primary lodges scattered throughout the six represented counties. When known residences were compared to known lodge affiliation, identified Orangemen were clearly linked to seventy-two primary lodges. Of these Saint John County housed the greatest number with 22, followed by Queens and Carleton with 13 apiece, York with 12, Kings with 9, and Sunbury with 3. However, for the purposes of this analysis, and in the interest of assessing information that is statistically significant, only those

TABLE 9
Primary lodge membership according to birthplace (with 5 or more valid members)

| Primary lodge number | New Brunswick–born | Other North American–born | Irish-born | Other European-born | Total valid |
|---|---|---|---|---|---|
| 1 | 3 | | 7 | 2 | 12 |
| 2 | 12 | 1 | 33 | 10 | 56 |
| 3 | 2 | | 6 | 2 | 10 |
| 6 | 3 | | 3 | | 6 |
| 7 | 1 | | 4 | 1 | 6 |
| 9 | 6 | | | | 6 |
| 11 | 4 | | 2 | | 6 |
| 13 | 1 | | 5 | | 6 |
| 16 | 3 | | 2 | | 5 |
| 20 | 2 | | 2 | 1 | 5 |
| 21 | 5 | 3 | 16 | 4 | 28 |
| 34 | 4 | 1 | 9 | 1 | 15 |
| 38 | 2 | 2 | | 1 | 5 |
| 59 | 8 | | | 2 | 10 |
| 61 | 6 | | 2 | 2 | 10 |
| 71 | 49 | | 3 | | 52 |
| 83 | 60 | 1 | 12 | 1 | 74 |

primary lodges that included at least five members with valid personal information are assessed.

When the members' birthplaces were assigned the role of governing variable, seventeen primary lodges produced enough members with the appropriate information. All but one indicated a cross-section of birthplaces, including New Brunswick, and at least one from a North American colony or state, Ireland, or other European country. Within this grouping all but three included members from each of the two largest clusters: the New Brunswick– and Irish-born. Two of those, no. 38 and no. 59, were located in Woodstock (Carleton County) and formed after 1846, while the other, no. 9 in Hampton Parish (Kings County), had six validated native-born members alone (see table 9). This strongly suggests that most primary lodges were not homogeneous, at

TABLE 10
Primary lodge membership according to occupational groups (with 5 or more valid members)

| Primary lodge number | Farmer | Labourer/ unskilled | Artisan/ skilled | Merchant/ proprietor | Profes- sional | Total valid |
|---|---|---|---|---|---|---|
| 1 | 1 | 1 | 7 | 2 | | 11 |
| 2 | | 18 | 24 | 8 | 4 | 54 |
| 3 | | 3 | 5 | 1 | | 9 |
| 6 | | 2 | 3 | 1 | 2 | 8 |
| 7 | | 1 | 6 | | | 7 |
| 9 | 4 | | 1 | | | 5 |
| 11 | | 2 | 3 | | 1 | 6 |
| 13 | | 1 | 3 | 1 | 1 | 6 |
| 21 | 2 | 7 | 9 | 2 | 1 | 21 |
| 34 | 11 | | 2 | | 2 | 15 |
| 38 | | 1 | 2 | 1 | 1 | 5 |
| 59 | 5 | | 3 | 1 | | 9 |
| 61 | 9 | 1 | | | | 10 |
| 71 | 52 | 6 | 6 | 2 | | 66 |
| 83 | 69 | 6 | 7 | 3 | | 85 |

least when the members' birthplaces are considered. Of course native-born members could have had Irish-Protestant roots, and without a doubt many did. Still the evidence from this file offers a clear indication that the ideological tenets of the Orange Order fashioned powerful bonds between potentially disparate individuals – in this case, groups with different birthplaces and/or ethnic backgrounds.

These essential points receive reinforcement when similar computations are performed, this time with the governing variable being the members' occupations. Of the fifteen primary lodges with five or more members with a confirmed occupation, none favoured a single occupational group. Seven had members from four of the categories, while four had members in three. One lodge, Portland's Wellington no. 21, covered all the occupational categories, including two from farming communities and one located in Portland (see table 10). Thus, a wide range of employment could be found in most primary lodges, a fact that undermines perceptions that the fraternal organization at the local level encouraged occupational or social homogeneity. Once again, Orange members in mid-century crossed powerful class and cultural boundaries to pursue more compelling interests.

Finally, microstudies of those primary lodges with the greatest frequencies in the pool cast the Orange portrait into even sharper relief. Four excellent candidates, with extraordinary numbers of valid names, emerged as a result of relatively complete membership rolls, accounting records, and correspondence files. Significantly, these lodges represented two of the regions under focus in this book: the urban environs of Saint John, including Eldon no. 2 and Portland's Wellington no. 21; and the predominantly agrarian York County parishes of Longs Creek no. 71 and Prince William no. 83.[87] Longs Creek and Prince William Lodges, both chartered at the height of Orange expansion in 1848, were located on the southern bank of the Saint John River, due west of Fredericton approximately sixteen and nineteen miles respectively. Eldon Lodge, New Brunswick's second primary institution when it was formed in 1833, held meetings in Saint John's Hibernian Hotel during the 1840s. Wellington Lodge, granted a charter in 1844, used a variety of locations in Portland during the decades around mid-century.

The two rural lodges of Longs Creek and Prince William exhibited, not surprisingly, an overwhelmingly rural population of farmers – approximately 80 per cent of the sample in both cases. Importantly, both also attracted significant numbers of men from other occupations, including general labourers, artisans, and a handful of merchants, all probably in numbers proportionate to the general population. Notable was the lack of professionals in both organizations, which can partially be explained by the fact that barristers, government officials, doctors, and publishers would not be residing in the agrarian communities, at least in significant numbers. The members of both were overwhelmingly New Brunswick–born; for example, Longs Creek reached well into the ninetieth percentile. Irish-born individuals accounted for virtually all the others in both cases, suggesting that the lodges

TABLE 11
Primary lodges nos. 2, 21, 71, 83 according to birthplace and
occupation of members

| | Eldon no. 2 | | Wellington no. 21 | | Longs Creek no. 71 | | Prince William no. 83 | |
|---|---|---|---|---|---|---|---|---|
| | N | % | N | % | N | % | N | % |
| BIRTHPLACE | | | | | | | | |
| New Brunswick–born | 12 | 21.4 | 5 | 17.9 | 49 | 94.2 | 60 | 81.1 |
| Other North American–born | 1 | 1.8 | 3 | 10.7 | | | 1 | 1.4 |
| Irish-born | 33 | 58.9 | 16 | 57.1 | 3 | 5.8 | 12 | 16.2 |
| Other European-born | 10 | 17.9 | 4 | 14.3 | | | 1 | 1.4 |
| OCCUPATION | | | | | | | | |
| Farmer | | | 2 | 9.5 | 52 | 78.8 | 69 | 81.2 |
| Labourer/ unskilled | 18 | 33.3 | 7 | 33.3 | 6 | 9.1 | 6 | 7.1 |
| Artisan/skilled | 24 | 44.4 | 9 | 42.9 | 6 | 9.1 | 7 | 8.2 |
| Merchant/ proprietor | 8 | 14.8 | 2 | 9.5 | 2 | 3.0 | 3 | 3.5 |
| Professional | 4 | 7.4 | 1 | 4.8 | | | | |

% = valid percentage

of the rural hamlets of Prince William and Longs Creek were
more homogenous, on average, than many of their provincial
counterparts (see table 11).

Further research indicated that the two lodges had a much
younger membership than the provincial average, with the majority taking initiation oaths in the year following the granting of
institutional charters (1848). Thus, the microstudy of two well-
documented rural lodges produced an image of members who
were relatively young, agriculturally oriented, and mostly native-

born. This profile attested to the fact that these lodges were in rural communities, essentially removed from the major immigration routes of nineteenth-century New Brunswick, and that they were created relatively late in the period.

The remaining lodges, Eldon and Wellington, cast a different image of Orangeism's character. The occupational groups tended to be more evenly balanced in both lodges, with most members holding jobs in either the labourer/unskilled category, with approximately one-third in each, or the artisan/skilled category, with 43 and 44 per cent respectively. Each attracted its share of merchants and élites; Eldon's four members from the professions made a notably large group compared to the provincial standards established in this analysis. This finding reinforces the notion of variety in the ranks of the Loyal Orange Order. In Saint John and Portland barristers and assemblymen, august members of colonial society, gathered on 12 July with draymen and stevedores to toast Queen Victoria, their long-dead hero King William, and the Glorious Revolution.

Compared to the aforementioned rural lodges, Eldon and Wellington provided a much sharper image of a vibrant, demographic dynamic in nineteenth-century New Brunswick. As a testament to general immigration patterns, the Irish-born population fell just short of the sixtieth percentile; members from Scotland and England also figured predominantly in the organizations, accounting for between 14 and 18 per cent of each. Almost one-fifth were New Brunswick–born, a figure that stands in stark contrast to the corresponding percentages of Longs Creek and Prince William. When all the variables are considered, the more established, urban lodges of New Brunswick lent more credence to the stereotypical image that tangible and powerful transatlantic roots governed the colonial Orange Order.

Lastly, the urban lodges displayed markedly different demographic characteristics from their rural counterparts. Eldon's members averaged a birth date of 1811, old by provincial standards, while Wellington's members were on average seven years younger. The greatest years of growth, according to the membership rolls, were 1842 and 1844 respectively; the average initiation date was 1842 for the former, while the latter's was 1851. The preceding figures can be explained largely by the fact that while Eldon's roll books were most complete for the 1840s, Wellington's records carried on with abundant information well into the 1860s. In sum, the microstudies indicate that New Brunswick's urban lodges tended to be more ethnically, demographically, and occupationally diverse. Sitting astride the busy immigration roots, they traced a more direct lineage to the parent organization across the Atlantic.

Two fairly clear portraits, each of different scale, emerged from this quantitative analysis of New Brunswick's Orangemen. On the one hand, a microanalysis and comparison of the various primary lodges exposed a diverse membership. A detailed assessment of individual variables, including birthplaces, years of birth, initiation dates, and occupations generated the primary colours that were then applied to this empirical canvas. Ultimately, the data suggest that the lodges that fanned out along the Saint John River system in the mid-nineteenth century left demographic evidence as distinct as fingerprints.[88] The economies and settlement patterns of local communities shaped the character of the Orange lodges as surely as did the members' ideologies and political persuasions.

Yet a second stunning image of the Orange Order emerged when the evidence was viewed on a larger, provincial scale. The fraternal organization, when judged by its membership patterns, grew and thrived in New Brunswick primarily fuelled by indigenous stimuli. Clearly the tenets of anti-Catholicism and loyalty to Britain provided an essential ideological glue for its members; however, powerful factors were also at work breaking down the normally unsurmountable barriers created by economic class, ethnicity, and social standing in an essentially hierarchical society.[89] Forged by the hands of fervent Protestants, both native- and foreign-born, shaped by an unswerving belief in the hegemony of British laws and institutions, and cemented by an almost mystical sense of righteousness, New Brunswick's Orange lodges provided an elaborate social network in the years around mid-century. These bonds held, with various degrees of intensity, the

1150 Orangemen who provided the grist for this quantitative analysis. They helped to explain the improbable image of men from different backgrounds and social standings coming together to sup, to raise a glass, to march with banners and weapons, and periodically to clash with the Irish-Catholic enemy. Collectively, they lent their shoulders to the task of Orange development in the years around mid-century.

The Orange Order undeniably enjoyed unprecedented growth in the 1840s, yet it did so under a constant barrage by an aggressive group of opponents. Prominent administrators and civil servants spearheaded the anti-Orange campaign, including Attorney General Lemuel Allen Wilmot, Supreme Court Justices George F. Street and James Carter, and Lieutenant-Governors Colebrooke and Head. Some Protestant clerics also provided a countervailing force, most notably the fervent Saint John minister Ezekial MacLeod of the Free Will Baptists, who threatened his parishioners with excommunication if they deigned to join the fraternity.[90] An interpretation that the Orange Order symbolized an 'evil tree,' successfully transplanted to New Brunswick and now spreading its 'moral pollution' throughout the once peaceful province, permeated the opposition's rhetoric.[91] Although these detractors generally attributed the violent excesses of Orangeism to traditional Irish grievances, they also recognized the organization's appeal to native-born Protestants who feared Irish-Catholics. Most important, they recognized the symbiotic relationship between the institution's maturation and the proliferation of social violence during the 1840s. By tracing the order's chronological growth, the critics arrived at antithetical conclusions to Orange perceptions. Whereas Orangemen characterized the organization as fundamentally reactive or defensive, cultivated mainly by the riots with Irish-Catholics, their opponents insisted that they contributed to or caused the violence by their belligerent rhetoric and annual processions. To these officials, the Orange Order represented a misguided vigilante group bent on 'scandalizing' and taunting hapless Irish-Catholics into armed confrontations.[92]

Though neither as prolific nor as zealous as their counterparts, some newspaper editors also added voice to the anti-Orange chorus. Two journalists in particular actively combated the Orange messages that emanated from the *Loyalist, Weekly Chronicle,* and *Carleton Sentinel*: George Fenety in the *Saint John Morning News* and James Hogg in the *New Brunswick Reporter*. Hogg bluntly stated in his premier issues that his newspaper would not participate in religious animosities.[93] Fenety mounted a more frontal assault on the violence between Orangemen and Catholics: 'Then they [Orangemen] bring their lodges to St. John. The *thistle* is transplanted from the beautiful vales of Erin, and made to take root on our forest shore, to destroy by its rankling effects, the blossoms of the field.'[94] A fairly even-handed condemnation of Catholics and Orangemen alike, however, inevitably tempered anti-Orange rhetoric. Impassioned pro-Orange editors never questioned the necessity of the Orange crusade; detractors lamented the belligerence of *both* parties.

This pattern remained consistent until the Irish-Catholic community grew sufficient to support its own newspaper. The *True Liberator*, a journal that lasted briefly in the late 1840s, championed the Catholic cause with an enthusiasm that, except for an absence of spurious rhetoric, matched the pro-Orange newspapers.[95] Timothy Warren Anglin, a Catholic Irishman who emigrated to Saint John in 1849, filled the void left after the *True Liberator*'s demise. Anglin's *Freeman* ran successfully for years, and while it applauded Catholic civil rights, it too fell short of the scathing propagandizing of such journals as the *Loyalist*. Anglin consistently called for Irish-Catholics to abstain from violence. Tolerance, he argued, remained the most effective antidote for Orange behaviour.[96] Taken collectively, therefore, journals critical of the Orange Order for the most part eschewed the vehement and scurrilous discourse of their counterparts.

Of all the critics aligned against the fraternity, those in the provincial legislature enjoyed the most tangible successes. Most assuredly, they acted well within the parameters of official British denunciation of the Orange Order. For twenty-five years, from 1850 to 1875, a coalition of Protestants and a few Catholic legislators blocked the passage of an Orange incorporation bill.[97]

The Orange debate traced its roots, however, to the 1848 session when Carleton County petitioned the province for assistance in meeting its military and judicial expenses following the 1847 disturbance. Legislators ultimately awarded the county a cash settlement, but more important, the February and March hearings signalled the advent of public dialogue about the Orange Order's worthiness. Legislators aligned into camps on either side of the issue. Although pro-Orange forces presented impassioned arguments, the session closed with a general condemnation of the Orange society and a resolution to discourage its further growth in the colony. Though Orangemen suffered a setback in this legislative test case of their legitimacy, influential members resolved to reformulate the issue.[98]

Two years later Orange forces brought the subject before the House of Assembly, this time in the form of an incorporation bill. Superficially, the bill was an innocuous document that articulated the financial benefits that an incorporated Orange society might enjoy.[99] Debate over the bill, however, focused entirely on the justification of the Orange Order. In effect the Orange Order stood in the docket, on trial for its very existence. Orangemen from across the province bombarded the legislature with petitions in support of the bill. Over 6000 signatures, collected on twenty-three documents, attested to extensive support in those counties with the greatest stake in Orangeism: Saint John, York, Carleton, Kings, and Queens. Even official acceptance of the petitions drew heavy fire from Orange critics who were determined to block the bill's passage at any cost.[100]

The major debate over Orangeism, which ran for three days in March and April, sparked a keen interest among New Brunswickers. Even heavy snowstorms did not deter the crowds. Observers jammed the galleries; tardy visitors gathered on the legislature's steps and eagerly waited for news of the bill's progress. Though the almost maniacal concern over the Orange question drew the occasional sarcastic barb from pundits who found the debate a colossal waste of time, New Brunswickers from all stations in life found themselves captivated.[101] After either directly or vicariously experiencing the series of wrenching clashes between Orangemen and Irish-Catholics in the last five years, New Brunswick's citizenry deemed the moment ripe for a vote of confidence on the Orange issue.

The House quickly divided along lines roughly analogous to those of two years earlier. Four legislators emerged as the champions of Orangeism. John Earle, member from Queens County and Grand Master of New Brunswick's Orange Order, coordinated the petition drive. Another lodge master, Charles Connell from Carleton County, argued eloquently throughout the debates. James Taylor from York and Barzilla Ansley from Saint John, both of whom admitted to no official Orange connections, consistently acted as spokesmen for Protestant rights. Debate focused on three issues. First, Orange forces insisted – with justification – that recent legislation incorporating the Roman Catholic bishop and a Masonic lodge in Saint John set a precedent that should be followed for the Orange Order.[102] When the consensus argument failed to persuade the moderates, Orange supporters concentrated on the bill's financial implications. This also proved fruitless. Then, striking to the heart of the matter, they focused on the vigilante rationale for Orangeism. In the absence of a Protestant bulwark, they maintained, Irish-Catholics would soon introduce an age of social chaos and political anarchy.[103] This avenue of attack, clearly designed for its emotional appeal, drew the most reproach. The Orange Order's bid for legitimacy temporarily foundered in the face of a counter-attack by moderates who called for religious and ethnic tolerance.

Orange opponents came to the battle well armed. Galvanized by lengthy speeches from Attorney General Wilmot and James Brown from Charlotte County, backed by English parliamentary transcripts and recommendations from the Home Office to discourage Orangeism, and fortified by the 1836 pledge from the Duke of Cumberland to dissolve the Orange Order, New Brunswick's moderate legislators hammered at three themes. If the Orange Order considered itself a 'loyal' organization, they queried, then why did it repeatedly ignore directives from the monarchy and colonial representatives to dissolve? Moreover, they accused Orangemen of making Irish-Catholics scapegoats for the colony's economic and social ills. The blame for the bloody confrontations of the 1840s, they reasoned, rested at least partially on the shoulders of the belligerent Orange society. Finally, they accused Orangemen of codifying prejudicial behaviour; an exclusively Protestant fraternity would surely serve as a perennial irritant to the disfranchised.[104]

The Orange opponents effectively killed the bill by postponing further debate. Passage failed because the Orange Order suffered negative publicity after the riots, and because proponents inadequately answered the searching questions posed by their opponents.[105] But perhaps most important, the Orange Order lost its initial attempt to incorporate because it suffered from a relatively narrow geographical base. Supportive petitions came from only five counties; moreover, the most adamant legislative proponents represented those same regions. If the Orange Order wished to win its bid for incorporation, it would have to extend its membership throughout the province.

New Brunswick's Orangemen grasped the lessons of 1850, despite the fact that it would take twenty-five years to enact the incorporation bill. The number of petitions trebled in 1851, and included respondents from Sunbury County for the first time. Orangemen subsequently introduced the bill on eleven occasions, triggering a variety of responses. Often it faced postponement, as in 1850, twice legislators blocked it from committee, and once in 1859 they categorically refused to consider it.[106] Yet Orangemen persisted. The emotionally charged separate-schools issue of 1871 finally galvanized Protestants to push the bill through the House of Assembly. Without a doubt Canada's achievement of dominion status four years earlier helped New Brunswick's Orangemen to distance themselves further from British disapprobation. Thus, after a quarter of a century, Orangeism basked in the sunshine of legal recognition. Yet even in the final phases of passage, the bill continued to run into vehement criticism. The Legislative Council grudgingly approved the legislation but labelled the ultra-Protestant organization both 'unnecessary and undesirable.'[107]

The Orange Incorporation Bill stood as an eloquent testimonial to the ascendancy of militant Protestantism in New Brunswick. Orangeism thrived not because of its Irish roots, but because it found fertile pasturage for growth among the descendants of Loyalists and Protestant immigrants. New Brunswick's Orange Order shaped, and in turn found itself moulded by, provincial factors. It led the nativist campaign against Irish-Catholic immigrants; it championed Protestant ascendancy and tirelessly advocated the maintenance of a British connection. But most important, the Orange Order adopted vigilante tactics to rid the colony of the 'uncivilized and lawless' Irish-Catholics whom it perceived to be a dire threat.

Ironically, by their own behaviour Orangemen shattered the peace and jumbled the order they sought. The rapid growth of the organization in the 1840s, and the increasingly belligerent actions of its members, encouraged equally aggressive Catholics to reciprocate. In a classic vicious circle, Orangeism functioned not as the solution to social discord, but as an instrumental part of it. The symbiosis of the fraternity's meteoric rise and the influx of destitute Irish-Catholics engendered several major riots from 1845 to 1849. In Woodstock, Fredericton, Saint John, and Portland, disturbances between Orangemen and Catholic immigrants would be attributed, at least partially, to the legacy of institutionalized nativism.

# PART THREE: THE RIOTS

# 5

# The hinterland:
# The Woodstock riot of 1847

Silent and rotted, scorched by the sun and ravaged by almost a century and a half of seasons, Loyal Orange hall no. 38 sits prominently on a gentle slope in Woodstock, New Brunswick. Its foundation is set symbolically on the site of the legendary – at least according to local mythology – Orange-Green disturbance of 1847. It is a sullen reminder of tensions between native-born Protestants and Irish-Catholics, a testament to the ascendancy of the Orange Order as both a fraternal entity and as an extra-legal arm of community magistracy and law enforcement in a hinterland community.

The 1847 riot at Woodstock, an agricultural and lumbering centre, fits well into patterns of social violence and the rise of the Orange Order in New Brunswick as a vehicle of institutionalized nativism. Like most colonial communities, Woodstock relied on its magistrates, sheriff, and constables for maintaining law and order. But the turmoil of the 1840s led many residents to question the effectiveness of their duly appointed protectors. As the Irish-Catholic population increased and became identified with the turbulent lumbering community, Protestants began to seek alternative measures to ensure peace. For example, in December 1846 justices worried about maintaining order, specifically during the trial of four men charged with felonies, appealed to the provincial attorney general for permission to expedite matters. Charles Peters denied the request, but the episode illustrated the point that the justices were convinced that public order should be maintained at all costs.[1] Although no conclusive evidence suggested that a single ethnic group predominated among lumbermen, many Protestants believed that Irish-Catholic immigrants instigated most of the county's violence.[2] Vigilantism appeared to be the most attractive solution, and the Loyal Orange Order duly responded to the call in September 1846 when it located its initial Carleton County lodge at Woodstock.[3] Less than a year later, during the organization's first public procession, and when Irish-Catholic famine immigration reached its apex, the community experienced a violent ethnic riot.

The Orange Order grew dramatically as it capitalized on Protestant fears of the increasingly visible Irish-Catholic community. The Spring of 1847 brought tensions between Woodstock's ethnic groups to a fever pitch, when on 21 April several Catholics molested a prominent Orangeman following his public pronouncement that the organization had scheduled a procession for the Glorious Twelfth. The incident touched off a flurry of letters to the provincial government petitioning for additional troops. Several magistrates correctly pinpointed the problem when they argued that the difficulties grew out of 'the rancorous feeling at present unhappily created, and rapidly increasing and extending between the Roman Catholic portion of Her Majesty's subjects and the Orangemen organized in this place.' Most of the letters, however, evinced a decidedly anti-Catholic tone. In fact, many of Woodstock's officials openly sympathized with Orange principles, and several had already taken the sacred oath of initiation.[4]

A fracas in a public house later in May further illustrated the growing rift between religious parties. Protestant and Orange requests for troop reinforcements intensified. Lieutenant-Governor Colebrooke, preferring to deal directly with Woodstock Sheriff John Winslow, emphatically rejected the petitions. Throwing the burden of defence back on the community, he recommended that the sheriff call a special session of magistrates to defuse the issue. Winslow followed the instructions, but the peevish justices promptly cancelled the meeting because Colebrooke had failed to contact them personally. The sheriff, who believed that the magistrates sympathized with the Orange Order, deduced that they did not want to risk interfering with the procession scheduled for the Twelfth.[5]

The incident illuminated Woodstock's deep-seated problems. Magistrates sworn to uphold justice supported Orangeism, the Fredericton government refused to intervene in community affairs, and the sheriff found himself caught in the middle.[6] While he would eventually empathize with the Orange Order and labour tirelessly to repress Irish-Catholics, Winslow exhibited frustration with official inactivity prior to the riot. In a bitter condemnation of the local justices he observed: 'I am of opinion that if the Magistrates in Sessions had earnestly and unanimously recommended both parties to desist from preparations for organizations on the 12th July – which are said to be going on – it would have had the desired effect ... and maybe have defeated attempts of ambitious persons who while professing a desire to assist the government would be destroying every thing in their way and would blame the Governor for not sending troops here.'[7] As of the Twelfth's eve, the warnings of a religious collision remained unheeded. The Orange Order still planned a massive procession, Irish-Catholics plotted a counter-demonstration, and Colebrooke placed the onus for keeping the peace on the shoulders of men who could not, or would not, attempt to defuse the powder keg.

As anticipated, Woodstock filled with people on the weekend before 12 July. Orangemen arrived from Carleton County and central sections of New Brunswick to celebrate with their Woodstock brethren. Lumbermen from the hinterland came to observe or to participate in the festivities. And finally Irish-Catholics, some reportedly from the United States and bordering counties, gathered to assemble a procession of their own.[8] Both sides came heavily armed, and neither bothered to hide its weapons. On the evening of 11 July four Catholic leaders met with the local priest, who warned them of the dangers if they continued their plans for a counter-demonstration. Apparently he argued persuasively, for the men left with a promise to cancel the rally. But the wheels of social conflict had been set in motion, and the efforts of a few individuals would be insufficient to alter its course.[9]

The Twelfth dawned bright and warm, and brought with it a confirmation that tensions had not abated. Armed men patrolled Woodstock's streets by 9:00, and by the time Orangemen emerged from their lodge an hour later, officials feared that a riot would erupt.[10] The Orange plans, ostensibly made to avoid a conflict in Woodstock, included a march to nearby Jacksontown for a sermon at the Baptist Church.[11] The approximately 200 to 300 Orangemen who assembled in front of the lodge quickly fell into military-styled ranks for the three-mile walk. Most carried either muskets or pistols.[12] Irish-Catholics gave the Orangemen a wide berth as they left Woodstock, yet they continued to muster their forces throughout the morning.

With the community temporarily devoid of Orangemen, the Catholics staged a procession of their own. They numbered roughly the same as their foe, and carried a variety of weapons that included muskets, pitchforks, scythes, axes, and wooden bludgeons.[13] After parading in the streets for a few minutes, they proceeded north of 'The Creek' for a half-mile and positioned themselves alongside the road to await the Orangemen's return. A team of five watchful magistrates accompanied the Irish-Catholics, including three Orange leaders: Carleton County's provincial legislator Charles Connell, George W. Cleary, and R.S. Demill. In addition, Sheriff Winslow brought a sixteen-man detachment of British garrison troops under the command of Lt. Wickham. Scores of curious townspeople also gathered along the road, anxious to witness the unfolding drama.[14] With the troops present for moral support, the magistrates informed the Catholics that it was illegal to carry arms and parade in public. Leaders in the Irish crowd quickly pointed out that the Orangemen, similarly armed, had been allowed to continue their procession unhampered. Given the proclivities of the magistrates, the Catholics' complaint of a double standard appeared justified. After much haggling, the authorities persuaded the crowd to retreat to Woodstock on the condition that the Orangemen would be prohibited from carrying arms and marching in ranks on their return from Jacksontown.[15]

After the crowd had dispersed, the delegation of magistrates proceeded to Jacksontown to inform the Orangemen. Orange leaders reluctantly agreed to cooperate, but only after devising a plan to retain their weapons. They would not 'march' back to Woodstock, but they would 'walk' in file. Their arms would not be carried, but would be placed in a wagon that would trail the procession.[16] The Orangemen, with the blessing of brethren magistrates, cleverly circumvented the spirit of the compromise while technically adhering to its tenets.

The Irish-Catholics, by contrast, ultimately chose to ignore the agreement. After an hour of milling and parading in Woodstock, they reconvened on the outskirts of town. With a sharp slope at their backs, they positioned themselves in a line parallel to and about fifty yards from the road to Jacksontown. Thus ensconced, they waited for the Orangemen's return. In open defiance of their bargain with the magistrates, the Irish-Catholics risked an official rebuke. It came moments after the authorities had arrived. One of the justices read the Riot Act, and the crowd was given the prescribed hour to disperse.[17] As a precaution, Lt. Wickham stationed his troops two hundred yards up the road in the direction of Jacksontown.

The troops successfully intercepted the returning Orangemen. Discovering the wagon filled with weapons, they instructed the magistrates to disband the procession. The Orangemen received the Riot Act, but after spying the Irishmen who were still entrenched along the road, they asked the magistrates for permission to arm themselves. After the justices denied the request, the Orangemen decided unanimously to continue their procession. Much as the Irish-Catholics had done hours earlier, the Orange brethren willingly prepared to meet their foe in battle.[18]

The great Woodstock riot thus commenced with both crowds acting in open defiance of the law. The Orangemen marched from the interception point with the troops until they were directly in front of the Catholics on the hill. Lt. Wickham, instead of positioning his detachment between the belligerent parties, remained at a right angle with the road at the rear of the Orange procession. When the Orangemen reached the street where their lodge was located, the Irish-Catholics purportedly opened fire. Whether or not the opening salvo came as a single shot or a volley remains unclear; regardless, it sufficiently provoked the expectant Orangemen. Quickly arming themselves from the wagon, they returned the fire and mounted an assault on the Irishmen's positions.[19]

Chaos broke out among the Catholics as soon as the Orangemen charged. According to traditional accounts, they broke ranks and desperately tried to escape. Orange leaders pursued their foe on horseback, bayoneting several and rounding up dozens for arrest. Scores of Catholics disappeared into the woods north of Woodstock, while some of their companions surfaced days later in Houlton. Still others fled across a log-jam on the Meduxnekeag River. Acting in concert, the British troops, civilian authorities, and Orangemen captured dozens of Irish-Catholics near the scene of the riot. While the crowds traded hundreds of shots, the soldiers abstained from firing their weapons and thus avoided triggering a military-civilian confrontation.[20]

By late afternoon, the rioting lingered only in sporadic skirmishes. Authorities placed captured Irish-Catholics under guard in Woodstock. Each crowd quickly removed its dead and wounded, thereby precluding an accurate assessment of casualties.[21] The handful of wounded in the initial reports later gave way to accounts of scores of serious injuries and up to ten killed.[22] While every account of the riot disagreed on casualty figures, no one questioned the fact that gunshot and stab wounds abounded. Moreover, observers unanimously agreed that the Irish-Catholics suffered most of the bloodshed and had the only confirmed dead.[23]

The inequitable casualty rates illustrated one of the many deficiencies in the available accounts of the Woodstock riot. A close inspection of the documents indicated the following: except for one brief eyewitness report in the *Morning News*, a Saint John newspaper, Orangemen or Protestants sympathetic to the Orange cause produced all of them. John Connell and several magistrates claimed Orange membership at the time of the riot. John Baird, John Dibblee, and Sheriff Winslow, while not being members, obviously sympathized with the fraternity's tenets and strongly disapproved of Irish-Catholic settlement in the Woodstock area.[24] The most extensive narratives available to the public appeared in the provincial Orange organ, the *Loyalist*, and in the pro-Orange *Woodstock Telegraph*. And finally, while Lieutenant-Governor Colebrooke attempted to produce a balanced assessment of the riot, his information came almost exclusively from the above-named sources.[25]

The aphorism that only victors write history applied well to the Woodstock riot. While much of the evidence is useful and informative, a careful analysis of the riot reveals the dubious nature of some of the pro-Orange accounts. They agree upon the following: both sides were roughly equal, the Irish-Catholics were armed before the riot and strategically occupied a high ground, and the Orangemen were unarmed and strung out in file only fifty yards in front of their enemy. But these descriptions raise nagging questions, especially from a technical standpoint. How did the Orangemen escape serious injury after the opening salvo, run back to the wagon, arm themselves, and then proceed to rout handily the Catholics? From a tactical point of view, this account stretches the limits of credibility. Yet what happened? Did the Irish-Catholics miss? Were they poor shots? Probably not, for some served as riflemen in the Woodstock militia unit, including a sergeant and several marksmen.[26] In addition, the Orangemen were fifty yards away, close enough for the Catholics to do great damage even without great accuracy. In order to wrest an unequivocal victory from such a unpropitious beginning, the Orangemen needed a phenomenal amount of luck – or different circumstances. Perhaps they were armed at the riot's outset. They may even have fired the first shots. At any rate, they clearly enjoyed superior weapons.[27] Given their overwhelmingly pro-Orange bias, narratives of the Woodstock riot should be approached with scepticism.

News of the Woodstock riot sent shock waves across the province. Rumours proliferated concerning the nature of Woodstock's problems and what transpired during the disturbance. Colonial newspapers evoked hyperbolic and centuries-old images of 'French and Indian' insurrection.[28] But clearly those closest to the epicentre found themselves galvanized and compelled to respond. Woodstock authorities buttressed the constabulary and steeled themselves for Irish-Catholic reprisals. On the evening of 12 July John Dibblee, a pro-Orange magistrate and major in the local militia, distributed fifty rifles and a keg of ammunition to Protestant residents. Sheriff Winslow swore in dozens of special constables, and two days later Dibblee released one hundred more rifles to outfit the growing constabulary. Most of these arms passed into the hands of Orangemen who neglected to return them. Clearly, the boundary between Orangemen and Protestants blurred and disappeared in an effort to prevent a possible Irish-Catholic offensive.[29]

Guarding the swelling numbers of prisoners also proved to be a logistical problem. The magistrates asked Colebrooke to reinforce the military detachment to discourage Irish-Catholics from trying to liberate their compatriots. Colebrooke posted twenty-one additional soldiers to Woodstock on 14 July with instructions that their presence should be entirely symbolic. The Lieutenant-Governor and his counsellors prudently wanted to avoid a direct confrontation between British regulars and Catholic settlers. The troops were to be used only if all other methods of preserving the peace failed. Woodstock received instructions to prevent future riots, guard the prisoners and ensure those accused of a judicious and pacific trial. Colebrooke's soldiers followed his orders to the letter; after three months of inactivity, they returned to their Fredericton base on 19 October.[30]

Woodstock's authorities, responding to Colebrooke's wishes, relied on the pool of local Protestants for support. They faced formidable problems. The Carleton County jail, destroyed by a fire in 1845, still awaited replacement.[31] The sheriff commandeered the top floor of the court-house in Upper Woodstock to hold the Catholic prisoners. His constabulary, now swollen to 112 heavily armed Protestants, blanketed the region hunting for suspects in the days following the riot. The repressive search among only Catholic households yielded immediate results. On 14 July officials counted sixty-six prisoners crammed into their temporary cells. Most had been arrested in the riot's aftermath on intelligence supplied by Orange participants. Seven more joined their hapless compatriots two days later. As the number of prisoners grew, so did the fear among Protestants that free Catholics would mount an assault on the court-house to aid their friends.[32] For while Colebrooke had implored the magistracy to act swiftly and with 'rigid impartiality in enforcing the law against all disturbers of the peace,' everyone knew that an Irish-Catholic repression was in progress.[33] Not one Orangeman was arrested for participating in the 12 July riot. However, Orange brethren participated in all levels of Woodstock's judicial system – the magistracy, constabulary, and militia. Moreover, on 28 July Colebrooke's Executive Council added an insidious wrinkle by appointing a special commission to gather evidence and testimony for the rioters' trial. Spearheading the panel were George Cleary, a local Orange master, and John Bedell, who publicly sympathized with Orangeism.[34]

Despite the inequitable nature of maintaining the peace after the riot, legitimate causes for alarm lingered. Sporadic violence erupted between Orange and Catholic individuals in the weeks after the Glorious Twelfth. On 21 July an unidentified assailant fired upon an Orangeman who had been involved in the riot as he left his home in Woodstock. Incendiarism reached epidemic proportions. A barn, grist mill, and oat kiln, all belonging to Protestants, met fiery destruction in July and August. While Orangemen blamed the Irish-Catholics, whom they branded 'Demons in human form,' for these attacks, authorities never discovered the guilty parties.[35] These incidents illustrated the tensions that pervaded Carleton County during the summer following the disturbance. As the trial date for the accused rioters approached, Protestants redoubled their efforts to prevent an Irish-Catholic insurrection.

On 8 September a special court convened for the trial of the Woodstock rioters. Justices brought true bills against all but three of the arrested Irish-Catholics, making a total of eighty-eight defendants.[36] Judges Robert Parker and George F. Street presided, while George Botsford and Solicitor General William B. Kinnear acted for the prosecution. The accused retained an impressive team of lawyers: Lemuel Allan Wilmot from Fredericton and W.J. Ritchie from Saint John designed the defence, assisted by Charles Watters and B.C. Friel from Saint John and Fredericton respectively. In an attempt to expedite the trial and undermine the rights of the accused to challenge the jurors individually, Kinnear dropped the normal felony charge for rioting to a misdemeanour.[37] All the defendants entered the trial with a 'not guilty' plea.

Ritchie opened the defence with a two-pronged attack on the arrangement of the jury. First he argued that Sheriff Winslow excluded all Roman Catholics in Carleton County when he had constructed the jury. He claimed, moreover, that the list of prospective jurors had been hastily assembled before the trial, in direct violation of a New Brunswick statute that set an annual 1 May deadline for such lists.[38] Thus, Ritchie argued, Winslow deliberately discriminated against the county's nearly eight hundred Catholic freeholders. While the prosecution conceded this point, they observed that no Orangemen were empanelled on the jury either. After several days of heated debate, Judge Parker handed down his decision. He found the sheriff's exclusion of Catholics justified because some of the Irish rioters were still at large, and the court should not risk the perversion of justice by having a participant serve on the jury. He did agree, however, with Ritchie's argument about the technical oversight. Over the objections of the solicitor general, who claimed that compliance with the jury list law had 'never been attended to in this province,' Parker postponed the trial until January.[39]

Prudence, rather than a desire for equality, shaped Parker's decision. The judges and the prosecution did not want to risk losing the case because of the skilful manipulation of a technicality by big-city lawyers.[40] Orangemen and Protestants, anxious for the incarceration of the Irish-Catholic rioters, bitterly lamented the postponement. The 'Mickey' lawyers invented the ploy, one argued, in order to drag out the proceedings so that they could extract more money from the 'miserable dupes' they defended.[41] Other zealous Protestants characterized Kinnear's motion to drop the felony charge as treasonous.[42] Despite the condemnation, the judges and prosecutors sought the same goals as the fervent Orangemen. Caution dictated the methodological parting of the ways.

The judge's decision to back a mere technicality in lieu of the major charge of discrimination reflected Carleton County's prevailing mood after the riot. Rather than agree with the defence lawyers, who clearly proved that the sheriff had no right to exclude pre-emptively a religious group from the jury, Parker applauded Winslow for making a wise decision. He rationalized that a fair trial would ensue without Orangemen or Catholics on the jury. With Catholics lawfully omitted, however, only Protestants would be eligible to serve. In such a Loyalist county, even disinterested Protestants would be more likely to favour Orangemen over Irish-Catholic settlers. Thus Parker's decision codified discrimination against Catholics.[43] While some Catholic supporters interpreted the postponement as a smashing triumph over the 'Bigots and Boobies of the intolerant Orange confraternity,' time would prove the tactic a Pyrrhic victory.[44]

The trial officially adjourned on 20 September after authorities brought an additional 51 bills for rioting, making the total 139 Irish-Catholic defendants. Friel attempted to introduce bills of indictment against Orangemen who participated in the riot, only to have his motions quickly thrown out by the jury. Winslow's handpicked panel obviously found the prosecution of fellow Protestants anathema.[45] A court decision to release any prisoner who agreed to sign a bond to appear at the next trial relieved the overcrowding at the court-house's temporary lock-up. The court set stiff bails, but granted prisoners the option to co-sign recognizances for one another.[46] Eventually, every alleged rioter took advantage of the program. Although the court appeared humane by freeing the Irish-Catholics, the decision also grew out of the desire to save the county the costs and hazards that would accompany a massive incarceration until winter.[47] Just over two months from the riot, the released prisoners and Carleton County's residents had settled into a restless wait for the rescheduled trial.[48]

The new year found the uneasy peace intact between Irish-Catholics and Orangemen. Petitions from both parties flooded Fredericton. In one case 108 freeholders of Carleton County lamented the increase in 'party feelings,' an expression that in this context implied ethnic tensions. They deplored the 'ruinous consequences' and the loss of the 'happy state of social and friendly intercourse' that existed prior to the riot. While decidedly Irish names clustered at the bottom of the petition, no signatures from confirmed Orangemen appeared. It stood as an eloquent reminder that many residents, in this case probably Irish-Catholics, lamented both the eruption of social violence and the vigilante impulse.[49]

By contrast, some petitions from community élites, including magistrates and Orangemen, attested to the growing desire to control tumultuous behaviour and address the community's general socio-economic distress. Requests for aid from the province to bring the transgressors to justice, totalling £1091, included the cost of a large number of special constables. The petitioners, including ten justices of whom at least three claimed Orange membership, complained of a depression in the lumber business, which 'bears most heavily upon all classes of its inhabitants.' The document provided excellent illustrations of the strengthening interrelationship between economic concerns, the suppression of certain ethnic groups, and a vaguely defined 'party spirit.'[50] Even more dramatically, Orangemen orchestrated a petition campaign that ultimately reached into York, Sunbury, Queens, Kings, and Saint John counties. Congratulating Carleton County's authorities, the petitioners acknowledged the 'prompt and energetic' containment of a potentially explosive evil. In fact, the 654 signatories enthusiastically signalled their approval of vigilantism. Expenses for the riot and its aftermath should be shouldered by the province, they argued, because Carleton County heroically staved off an anarchist impulse. The petitions stand as vivid testaments to the cementing of purposes between New Brunswick's Orangemen and community leaders.[51]

The trial, which had originally been slated for the winter, again faced postponement until 29 June owing to the death of Attorney General Peters.[52] Tensions mounted as the date approached. The Orange Order, capitalizing on rampant Protestant fears of Irish-Catholic insurrection, continued to expand its membership and lodges. For example, over two hundred Orangemen marched through Woodstock on 1 June to commemorate the opening of a new lodge. While authorities knew that a procession so close to the trial could rekindle violence, they did nothing to stop the proceedings. Indeed, three of Woodstock's influential magistrates participated in the festivities: George Cleary, who was still acting as a special commissioner for the trial, R.S. Demill, and Henry Baird. When Sir Edmund Head, the newly appointed lieutenant-governor, questioned the wisdom of their actions, their proud and emphatic response invoked their 'duty' to protect 'God and Loyalty' against Woodstock's 'Romans.'[53] Head mildly admonished the justices, but he refused to remove Cleary from the trial commission.[54] By failing to act decisively in the face of such blatant inequities, the Fredericton government tacitly approved Carleton County's policy of Orange favouritism.

Linkages between Orangemen and authorities crystallized on yet another level. Some magistrates and citizens, most of whom belonged to the Orange Order or openly sympathized with it, petitioned Head to send a detachment of troops to Woodstock for the trial's duration. They reasoned that extra protection would be needed when the Irish-Catholics returned to jail to stand trial.[55] Although the probability of the defendants acting raucously was minuscule, primarily because they would appear under their own recognizances, Head agreed that a military unit would be a significant deterrent to any Catholics who planned violence. He dispatched a small detachment to Woodstock with instructions similar to the previous year's. The soldiers were to be called only in an emergency, and to diminish the possibility of a military-civilian confrontation, he included instructions to quarter them in a compound on the outskirts of town.[56] Still, Orangemen and Protestants applauded their symbolic presence.

The community's hostility against Irish-Catholics, as evidenced by the linkages between Orangeism and the magistracy and by the presence of troops at the request of Orangemen, became sharply focused during the riot trial. The brethren announced in June that they planned two weeks of celebrations to run concurrently with the proceedings. The festivities would culminate in a grand procession on the riot's anniversary. With Woodstock's citizens engaged in a celebration of Orangeism while court officials decided their fates, the defendants knew that they faced overwhelming odds against receiving even a modicum of impartial justice.[57]

Finally, the defendants absorbed another crippling blow when they appeared for trial. The fifty-seven who presented themselves to the special commission in late June discovered that the jury did not differ substantially from that of the previous September. All Catholics had been excluded; moreover, Sheriff Winslow appointed jurors only from Woodstock and nearby towns where prejudice against the rioters was the greatest. The defendants presented their case to Head, who agreed to have Winslow call another panel.[58] The shuffle caused the trial's opening date to be moved to 11 July, one day before the planned Orange demonstration. The Catholic defendants once again appealed to the lieutenant-governor, this time to have the trial postponed until later in July or August. Head, who did not want to 'interfere in favour of persons who were probably guilty of a very gross outrage,' denied the petition.[59] The trial of the Irish-Catholics would commence on the eve of the anniversary of the Battle of the Boyne.

The defendants realized their worst fears as the clerk read the charges on 11 July and their counsellors prepared their final arguments. On the morning of the Twelfth, Orangemen from every corner of Carleton County gathered in Woodstock. Sentiments against those on trial, and indeed all Catholics, ran 'exceedingly strong.' A large and colourful procession snaked among Woodstock's streets, ultimately arriving at the court house.[60] After such an inauspicious prelude, the rioters finally faced their day in court.

While traditional accounts portray the accused as being representative of the 'lower orders' and largely transients without a stake in the community, a careful assessment of trial accounts, arrest records, and the provincial census of 1851 suggests otherwise. Of those indicted for the riot, 115 – 83 per cent – were clearly traced to a Carleton County residency. The remainder undoubtedly included transients, American citizens, and visitors from bordering New Brunswick counties. Of the resident group, sixty-eight individuals emerged in the 1851 New Brunswick census, while the remainder either left the region or died in the intervening years between the riot and the census.

The profile of those traced to the census, admittedly the most persistent individuals, suggests that they were neither despondent nor unininvolved in community affairs. While almost half lived in Woodstock Parish, all of Carleton County's parishes were represented, in addition to four from neighbouring Victoria County. Irish-born accounted for 85 per cent, with all but one of the remaining New Brunswick–born. Immigration dates of the Irish-born ranged from 1811 to the year of the riot; the overwhelming majority, over 75 per cent, had been in the province at least twelve years.[61] Thus, the arrested Irish-Catholics included a significant number of entrenched residents, men whose participation in the 1847 riot represented a risk to their community status, their families, and their jobs.

Perhaps more compellingly, an assessment of the group's ages and occupations dispels images of a rebellious and youthful cohort. Ages at the time of the riot ranged from 66 to 11; 32 emerged as the average, while 13 individuals constituted the most frequent age group, 36.[62] Contrary to contemporary accounts, the portrait of arrested rioters does not render a youthful visage; indeed seven were in their fifties.

An occupational evaluation further calls into question the 'lower orders' characterization. Sixty-three per cent earned their living as farmers. Labourers, including farm-hands, made up the second-largest group with fourteen. Shoemakers, several merchants and innkeepers, skilled craftsmen, and a sailor accounted for the remaining eleven. This was not an indigent group, and while admittedly transients remained elusive because they did not appear in the 1851 census, surely any assumptions that the arrested Irish-Catholics had no stake in the community need to be reassessed carefully, and perhaps abandoned. Plausibly, many arrested individuals railed against socio-economic repression; rather than spoiling for a 'good fight' they may have left their farms and jobs to protest what they perceived to be a menacing impulse: the growth of Orangeism in Carleton County. Thus, the individuals who faced the unlikely chances of having an all-Protestant jury render them an impartial decision included a significant number of entrenched, middle-aged, and gainfully employed men of Irish-Catholic extraction.[63]

Kinnear and Botsford once again handled the prosecution, but the defence had replaced Wilmot and Ritchie with John A. Street from Northumberland County. Immediate appeals by the defendants to postpone the trial yielded an emphatic denial. The prosecution moved swiftly through the docket, considering the large number of accused. By the time Judge Parker dismissed the jury on 20 July, 35 of the 49 defendants who stood trial had been convicted.[64] The seven found guilty of rioting received sentences from four months to one year with hard labour in the provincial penitentiary. The group included farmers, a shopkeeper, and an artisan from the Woodstock area who had allegedly been the leaders or armourers of the Irish-Catholic rioters. They ranged in age from 26 to 52, including the father-and-son pair of Owen and James Finnegan. On average they arrived in New Brunswick in 1833, fourteen years before the riot. Jurors found the remaining twenty-eight guilty of unlawful assembly and the judge bound them over to the county jail for sentences ranging from one to six months. The overwhelming majority of these were farmers from Carleton County; also included were labourers, artisans, and another innkeeper.[65] All were Irish-born, and had resided in the province an average of fifteen years. Their ages ranged between 13 and 52, the average being 27.[66] Once again, the emerging picture suggests that those sentenced for unlawful assembly were well-established individuals representing a variety of ages and occupations.

The low number of those appearing for trial, roughly half,

caused prosecutors concern. They concluded that those absent were guilty of the more heinous crimes and had probably absconded to the United States or other British colonies.[67] Evidence corroborated this view in a few cases, but at least twenty Irish-Catholics who failed to appear still resided in Carleton County in 1851.[68] Considering the above analysis of those who chose to face their accusers, no evidence suggests that this group was unrepresentative of Carleton County's Irish-Catholic population. Affixing the burden of blame to those who failed to appear apparently was more satisfying for authorities and residents alike as they tried to make sense of the riot and fit the causes into their paradigms of Orange ascendancy, vigilantism, and Irish-Catholic intimidation. Apparently only the more fervent Orangemen wanted to mount an intensive search for the missing defendants. Most of the county officials welcomed the estreated recognizances as a source of funds to offset the trial costs.[69] The few attempts to extradite rioters failed; by the winter of 1848, only a handful had been conclusively traced to the United States and none had been returned.[70]

In the meantime, Kinnear remained firm in his commitment to collect the bonds from all of those who failed to appear as well as from the co-signers. As the campaign progressed, distraught Irish-Catholics who were being forced to pay for their friends who had absconded deluged the lieutenant-governor's office with petitions. Over Kinnear's objections, Head suspended the suits against all outstanding debtors in October.[71] The following March, in an effort to suture Woodstock's wounds, Head yielded to another Catholic petition drive and released the five prisoners still serving prison sentences.[72] His executive order officially closed the chapter of the Woodstock riot of 1847.

Yet the riot spawned a legacy that would shape the lives of Carleton County's residents for years to come. The Irish-Catholic minority, for example, clearly suffered substantial losses during and after the conflict. They probably accounted for most of the dead and wounded at the riot, and certainly all of the arrested. New Brunswick's legal system denied Catholic freeholders the right to serve on the jury during the trials.[73] Those who faced the all-Protestant jury endured a high rate of conviction. Even those found innocent suffered the abuse and boycotts of their Protestant neighbours.[74] Irish-Catholics who left the county under a cloud of suspicion often lost their property holdings.[75] But most profoundly, the 1847 Woodstock riot underscored the second-class citizenship of Irish-Catholics in a Protestant-dominated region of Loyalist foundation. The local constabulary and magistracy, as well as the provincial executive and legislative branches, uniformly favoured the Orangemen in their struggle against Catholicism.

Moreover, Orangeism enjoyed exponential growth in Carleton County as a result of the riot. Only a handful of members staffed a single lodge in September 1846. A year later, thanks to a sympathetic population, over 1200 Orangemen belonged to a dozen lodges across the county. Orange processions and festivals became a familiar sight in Woodstock. The phenomenal success of Orangeism was perhaps best illustrated in October 1847. Over five hundred county members attended the ceremonies to dedicate a cornerstone for a new lodge in Woodstock, the one mentioned at the outset in this chapter. The building would be constructed on a symbolic piece of ground – the site of the Orange 'victory' over the Irish-Catholics in July.[76] The riot's most important contribution to Orangemen was the confirmation that vigilante tactics were effective in the suppression of the 'brutal ... and ignorant' Irish-Catholics.[77] To resident Protestants shocked by the riot and bloodshed, the Orange Order appeared the champion of law and order. Rather than acknowledging the Orangemen's violent contributions, the descendants of Loyalists and other Protestants looked to the fraternity to maintain peace in their hinterland society.[78] Carleton County would become one of New Brunswick's Orange bastions as the nineteenth century progressed.[79]

# 6

# The capital:
# Confrontations in Fredericton

Woodstock was not the only New Brunswick community to have a riot between Orangemen and Irish-Catholics in 1847. Another major disturbance broke out in the provincial capital of Fredericton, where during the 1840s Irish immigration had dramatically affected the demographic balance and triggered the development of the Orange Order. The first warranted lodge appeared in July 1844 under the direction of Thomas Hill, the fiery co-editor of the anti-Catholic *Loyalist*. Although Irish-Protestants built the foundation of Graham Lodge, its rolls quickly swelled with native-born Protestants, including the descendants of Loyalists.[1] With the *Loyalist* acting as a catalyst, Irish-Catholics and Orangemen would soon rend Fredericton's relatively congenial social fabric.[2]

In keeping with Orange tradition, Graham Lodge members planned an excursion in 1846 to celebrate the Twelfth with their brethren in Gagetown. As they collected at the wharf to board the steamer *New Brunswick* for passage to Gagetown, they encountered a restless crowd of Irish-Catholics. At first the groups remained apart, trading an insult or two. But when Robert Rosbury appeared with some orange lilies for the journey, the tenuous peace disintegrated. An aggressive Catholic bystander tried to snatch the offensive flowers from Rosbury's hand, only to be rebuffed by a group of vigilant Orangemen. Fist fights immediately broke out between the Orangemen still on the wharf and the Irish-Catholic crowd. Orangemen already on the steamer brandished the weapons they had brought for 'self-defence.' A major riot was averted, however, when Fredericton's deputy sheriff and the steamer's captain persuaded the Orangemen to shoulder their firearms. Orangemen and Catholics gradually disengaged from their fights, leaving bloody noses and black eyes as the most serious injuries. The Catholic crowd dispersed as the steamer disembarked, bringing an end to the disturbance.[3]

The incident raised a storm warning in Fredericton's ethnic and religious communities. Little over a year old, the Orange Order had sparked a religious feud. As a local newspaper editor lamented, 'The introduction of Orange Societies is but of recent origin in this community ... and is calculated to foster a spirit of animosity among the inhabitants of this city.'[4] Catholics and Orangemen used the 1846 disturbance to gauge each other's strength; both would be better prepared for the next symbolic holiday.

The spring of 1847 brought plans for an Orange meeting and procession on 12 July. Violence between Catholics and Orangemen mounted as summer approached. In June the York County Grand Jury noted the proliferation of disturbances, though it stopped short of blaming a particular group: 'We allude to the extreme disorderly conduct so frequently occurring on the part of persons ... frequently firing shots – in the most public places and sometimes through the windows of the inhabitants – and thereby endangering the lives of their neighbours and by their bad example tending to increase a party spirit in this community from which until recently it was most happily free.'[5] Unlike Woodstock, where alarmed magistrates called for military intervention before the Twelfth arrived, Fredericton made no official attempts to avert a confrontation. Perhaps the large British garrison stationed in town gave its residents a false sense of security. At any rate, social violence continued apace until the eve of the Orange holiday.[6] It was but a portent of things to come.

The early morning of 12 July found Irish-Catholics and Orangemen from outlying regions converging on the city. A large Catholic crowd had gathered along the downtown waterfront by 9:00 AM. Small groups of Orangemen traded taunts and insults with the Irishmen as they made their way to the Orange Hall on Queen Street.[7] Just as at Woodstock on the same morning, both belligerent parties were measuring the strength of their enemy. Yet unlike the Woodstock riot, which followed a deliberate, almost premeditated pattern, the disturbances that were about to unfold in Fredericton would be spontaneous and chaotic. The Catholic crowd would ebb and rise as the day progressed; it would lack both the leadership and sense of mission exhibited by its Woodstock counterpart.

The first reported disturbance occurred shortly after 9:00 AM at the steamboat wharf near the foot of Regent Street. Bands of Orangemen and Catholics attacked one another with fists and sticks. Although the fighting took place in small pockets, often with only two or three combatants in a group, it was none the less brutal.[8] Within an hour most of the Irish-Catholics had moved the short distance from the wharf to station themselves in front of the Orange meeting room near the intersection of Queen and Carleton streets; they also directly faced the barrack's gate to the British military compound on Queen Street. Most of the violence during the day would take place within a one-block radius of this location.[9] The crowd now numbered approximately three hundred, including men, women, and boys.[10] Judge George F. Street and some Fredericton magistrates soon arrived to defuse the powder keg. While they couched their warnings in strident language, they chose not to read the Riot Act. As a result, the Irish-Catholic crowd continued to mill in the street under the windows of the Orange Hall. As one angry Irishman told the magistrates, the crowd would not let the Orangemen 'trample' on their rights any longer.[11]

Most of the Orangemen were already ensconced in the hall when the crowd appeared. They clustered at the windows facing the street, brandishing the firearms they had bought for just such an occasion. One Orangeman proudly displayed a blunderbuss that he affectionately called a 'toothpicker.'[12] As the morning wore on the enemies traded insults and threats. Soon both sides tired of the verbal warfare. Lieutenant-Governor Colebrooke arrived shortly before noon to coordinate the efforts of the magistrates and constables to prevent a major disturbance. Under his direction, Sheriff Edward Miller escorted some women to safety who had been participating in the Orange festivities when the crowd had arrived.[13] With the hall cleared of women, both sides intensified their belligerent rhetoric.

Frustration grew in the Irish-Catholic crowd because the Orangemen remained in the building. Fights broke out with bystanders; crowd members assaulted several men because they suspected them of Orange connections or sympathies. The mood turned uglier as orange lilies thrown from the building settled among the Catholics on the street.[14] The crowd taunted the Orangemen, begging them to come down and face them in open battle. Most prudently ignored the challenge, but enough responded to cause a resurgence of fighting. Early afternoon found dozens of fist fights ranging along Queen Street and adjacent alleyways. Frustrated Catholics instantly assaulted tardy Orangemen as they arrived, many of them dressed in full regalia and expecting a procession. One constable who tried to arrest an assailant received a thrashing with sticks from his compatriots.[15] Several vicious skirmishes erupted near the military barracks gate. Members of the British detachment participated in some of the struggles, always on the side of the Orangemen. For example, Captain Walker of the 33rd Regiment drew his sword and entered the fracas to aid a beleaguered Orangeman. Walker beat a hasty retreat and sought refuge in a nearby shop after the crowd set upon him with enthusiasm. Although soldiers became involved in the riot, they did so individually. The troops averted a large-scale and armed confrontation with civilians because the bulk of the detachment never left the parade ground.[16]

The Fredericton 'riot' in fact consisted of a series of individualized assaults. With only one exception, all the testimonies and indictments described encounters that involved fists, stones, and sticks. The most dangerous weapons used by the Irish-Catholic crowd consisted of stockings filled with rocks. Apparently women favoured this device.[17] Although the testimonies of Orangemen and the authorities included no references to firearms, at least one man received a fatal gunshot wound. An Irish-Catholic named Thomas Welch was struck by a bullet while demonstrating in front of William Armstrong's house on Carleton Street. Authorities questioned Armstrong, undoubtedly an Orangeman, and promptly released him despite the fact that the unarmed Welch had remained on the street, well clear of the house, throughout the interchange.[18] Although authorities never established whether or not Welch threatened Armstrong or his property, the incident was clearly linked to the general disturbance. Welch's death accounted for the only recorded fatality of the Fredericton riot.[19]

Prolonged skirmishes prompted the magistrates to appoint special constables for duty along Queen and Carleton streets, where the afternoon fighting was most intense. The constables arrested several Irish-Catholics; a crowd liberated at least two before their captors reached the jail. While the dogged constables eventually recaptured the suspected assailants, the incident strikingly illustrated the crowd's fraternal and cohesive nature.[20] Fighting continued in individualized pockets throughout the afternoon, but by nightfall most of the crowd had dispersed and the Orangemen had vacated the hall. Constables arrested suspected Irish-Catholics long into the evening, and by the following morning Fredericton once again assumed the mantle, or more accurately the illusion, of a peaceful government town.[21]

The Fredericton Orange-Green confrontation, while a tumultuous and bloody event for some participants, fell well short of being an episode of social violence on the scale of Woodstock's. Notwithstanding contemporary interpretations, the encounter probably did not deserve to be characterized as a riot. A large crowd of Irish-Catholics indeed gathered to protest the Orange meeting and prevent a procession, but the enemies never directly engaged in battle. Not one of the accounts or testimonies recorded property damage. The crowd never stormed the Orange Hall and, conversely, an Orange procession never materialized to fan Catholic passions. And while some people received serious injuries, most notably Orangemen caught on the street along with several bystanders and the one Irish-Catholic who died as a result of a gunshot wound, casualties were probably limited because the disturbance did not involve the authorities to the extent that the Woodstock riot did. For undisclosed reasons, the attending justices abstained from reading the Riot Act. Similarly, they chose not to appeal to British troops for aid despite the fact that most of the fighting erupted directly in front of the barracks gate.[22] The Fredericton 12 July disturbance should be recorded, therefore, as a series of individualized and small group clashes between Orangemen and Irish-Catholics.

An analysis of the crowd provides clues as to why a riot never erupted. Local newspapers claimed that the crowd consisted entirely of the 'lower orders' of Roman Catholics – both men and women – but evidence gleaned from arrest records proves otherwise.[23] To begin with, only Irish-Catholics were apprehended. Of the thirty-four who received indictments, half referred to themselves as 'labourers.' In the language of the mid-nineteenth century, this would have included unskilled and skilled workers as well as the unemployed. But the arrest lists also included shopkeepers, masons, shoemakers, proprietors, and farmers.[24] Three of those in the former category had been previously arrested for assaults; the remainder faced charges for their first offence.[25] Finally, while those seized for their participation in the Fredericton disturbance might accurately be termed members of the working class, most lived in the vicinity of the Orange Hall on Queen Street. This fact undermined contemporary arguments that the crowd consisted of 'dangerous' strangers and itinerant 'lower orders.'[26] Much like the Irish-Catholics arrested in the wake of the Woodstock riot, many of Fredericton's prisoners were actively employed, local residents.

Unlike the hinterland community, however, Fredericton quickly regained its equanimity after 12 July. City records remained devoid of reports of violence between Orangemen and Catholics, including personal assaults and incendiarism. The relatively disorganized nature of both crowds probably accounted for the lack of post-riot disorder. The Irish-Catholic crowd had been cohesive in its purpose of preventing an Orange procession, but it neither functioned as a unit nor shared a common leadership. And unlike the massive battle at Woodstock between clearly defined enemies, the Fredericton disturbance consisted of small, autonomous groups searching the streets for Orangemen or Protestant sympathizers. For example, an excited Irishman demanded of bystander Charles Bailey, 'Damn you, are you one of them too?' just before he assaulted him. Another Orangeman reported a triumphant comment from a crowd member: 'Will you laugh or grin at me now?'[27] These queries illustrated the nature of Fredericton's social violence. Members of the Irish-Catholic crowd either targeted known Orangemen or assaulted those whom they suspected of connections with the fraternity.[28] But most of the Orangemen remained in the relative sanctuary of their lodge on Queen Street, forcing the frustrated Irish-Catholics to roam the adjoining thoroughfares looking for individual fights. Thus, the Fredericton disturbance paled when measured against the scale of Woodstock's battle.

The post-riot trials moved swiftly in Fredericton; postponements and arguments over technicalities did not bog down the judicial proceedings as they did in Woodstock. Justices bound over the thirty-four arrested Irish-Catholics for a trial that convened in early November. Thirteen did not appear and thus forfeited their recognizances. None of their names emerged in the 1851 census, suggesting that they may have been itinerant labourers or residents who absconded to avoid trial.[29] If they left because they questioned the likelihood of a fair hearing, their decisions were prudent.

Fredericton in November did not elicit a favourable environment for the trial of the Irish-Catholic defendants. They faced an overwhelming array of power. All but one of the sixty witnesses called for statements and trial testimonies spoke against them. Prosecutor John A. Street's deponents included dozens of Orangemen, British soldiers, magistrates, and even newspaper editor James Hogg, a recent Orange convert who had been convinced of the righteousness of its cause as a result of the disturbances.[30] Judge James Carter sat on the bench, fresh from the aborted proceedings in Woodstock. He asked the jurors to be impartial, to rise above religious antagonisms. However noble his sentiments, a confluence of circumstances prevented impartiality.

Justice would be meted out by Protestant jurors to only one offending group – the Irish-Catholics.[31]

The jurors wasted no time in formulating their decisions. Within five days they found two-thirds of the defendants guilty of offences ranging from assault to unlawful assembly. Four received stiff sentences of one year in the provincial penitentiary with hard labour, another five drew six months under the same conditions, and the remaining five were sent to York County jail for four months.[32] Given the fact that felony charges for rioting could not be brought because the Irish-Catholic crowd had never received the Riot Act on 12 July, the harsh penalties smacked of repression. Defence attorney Lemuel Allen Wilmot's impassioned pleas for leniency went unheeded. Perhaps his dubious assertion that the most guilty rioters had absconded undermined his more convincing argument that the disturbance had never achieved the dimensions of a full-fledged riot.[33] Moreover, Street successfully rebuffed assistant defence attorney William Watt's claim that Orangemen provoked the disruption by pointing out that a procession never materialized. With the majority of the Orangemen remaining in the hall, the blame for every fight fell on the Irish-Catholic crowd.[34] Street and the avalanche of pro-Orange testimony carried the day; the all-Protestant jury convicted fourteen and turned them over to Judge Carter for sentencing.

Carter's two speeches at the Fredericton riot trials – the first his charge to the jury and the second his sentencing of the accused – illustrated both the depth of religious antagonisms and the complex nature of the problem that all judicious citizens faced. While he acknowledged that only Irish-Catholics stood trial, he attempted to salve their bruised spirits by insisting that had any Orangemen started a fight or assaulted a Catholic, then they too would face justice in the dock.[35] His assurance rang hollow, however, because the prisoners knew that authorities immediately dropped the charges against William Armstrong for murdering Thomas Welch despite the coroner's recommendation.[36] Carter also placed equal blame for the fracas on each contending party and then paradoxically passed judgment on only the Irish-Catholics for perpetrating the 'grossest misdemeanor ever attempted' in York County.[37] While Carter had recognized the two-edged sword of religious conflict, he had fallen prey to the irresistible pull of the Protestant majority. Fredericton's Orangemen emerged unscathed from the judicial process just as their Woodstock brethren had. This example illuminated one of the profound problems of the 1840s: while many sagacious people perceived the fundamental causes for religious violence, their actions either deliberately or inadvertently contributed to the repression of Irish-Catholics.

Fredericton's Orange-Green disturbance officially came to a close two days after the prisoners received their sentences. The nine Irish-Catholics bound for incarceration at the provincial penitentiary at Saint John boarded the steamer at Fredericton's slip. Crowds of Orangemen and Protestants lined the wharves and banks of the Saint John River. Spontaneous cheers erupted as the steamer disembarked, a joyous outburst that symbolized the popularity of Orange principles in the province's capital.[38] Woodstock's Irish-Catholics would share a similar fate the following July, but whereas those serving the longest terms received commutations, the Fredericton rioters served the full terms of their original sentences.

The Fredericton disturbance left a wake larger than the steamer that carried the wretched Irish-Catholic prisoners to Saint John. Anti-Catholic fervour peaked after the 12 July riot, spearheaded by the burgeoning Orange Order. The number of lodges in Fredericton and its environs in York County multiplied after 1847.[39] The swelling membership would insist on proper observances of the Glorious Twelfth. In 1848, to celebrate the anniversary of the conflict, approximately eight hundred Orange brethren from as far away as Saint John gathered in the capital. Bedecked in full regalia and heavily armed, they paraded for hours through the city's streets.[40] No Irish-Catholics challenged the procession, a tribute to superior Orange numbers and the support they enjoyed from the Protestant majority. Echoing the vigilante spirit exhibited in Carleton County, the capital region's Protestants joined the Orange Order because it represented an alternative to maintaining law and order in the face of an inadequate civil authority.[41] The Orange Order, according to Fredericton Grand Master George Anderson, stood paramount as an armed defensive organization, ever vigilant, ever ready to cry 'No Surrender.'[42]

The collective conflict also contributed to the fortification and then institutionalization of the local constabulary. Just before 12 July York County's Grand Jury recommended replacing the annually appointed constables, who worked only when called or available, with a more permanent force.[43] In 1848 the City Council received the charge to improve law enforcement as one of its first orders of business.[44] Magistrates appointed a city marshal in June 1848 for £15 a year; in addition they assigned eight constables, at a stipend of £10 a year, to each of the city's wards. Included that first year were at least two prominent Orangemen, Nicholas Wheeler and James E. Perley, of Wellington and Queens wards respectively. Orangeman Thomas L. Simmons joined their ranks later.[45] In 1850 almost fifty residents petitioned the city council that representatives 'may be embodied as a police within the city.' Although councillors tabled the measure, the idea persisted.[46]

In 1851, partly as a result of the religious violence that underscored the deficiencies of the antiquated system, the city council of newly incorporated Fredericton established a regular police force. At the order of Orangeman James S. Beek, 'special police' were added to the constabulary rolls that year, including at least two additional Orangemen, Robert Wiley and John Mullin.[47] By the following year, councillors had passed a resolution creating a permanent police constable for each ward. The new constabulary included notable Orangemen such as William Armstrong – the veteran of the Welch murder incident – for Queens Ward.[48] By 1854 salary schedules had improved dramatically; now two 'city constables' received £50 for a two-year commitment, while the city marshal commanded twice that sum. The mayor and city council controlled the squad for years until they adopted Saint John's model and appointed a police magistrate in late 1857. The creation of this position, which yielded a handsome salary of £150 a year, signified the successful genesis of an institutionalized force.[49] In sum, various precipitating factors contributed to the professionalization of Fredericton's constabulary. The fear of collective civil disorder, exacerbated by 1847's Orange-Green conflict, was one of the more important ingredients of that evolution. Significantly, a recognizable and symbiotic relationship between the nascent police force and the Orange Order also helped to explain the process.

Also directly attributable to the Fredericton disturbances of 1847 was the codification of legislative measures designed to curtail vagrancy and buttress vigilante behaviour. An appeal to tighten a 'nuisance law,' ostensibly to give authorities more effective control over individual and collective conduct, appeared as one of the first orders of business for the Fredericton City Council in 1848.[50] In addition, the grand jury complained about vagrants and the 'prevailing custom of ... dissolute persons male and female congregating in certain parts of the streets to the great annoyance of the public.' They recommended greater vigilance and supervision of the lower classes, potentially the spawning grounds of social disorder.[51] The grand jury's recommendations succinctly illustrated the confluence of the agendas of Fredericton's authorities and the Orange Order. By the late 1840s each advocated systemic control over the movements of the potentially dangerous 'lower orders,' especially Irish-Catholics.

Tangible linkages between the Orange Order and Fredericton's political machinery emerged in the late 1840s, and in the decades after mid-century the two thoroughly intermeshed. Prominent Orange members regularly sat on the city council, most notably representing Wellington, Queens, and St Anns wards. Throughout the 1850s the council contained at least two confirmed Orangemen in any given year.[52] Representative of this pattern were John L. Marsh, Robert Gowan, James S. Beek, William Segee, William Grieves, and Robert Wiley. Moreover, two members of the upper echelons of the Provincial Orange Order became mayors during the same decade. William H. Needham, mayor from 1855–8 and through much of the 1860s, achieved notoriety as the fraternity's first Grand Master in 1847.[53] On Needham's footheels came Irish-born James S. Beek, a magistrate, general merchandiser, legislative librarian, provincial auditor general, prohibitionist, and member of the Church of England. Beek, who served three terms from 1859–61, tirelessly lobbied for the incorporation of the Orange Order and served in a variety of leadership positions during the same years.[54] The unanimity of purpose of those in authority and the Orange Order held dramatic consequences for Irish-Catholics in Fredericton and greater York County.[55]

A series of hotly contested elections for city councillors during the 1850s served to harden the lines already drawn between the competing religious groups. Inevitably candidates from the most contentious wards, particularly Wellington and St Anns, accused their opponents of pandering to the voters by manipulating an ill-defined 'party spirit.' In this context, as was true in the other communities under discussion, this phrase might be interpreted to mean socio-economic, ethnic, or religious alignments. With monotonous regularity losing candidates complained that their opponents gleaned ballots from ineligible voters, purportedly those with insufficient property holdings or financial qualifications.[56] In 1858 the religious tensions in St Anns and Wellington wards percolated to the surface and received the direct attention of candidates. John L. Marsh, Jr, an active Orangeman, presented a case to voters during a contested election to create a city 'council for Protestants.'[57] Marsh and his Orange contemporaries essentially gained the high ground; they may not have mustered enough votes to codify religious and ethnic segregation, but their efforts effectively blocked Roman Catholics from serving as city councillors during the decade.

The disturbance shaped the futures of York County's Irish-Catholics in other ways. Not surprisingly, those arrested for participating in the 12 July affray found themselves most directly affected. After being released on bonds they faced the Hobson's choice of permanently leaving the area, and probably New Brunswick, or standing a trial that was practically guaranteed to be inequitable. Thirteen chose the former strategy. Undoubtedly, general migration patterns of Irish-Catholics through the Maritimes would have eventually carried some of the itinerant labourers south to the United States or west to other British colonies.[58] But the defendants' dismal prospects offered them little incentive to remain. Among the fifteen who were convicted and served sentences, nine chose not to return to York County after their release. Of the five who did, all but one were skilled labourers or proprietors who had financial inducements to attempt a reintrenchment.[59] Yet those who returned – and indeed the entire Irish-Catholic population – faced harassment from the Protestant majority.

Economic prejudice emerged as an important manifestation of this harassment, much as it did in Woodstock following the riot. Boycotts and competition shaped purely by religious affiliation, noticeable before the 12 July disturbance, reached epidemic proportions afterwards. One Fredericton teamster, who also served as a special constable during the riot, acknowledged that his employers forbade him to haul goods for Roman Catholics.[60] Orange Order propaganda helped to drive this wedge between religious groups. Officials espoused a separate but equal policy, encouraging their followers to avoid dealing with Catholics in every aspect of their lives.[61] The 'equality' part of the equation served as mere rhetoric; in practice the Orangemen and militant Protestants wanted to drive Catholics from the province using the boycott.

Finally, the Fredericton conflict left many unanswered or unanswerable questions in its wake. To begin with, anti-Catholic sources generated virtually all accounts of the disturbance and the proceedings of the trial. As was the case in Woodstock, contemporary accounts were written by Orangemen, sympathetic Protestants, victims of assaults by Irish-Catholics, magistrates, constables, British officers and troops, and a uniformly hostile press. To these people, the Fredericton disturbance represented a riot that approached the magnitude of an insurrection. But were the Irish-Catholics a crazed mob, bent on destroying New Brunswick's political and social framework? As defence attorney Wilmot pointed out, the crowd was loosely constructed, it carried weapons no more potent than a rock, it caused no property damage, and it never stormed the Orange Hall. Moreover, why would Irish-Catholics engineer a riot in full view of Her

Majesty's Regulars? And if the affray approached an intensity of cataclysmic proportion, as authorities subsequently insisted, why was the military, or at least a local militia detachment, not mustered to aid the constabulary? Lastly, Lieutenant-Governor Colebrooke, Sheriff Miller, and several magistrates addressed the crowd on several occasions. If they judged the situation to be volatile, then why did they fail to follow standard nineteenth-century procedure and read the Riot Act? Clearly the 12 July Fredericton disturbance never became a riot in either a legal or social sense, notwithstanding the assessments of abundant and sometimes apocryphal contemporary accounts.

The nature of justice in Fredericton and York County illustrated the linkages between Orangemen and local authorities. In a sense the Orange Order emerged as an unofficial arm of social control as a result of the 1847 conflict. Just as at Woodstock, only Irish-Catholics faced arrest and prosecution. Dozens of Orangemen admittedly participated in the fighting, but the judiciary never seriously questioned their justifications. Officials blithely ignored even the most glaring offences. For example, an Orangeman named John Pendergast enthusiastically disclosed information about his involvement in both the steamboat incident of 1846 and the 12 July conflict the following year. Authorities encouraged him to submit testimony against his Catholic enemies but failed to ask him probing questions about his preparation for violence – he carried weapons during both incidents – and his obvious relish for fighting.[62] Orange deponents uniformly admitted to authorities that they brought firearms to the lodge and bore them into battle, thus clearly defying New Brunswick statutes. The judiciary took no official notice of this either.[63] And most blatant of all, when an Irish-Catholic was shot and killed the investigation went no further than a coroner's jury. Witnesses positively identified the owner of the house whence the shot came, yet he was never indicted.[64] Irish-Catholics would shoulder the entire blame, at least in the judicial system, for the Orange-Green collision.

# 7

# The ports:
# Orange-Green disturbances in
# Saint John and Portland

In March 1839, the St Patrick's, St George's, and St Andrew's societies held a collective meeting in Saint John. Delegates noted and condemned the Protestant-Catholic confrontations that appeared to be endemic in Boston and other unfortunate American cities. In a spirit of congeniality, they applauded themselves on the good fortune of living in a British colony free of such acrimonious religious strife. Delegates proposed generous toasts to Queen Victoria, to Lieutenant-Governor Harvey, and, most effusively, to each other.[1] Eight years later, after Saint John and neighbouring Portland had experienced a series of bloody riots involving Orangemen and Irish-Catholics, those sentiments would be recalled with bitter irony. Sarcastic comparisons would then be drawn between Saint John and New Orleans, a tumultuous city with a reputation for collective violence.[2]

What happened to shatter the calm, and why would the toasts of 1839 turn out to be so farcical in the light of events during the 1840s? Why would Saint John and Portland, both relatively stable communities that had escaped major incidents of social violence prior to the 1840s, become ethno-religious battlegrounds involving natives and immigrants? The disturbances in the port communities eclipsed Woodstock's and Fredericton's riots by most standards of measurement. Ranging from the isolated incidents of the late 1830s to the massive 1849 riot at York Point, the

Orange-Green confrontations in Saint John and Portland epitomized New Brunswick's social violence.

Along with economic dislocation, a dramatically altered ethnoreligious composition, and the rise of the Orange Order, the 1840s introduced an era of collective violence. For authorities charged with maintaining civil order, change loomed ahead as a bewildering and terrifying prospect. Many of these incidents were socially or religiously defined, and they will be discussed in detail below. But an increasing number found their roots in the proliferation of crime and the popularity of collective demonstrations. For example, a circus in the summer of 1841 touched off several days of rioting in York Point and neighbouring districts. Gangs of 'young rowdies' destroyed fences and windows and made dozens of random attacks on bystanders.[3] Similarly, the theatre presentation of a farce that satirized several Saint Johners led to a raucous night. Scores of people suffered wounds and the theatre received extensive damage before authorities could restore order.[4] At least two major clashes broke out between off-duty British troops and civilians during the 1840s.[5] Judicial records clearly indicated the prevalence of collective violence: between 1841 and 1844 city officials arrested dozens for rioting and unlawful assembly; seven of the defendants received major sentences at the provincial penitentiary or the county jail.[6]

The apparent connection between the dramatic increase in crime and collective violence and Irish-Catholic immigration alarmed the residents of Saint John and Portland. Just as in Woodstock and Fredericton, the Orange Order channelled the energies of disparate Protestants into a single nativist organization. According to Orange rhetoric, the construction of an extralegal bulwark against Irish-Catholic encroachment became the organization's paramount challenge. If the duly appointed authorities exhibited reluctance to use force, for fear of dividing the community even more, then vigilant Orangemen were prepared to impose their will with extra-legal behaviour. From a foundation of a handful of lodges in Saint John and Portland in the early 1840s, Orangeism would blossom to 'preserve and defend' Protestant and Loyalist principles.[7]

Instead of providing the solution to rampant crime, the Orange Order became a midwife for social violence. In 1840 Saint John's still modest Irish-Catholic community read with distress the publicized festivities for the anniversary of the Battle of the Boyne. Orangemen abstained from processions for several years, but this would change as they became stronger and Irish-Catholic immigration peaked.[8] The ethno-religious holidays of 12 July and 17 March would bring numerous conflicts, rising in intensity as the decade progressed. Each side became more identifiable and more antagonistic as its membership swelled with co-religionists. Orangemen and militant Irish-Catholics fostered the demise of any semblance of religious tolerance. Ironically, the assaults, larcenies, and gang fights that Orangemen so dearly wished to eradicate would appear trivial when compared to the massive riots that would erupt with such disturbing regularity in the late 1840s.

Collective social violence in Saint John and Portland grew in direct proportion to Orange membership and the level of Irish-Catholic immigration. Early examples of hostility vaguely resembled the riots of 1847 and 1849, but they served as important training grounds for learning the craft of urban warfare. The first clearly identifiable incident of collective violence between Orangemen and Catholics in Saint John occurred on 12 July 1837. Small Catholic crowds forced entry into two merchants' stores and attempted to burn them.[9] More traditional rioting quickly eclipsed incendiarism. The spring of 1841 found Irish-Catholics clashing with Orangemen in Saint John's streets. At issue was an Orange commemorative arch the latter erected to celebrate the visit of the newly appointed lieutenant-governor of the united Canadas.[10] The violent reaction of a crowd to symbolic stimuli, in this case an Orange arch, sparked many of the religious confrontations of the 1840s.

Saint John's first riot on the anniversary of the Battle of the Boyne in 1842 underscored this point. Two to three hundred angry Irish-Catholics gathered outside a home that displayed a Union Jack festooned with orange ribbons. After an exchange of threats with the owner, the crowd purloined the flag and proceeded to King Square. General fighting ensued later in the afternoon as Orangemen arrived from regional lodges. Mayor William Black, several magistrates, and the sheriff unsuccessfully appealed to the crowd to disperse. As a result, they called for special constables. One hundred and fifty Protestant volunteers, eager to crush the Catholics, assembled within an hour. The crowd rapidly dissipated when the constables reached King Square, but not before several of its members had been captured. Officials convicted at least three of the six arrested of unlawful assembly.[11]

Although the disturbance caused little damage, it left a bitter legacy and established patterns that would be repeated throughout the decade. Protestants were shocked by the crowd's ill treatment of the Union Jack and the mayor, both symbols of authority. The Catholics' cheers for 'Bloody Queen Mary and the Green Flag' struck terror into the minds of Saint Johners, and would echo through the streets for years to come.[12] But most important, Orangemen improved their image because they had abstained from holding a procession to counter the Catholic crowd. One newspaper implored anyone 'who has a drop of British Blood in his veins' to show respect for the Orange Order's restraint.[13] In 1842 ordinary citizens began to perceive Orangemen as the defenders of Saint John's Protestant and Loyalist traditions. The disturbance set into motion one final, over-arching pattern: throughout the 1840s, an exclusively Protestant constabulary and judiciary would consistently arrest and convict only Irish-Catholics for disturbing the peace.

The next two years, coinciding with the first substantial waves of Irish-Catholic immigrants and the attendant surge of Orangeism, brought more episodes of social violence. The Twelfth in 1843 witnessed several clashes between religious crowds in Saint John and Portland, although an official Orange procession never materialized.[14] A more serious incident transpired in March of the following year. Squire Manks, Worshipful Master of the recently established Wellington Orange Lodge and a belligerent man with a history of assaults, mortally wounded a Catholic Irishman at York Point. When officials collected Manks at his home in Portland the following day for questioning, an enraged Catholic crowd lined the Portland Bridge and the streets of York Point, chanting 'Down with the murderer.' Authorities placed Manks in jail, primarily for his own protection, and after the fervour abated an examining board of city magistrates exonerated him. The verdict: self-defence.[15] Holding true to patterns established the previous year, authorities proved reluctant to convict Orangemen for crimes against Irish-Catholics.

The year closed with a series of riots that lasted from Christmas until after New Year's. Crowds of up to three hundred Irish-Catholics roamed throughout York Point and Portland's wharf district, attacking Orangemen and their property. The Orangemen enthusiastically reciprocated. When a local cabinetmaker named John Allingham died during a fracas on the Portland Bridge in late December, a new wave of violence spread over the region.[16] Two companies of British regulars finally succeeded in quashing the disturbances, but not before dozens more had received serious injuries. Although uninvolved residents bemoaned the apparent state of anarchy, the rioting proved neither indiscriminate nor uncontrolled. Catholics and Orangemen carefully picked fights only with 'certain ... obnoxious individuals.'[17] The hostilities that ushered in 1845 were but a portent of the violence that Saint John and Portland would experience over the next five years.

Protestant-Catholic relations deteriorated later in January as a result of the murder of a local hotel owner named Charles Yerxa. While religious or ethnic differences may not have provoked the incident, the community believed that it indicated the entrenchment of social violence. Authorities expeditiously brought three Irish-Catholic labourers from York Point to trial despite their attempts to abscond. The hearings caused a mild sensation; visitors packed the court room in Saint John and crowds waited outside in the cold for the verdicts. Significantly, both the defence and the prosecution claimed that the murder grew out of religious tensions and constructed their arguments accordingly. One of the three defendants received a sentence for wilful murder.[18] The incident indiscriminately whetted the appetites of belligerent Orangemen and Irish-Catholics. As one contemporary noted, clashes between religious 'mobs' erupted with appalling regularity during the winter of 1844–5.[19]

The tensions of the winter culminated in a St Patrick's Day riot that eclipsed all preceding Orange-Green disputes. Even an attempt by Saint John's mayor to avert a confrontation failed. The week before the Catholic holiday, informants apprised Lauchlan Donaldson of the plans for a public celebration, as well as those for a proposed Orange counter-demonstration. Contacting Saint John's only Catholic magistrate and a local priest, he asked them to use their influence and have the plans cancelled. After receiving their assurances to do what they could, he took the added precaution of banning public processions two days before the seventeenth.[20] His efforts, although resourceful, failed to mitigate religious antagonism.

On the afternoon of 17 March Portland Orangemen fired upon a group of Catholic revellers. The incident touched off a wave of reprisals; by nightfall general rioting between Orangemen and Irish-Catholics had spread throughout the wharf district and York Point. The foot of Fort Howe Hill in Portland witnessed the most intense fighting.[21] Two radically different accounts underscored the difficulty of ascertaining what had happened. The Catholic viewpoint, forwarded by magistrate James Gallagher, maintained that Orangemen fired upon four Irishmen without provocation.[22] A dramatically different story appeared in the pro-Orange *Loyalist*. A Catholic amateur band, ostensibly in an advanced state of intoxication, paraded through the streets of York Point and Portland. Its belligerent posture, according to the *Loyalist*, convinced vigilant Orangemen that they must act swiftly to protect Protestant citizens.[23] Regardless of causation, the battle still raged by nightfall.

Mayor Donaldson, alarmed at the intensification of hostilities, petitioned Major Whingate at the British garrison to intervene. Whingate reluctantly agreed and ordered two companies of soldiers and an artillery piece to be stationed in Portland near the head of the harbour.[24] The military's presence had the desired effect of discouraging further bloodshed, but not before the rioters inflicted heavy casualties. At least four men had fallen with serious gunshot wounds, while scores more received superficial injuries. Two doctors, harassed by the crowds as they made their way to the wounded, arrived too late to save a Catholic band member. Another critically hurt Irishman, dubbed a 'ringleader' by the anti-Catholic press, later recovered from his wounds.[25] Despite the bloodshed, the military never became directly involved in the riot. Lieutenant-Governor Colebrooke and the British commanders understandably feared a military-civilian confrontation.[26] Military intervention was 99 per cent symbolic.

The examinations and trials in the riot's aftermath followed the patterns established in 1842. Although authorities arrested several Orangemen, including two suspected of murdering a Catholic 'ringleader' named McGrath, Saint John's all-Protestant grand jury pre-emptively threw out the bills before the cases could be brought to trial. Instead the jury returned bills for several Irish-Catholic rioters, two of whom were ultimately found guilty and sentenced. The swift vindication of Orangemen by the grand jury, despite an abundance of damaging testimony, illustrated the reluctance of Protestant authorities to condemn Orange violence and their continuing propensity to convict only Irish-Catholics for crimes against the public peace.[27]

The St Patrick's Day riot sounded alarm bells addressing the ineffectiveness of Saint John's and Portland's constabulary. Both communities laboured under an antiquated network that included a sheriff, no more than twenty-two annually appointed constables, a poorly paid and unreliable night watch, and the occasional services of stipendiary constables.[28] The Orange-Green disturbances, growing more intense every year, sparked public debate over whether to establish a tax-based, professionalized police force under the authority of a police magistrate. The plan took several more years to germinate, and each successive religious disturbance added credence to the proponents' assertions.[29]

Saint John and Portland escaped collective violence for the next two years, but the hiatus did nothing to diminish enmity or foster peaceful linkages between Orangemen and Irish-Catholics. The latter abstained from public displays on the St Patrick's Days of 1846 and 1847. Orangemen quietly observed 12 July in their lodges in 1845; the following year they took a steamer to Gagetown for a procession with their brethren from Queens, Kings, and York counties.[30] In 1847, with famine immigration reaching its zenith, Orangemen all across New Brunswick chose to celebrate locally. Their decision to assert control over the Irish-Catholic immigrants had profound implications for Woodstock and Fredericton, as has already been established; it would be no less important for the port communities of Saint John and Portland.

For 12 July, Saint John Orangemen invited neighbouring brethren and staged the largest procession since the organization's inception. As in 1845, violent skirmishes preceded the festivities.[31] On 14 July, a city newspaper trumpeted the now familiar requiem for the Orange holiday: 'Dreadful Riot! The Disaffected District [York Point] again in Arms – Shots Fired – Several Persons Dreadfully Wounded – the Military Called Out.'[32] The two-year truce had yielded only larger numbers of Catholic immigrants and nativist Orangemen, and a more sophisticated network for the combatants in both groups to utilize in battle.

The anniversary of the Battle of the Boyne dawned quietly enough, but as Saint John's and Portland's Orangemen began to make their way to their lodges, crowds of wary Irish-Catholics spilled into the streets. One of the larger Portland lodges, probably Wellington, entertained the amateur band from the local Mechanics Institute. All the band members belonged to the Orange Order. In the early evening, the group led a procession of Orangemen and on-lookers through the streets of Portland, across the bridge, and into the heart of the Roman Catholic enclave at York Point.[33] The tunes they played, like most Orange favourites, were designed to offend Irish-Catholics.[34] At the foot of Dock Street, the crowd attacked the procession with sticks and bricks, smashing many of the band's instruments and forcing the revellers to flee back across the Portland Bridge. Gathering reinforcements and firearms from their lodges and homes, the undaunted Orangemen quickly returned to their enemy's stronghold.[35]

The Irish-Catholic crowd, which by now had grown to several

hundred, also made use of the respite and collected weapons in the event of a reappearance of the humiliated band members and Orangemen.[36] The buttressed Orange legions did attempt to revive the procession and music when they reached York Point. A battle was inevitable. Volleys of shots from both parties shattered the summer air, leaving scores of wounded lying in the streets along the procession route. The mêlée continued throughout the evening, with most of the bloodshed occurring along Dock and Mill streets and the bridge. At midnight detachments of the 33rd Regiment, dispatched at the mayor's request, converged upon York Point only to find the streets deserted. Rather than chance an engagement with the military, both sides ceased hostilities.[37] Aided by the darkness, the Irish-Catholics escaped capture and returned to their homes. The constabulary failed to make any arrests after the riot, and the grand jury issued no warrants.[38]

The secretive removal of the dead and wounded by both parties, particularly the Irish-Catholics, hampered an assessment of the riot's severity. Official tallies included only one Catholic killed and several seriously wounded, but participants and witnesses suspected that many had died during the encounter.[39] The significance of the conflict, however, emerged unclouded in the following months. Both sides were organized, well stocked with weapons, and clearly prepared to kill for their beliefs. Catholics had gathered hours before the Orange procession had entered York Point, motivated by a desire to 'defend' their 'territory.' Orangemen willingly provoked the enemy by twice marching in procession and playing noxious songs through the most Catholic district of Saint John. An undeniable linkage also emerged between the Orange Order and the Mechanics Institute, symbolizing the nativist attraction that Orangeism had to economically beleaguered Protestant workers who faced stiff competition from famine immigrants. Finally, the riot underscored the Orange belief in vigilante justice. The procession's return to York Point symbolized a 'heroic' and selfless action to remove a dangerous Catholic 'mob' from Saint John's thoroughfares. The anemic state of the city's constabulary justified Orange vigilantism.[40]

In retrospect, the riot of 1847 illuminated the entrenchment of social violence as a perennial method of interaction between Orangemen and Catholics.[41]

A year of bloody skirmishes was the riot's true legacy, for neither side had emerged with a definitive victory on the Twelfth. A wave of assaults and murders swept Saint John and Portland during the weeks that followed; Orange and Catholic vengeance supplied the motive for all of them. On 17 July an Irishman who had been involved in the attack on the Mechanics Band five days earlier was shot in the leg while leaving a meeting at Portland's Mechanics Institute.[42] A murder of one David Campbell on 25 July was also clearly attributed to religious revenge, although authorities never apprehended the suspects. The deceased's mother provided the linkage when she reported that her son and his friends were engaged in a reminiscence of the Orange procession through York Point.[43]

One of the clearest examples of post-riot religious tensions occurred later in July. Three men accosted a visitor from Maine's Aroostook County as he entered York Point. Placing a pistol to his head, one enquired, 'Are you the damn'd rascal that passed along here with ribbons the other day?' Perhaps because he was unsure, or because his bravado was greater than his resolve, he let the startled Mainer go with a parting 'If I was certain I'd put this ball through you.'[44] Violent skirmishes continued to flare throughout the summer in York Point, Portland's wharf district, and especially at the bridge. As one newspaper observed with a grim metaphor: 'Napoleon did not cross the Bridge of Lodi with more danger, than is to be apprehended from crossing the Bridge of Portland at night.'[45]

The murder of a suspected Orangeman on 6 September brought religious antipathies to a fever pitch. James Briggs, Jr, the son of a prosperous Portland shipbuilder, was leaving a Sons of Temperance meeting when several men approached him. After a brief scuffle, Briggs was struck in the head by a bullet. His brother and another member of the group also sustained wounds. The incident shocked the community far more than any of the summer's assaults and murders and in a sense more than the 12 July riot itself. The press characterized the 23-year-old Briggs as a respectable – indeed irreproachable – lad: he came from a fine family, served as a teacher and choir member at St Luke's Church, and attended meetings of the Total Abstinence Society. He was also undoubtedly an Orangeman.[46] Briggs had been shot in Portland's ghetto, and authorities quickly captured two Irish-Catholic suspects. Inundated by sensational press coverage, the city's inhabitants anxiously awaited the trial.

The scores of testimonials and eye-witness accounts generated by the trial revealed the venomous state of ethno-religious relations and social tensions in Saint John and Portland. Informants clearly exposed paramilitary networks operated by militant Orangemen and Catholics. Personal revenge on an individual scale appeared to be the favourite tactic of the weaker and outnumbered Irish-Catholics. Orangemen, enjoying the support of a Protestant majority, preferred a collective vigilantism whereby they dispensed extra-legal justice while acting as an unofficial watchdog of the Irish districts.[47]

The two Portland Catholics arrested, Dennis McGovern and Edward McDermott, were apparently loitering to identify local Orangemen as they left their lodges on the night Briggs met his death. Evidence failed to establish conclusively whether Briggs and his friends had attended an Orange Order or a Sons of Temperance meeting. However, most of the testimony against McGovern and McDermott came from known Orangemen. For example, Squire Manks, the notorious Orange belligerent, volunteered an extensive statement for the prosecution. The eventual release of the prisoners – because witnesses could not positively identify either – inflamed Protestant passions.[48] By the year's end, the Orange-Catholic struggle had escalated. Both sides habitually armed themselves if they ventured into unfriendly districts; each tried desperately to identify its most virulent enemies; and in many cases, both were prepared to kill for their causes.

The Briggs murder provided the capstone for a summer of unprecedented violence in the histories of Saint John and Portland. It also served as the catalyst for the establishment of professionalized police forces. As discussed above, pressures to supplant the ineffective constabularies had been steadily mounting since 1841.[49] Saint John had come close to instituting a force in 1845, when Irish-Catholic immigration had blossomed enough to provoke widespread fears. As Mayor Donaldson had observed in his petition for professional police, 'a population has been introduced of opinions and manners differing from the former inhabitants; force must now be employed to keep order.' While Lieutenant-Governor Colebrooke philosophically agreed with the proposal, Saint John's Common Council had rejected it because it would increase taxes.[50] The social violence of the summer of 1847 rekindled the debate. Public clamour for a police force intensified after the Briggs murder, while Portland's Irish district served as the lightning rod.[51]

In October Colebrooke bowed to public pressure and asked Portland's magistrates to form a police force. A few justices – particularly Jacob Allan – responded favourably and petitioned Colebrooke for a £500 advance from the provincial treasury to pay the initial costs. Colebrooke baulked at the request but the magistrates went ahead with the groundwork, confident that their expenses would eventually be covered or that legislation would be enacted giving them the means to levy new taxes.[52] On 8 November magistrates swore in a temporary police force 'consisting of ten good Protestants,' and Jacob Allan assumed the position of police magistrate.[53] The cooperation between provincial and town governments offended some of the magistrates, who claimed that the new institution usurped their powers. One resigned in protest. Yet Colebrooke and Allan prevailed; in the closing months of 1847 New Brunswick moved closer to the creation of its first professional police force, modelled on England's urban contingents.[54]

Residents in Portland and Saint John applauded the innovation, but the agency's religious composition angered the Irish-Catholic communities. Tragedy struck less than a month after the establishment of the force. A crowd of vigilant Irishmen attacked three policemen when they attempted to arrest a drunk in the seedy wharf district. Because regulations restricted them to the protection of only night sticks, all three received serious stab wounds. One lingered for several days before succumbing.[55] Authorities arrested two of the attackers and sentenced them to prison, but the purported ringleader absconded to the United States and never faced trial.[56]

The incident sparked a wave of anti-Catholic sentiment in Portland and Saint John. Sceptical Protestants became convinced of the need for the paramilitary Orangemen. In addition, the police force became even more solidly identified with Protestantism. Colebrooke visited Portland only days after the affray and authorized swords and pistols for policemen on duty. Magistrates added five more Protestants to the force. Ultimately, the fears of Irish-Catholic civil disorder helped to entrench the spirit of nativism in the region.[57]

Portland's enthusiasm for the temporary police force, coupled with an effective lobbying campaign by magistrates, led to New Brunswick's first professional police statute. The executive council swung behind an enactment in February 1848 after Jacob Allan threatened to disband the force without either the immediate assurance of provincial funds or the permission to levy taxes.[58] On 30 March the New Brunswick legislature passed an act 'to establish and maintain a Police Force in the Parish of Portland.' The statute called for an executive-appointed police magistrate, who in turn retained the power to assign a police commissioner, and authorized a force of up to fifteen men, the current total. An authorization for police to take into custody any disorderly or suspicious person without a warrant emerged as the most effective clause for curtailing violence.[59] This stipulation, coupled with the immediate reappointment of Allan as police magistrate, ensured that a Protestant body of law enforcers would have the essential tools to supervise Portland's poorer Catholic neighbourhoods.[60]

In the meantime, Saint John struggled to follow Portland's lead and buttress its own forces. Following the December recommendations from the Saint John grand jury to assign a lieutenant, twelve policemen, and a stipendiary magistrate, the legislature passed a bill that addressed the constabulary.[61] While it provided for a larger night watch and day police, the measure fell short of the sweeping reforms of the Portland act.[62] Key architects in this change included two of New Brunswick's most prominent Orangemen, Cornelius Van Horne and William Needham.[63] The difference between the bills can be explained by the Saint John Common Council's continued reluctance to fund a professional force with tax revenues, and more important, by the demographic compositions of the two communities. Portland's larger proportion of Irish-Catholics explained their ubiquitous visibility; by contrast, Saint John's immigrant population clustered primarily in one section of the city – York Point. The threat to established order from Irish-Catholics in early 1848 failed to provide enough justification for the passage of a comprehensive police bill for Saint John. Only after social violence reached a zenith at the 12 July 1849 riot would popular support be substantial enough to demand a professionalized police force. By the spring of 1850, Saint John had followed its suburb's lead and was operating under the protection of a permanent police force.[64]

The establishment of police forces in Portland and Saint John, intended to curtail social violence, attacked only the symptoms of a profound problem. Indeed, by staffing the forces entirely with Protestants, the communities escalated ethno-religious tensions. Structural inequities remained unaddressed. Social violence was rampant in 1847 because of increased famine immigration, the concomitant growth of Orange lodges, and a depressed economy that made competitors out of native-born and immigrants. The linkage between the Mechanics Institute and the Orange Order, exposed in the 12 July riot, and the apparent connections between the Sons of Temperance and Orangeism, as depicted in the Briggs murder, pointed to a solidification among Protestants to ward off Irish-Catholic cultural and economic encroachment. To the Orangemen and Protestants, crime and violence were becoming virtually synonymous with the ghettos of York Point and Portland. Protestant citizens heaped the entire blame for social disorders on Irish-Catholics, when in fact they shared at least half the responsibility.[65] The injection of destitute Irish-Catholics into the Protestant-Loyalist strongholds of Saint John and Portland created the milieu for social violence.

For the first eight years of the 1840s, confrontations between Irish-Catholic immigrants and Protestants – both native-born and immigrant – increased at a staggering rate. Sporadic assaults because of religious preferences rapidly gave way to larger episodes involving organized crowds, particularly on days of religious or historical significance. Riots broke out in 1842, 1845, and 1847, each marking an increase in the number of participants and an escalation in intensity. In essence, collective conflict had become a ritualistic form of interaction between Catholics and Orangemen, with York Point and Portland's wharf district the arenas. Communities that once prided themselves on their ethnic and religious tolerance now resembled armed camps.[66] Yet as deplorable as this history of social violence appeared in 1848, Saint John and Portland stood on the brink of New Brunswick's worst armed confrontation of the nineteenth century – the 12 July riot of 1849.

# 8

# Social violence peaks:
# The York Point riot of 1849

The York Point riot of 1849 eclipsed the collective violence that New Brunswick experienced throughout the 1840s. Saint John and Portland were quiet in 1848, much as they had been in 1846, because Orangemen travelled to Fredericton on 12 July to participate in a massive demonstration.[1] But religious feuds continued to fester; for example, authorities arrested an Orangeman named John Young for assaulting an Irish-Catholic with a gun in early March of 1849.[2] As spring approached, Orangemen and Irish-Catholics embarked on a belligerent course that brought them to the worst riot in New Brunswick's history.

Following the orderly election of a city councillor, a large crowd gathered in front of Nethery's Hotel on Church Street in Saint John on 6 March. The hotel, owned by a prominent Orangeman, served as a local lodge's regular meeting place. Shouting for the destruction of the building, the Irish-Catholic crowd soon attracted hundreds of angry participants. Its truculent mood prompted the mayor to request the intervention of troops from the British garrison. They arrived too late to prevent a furious exchange of gunfire that left wounded littering the street and an Irish-Catholic butcher from Portland dead.[3] The incident sparked an investigation and kindled fears of the upcoming ethno-religious holidays.[4] In an effort to avoid a confrontation, the city's St Patrick's Society postponed its plans for a 17 March dinner until the summer.[5] Perhaps the delay produced the desired results; Saint John was free of collective violence for the remainder of the spring.

Tensions began to mount again, however, as the anniversary of the Battle of the Boyne approached. For the first time in local history, Orangemen advertised their plans for an elaborate procession. They even invited brethren from across the province.[6] This clearly signalled a new boldness among Orangemen; their numbers had increased dramatically as a result of the 1847 riot, and they now perceived themselves strong enough to withstand assault if they celebrated publicly. In regional lodges such as Wellington in Portland, Orangemen attended special meetings to tackle the logistical problem of coordinating a large gathering.[7]

The Orangemen's temerity triggered emotional reactions from many Saint John and Portland residents. With the memory of altercations between Catholics and Orangemen in 1842, 1845, and 1847 still fresh in their minds, concerned citizens knew that the scheduled procession invited violence. Several Saint John magistrates implored the mayor and Common Council to prevent the procession by edict, but the effort failed because a majority of the justices refused to sign the petition. According to a local newspaper, the abstainers preferred to let the pugnacious parties 'fight it out the best way they can.'[8] Mayor Robert D. Wilmot did make one attempt, however, to defuse the issue before the Twelfth. On the holiday's eve he met with local Orange officials and asked them to abandon voluntarily their plans to march. But the Orangemen, well versed in their rights, rejected the suggestion because no provincial statute gave civilian officials the authority to ban public processions. The march, they insisted, would proceed as planned.[9]

With a measure of fatalistic acceptance, the adversaries prepared for the occasion. While Carleton and York County Orangemen boarded the steamer in Fredericton for the all-night trip to join their brethren in Saint John, Catholics grimly prepared for a counter-demonstration. In a store on Market Square, a clerk sold a dozen flints to an Irishman who muttered that he 'did not approve of ... the Orange procession tomorrow.'[10] Officials mounted their final attempts to defuse a riot in the early morning hours of 12 July. Wilmot, acting under the only legislative guidelines at his disposal, tried to muster a contingent of special constables. Few responded to the call; partisan feelings and fear kept Saint John's eligible citizenry away.[11] Similarly Portland's Captain of Police, Francis S. Jones, met with his young squad at 9:00 AM. Jones briefed his men about the possibilities of a riot in Portland, for he had heard that the Orangemen intended to include his district in their processional path.[12] Yet even as Wilmot and Jones steeled the constabulary to prevent a battle, shop-keepers along Prince William Street, King Street, and Market Square boarded their windows and decided to declare a business holiday.[13]

Shortly after dawn hundreds of Orangemen began to gather at Nethery's Hotel, the scene of the March disturbances. Resplendent in their regalia and accompanied by a band and colourful banners, the Orangemen milled about until 9:30 AM, when a large contingent of Portland brethren joined them.[14] Many of the rank and file carried muskets on their shoulders and pistols stuffed into their belts and pockets; several of their leaders wore swords.[15] Just prior to departing the hotel the Orangemen learned about a green arch that Catholics had erected over a York Point street, spanning the Orangemen's intended route. They faced a symbolic surrender if they marched under the bough and risked a confrontation if they attempted to remove it. Yet they refused to alter their plans – they would rise to the Catholic challenge.[16]

The Orangemen, numbering well over one hundred, departed on the first leg of their journey at approximately 10:00 AM. With their weapons, band, and banners, they resembled infantry on the march. They quickly covered the distance to the foot of Princess Street, where they greeted the steam ferry from Carleton. A delegation from western Saint John and nearby Pisarinco disembarked. Among the new brethren was Joseph Coram, a Carleton carpenter and Senior Deputy Grand Master of the New Brunswick Lodge. As the procession leader, Corum would have the honour of representing King William by riding a white horse.[17] Thus reinforced, the procession began the long march to Indiantown, a small community on Portland's eastern boundary where the Fredericton steamer docked. The Orangemen's intended route would take them through the Irish-Catholic ghettos in York Point and Portland.

The information received prior to the departure from Nethery's Hotel proved accurate. A large green arch, probably constructed of pine boughs, stood across Mill Street near its junction with Union Street. A crowd of approximately two hundred jeering Irish-Catholics protected the arch, which effectively guarded the entrance to York Point. Although Mill Street served as the major thoroughfare leading to the Portland Bridge, several alternative routes down side streets were available to the Orangemen. Yet without hesitation the procession headed towards the arch. Mill Street loomed ahead unobstructed by people, but the bough had been cleverly designed. It was between seven and eight feet tall in the middle. Orangemen could easily pass underneath, but those carrying flags and banners would be forced to crouch down or drop their charges sideways. In effect they would have to dip their colours, an international sign of respect or defeat.[18]

Irish-Catholics lined the procession route, taunting the Orangemen and imploring them to march under the bough. Outnumbered for the moment, the Protestants accepted the humiliation. A flurry of stones and pieces of bricks accompanied the insults as the procession completed its passage through York Point. Several Orangemen responded by firing their pistols or muskets into the air. In spite of the provocations, both parties avoided a direct confrontation. The Orangemen, still in procession and without injuries, emerged from York Point and crossed the bridge to Portland.[19] Roughly seventy more brethren joined the marchers on the northern end. With their spirits buoyed by the reinforcements, they headed west for Indiantown. The Irish-Catholics prudently declined giving chase.[20]

At Indiantown, the Orangemen met the steamer from Fredericton. The northern contingent, from as far away as Woodstock, brought additional armament. Another pivotal Orange leader arrived with the newcomers, a man who would be second-in-command for the day's proceedings. George Anderson, a Presbyterian grocer from Fredericton and Orange Master, was a veteran of several disturbances in his home town. Carrying a sword that symbolized his rank, Anderson joined Corum at the head of the procession. A wagon filled with weapons and supplies driven by Alexander Boone, an Orange employee of the steamship company, assumed a position at the rear. The ranks of brethren followed – now numbering about four hundred. Most bore muskets on shoulder straps. Finally, several men brought axes to destroy the bough when the procession returned to York Point. Now that they enjoyed reinforcements, the Orangemen had every intention of engaging their enemy in battle.[21]

While the Orangemen had been occupied on their journey to Indiantown, attempts had been made in Saint John to remove the possibility of a riot. Upon hearing of the near confrontation at the arch, Mayor Wilmot headed for York Point accompanied by a city constable and a magistrate. Confronting the Catholic crowd, Wilmot insisted that the bough be removed. When the Irish demanded to know the reason, the mayor claimed that the arch obstructed the passage of hay wagons. Wilmot's lack of candour enraged the crowd. When the constable moved forward to dismantle the offending structure, groups of angry Irishmen surrounded the supporting poles. Wilmot tried to aid the constable, only to be physically repulsed. Magistrate James Gilbert and his son Henry captured a teenager immediately after he had struck the mayor with a stick, but after a brief scuffle the crowd liberated the offender. Although the Irish-Catholics continued to protect the poles, they did no further harm to the small party of officials.[22]

The attempt to remove the arch failed miserably; it also alienated the mayor from the Irish-Catholics and strengthened his sympathies for the Orange Order. The crowd was incensed that the authorities would direct their energies to dismantling their bough while allowing the Orangemen to march in an armed procession. Moreover, the crowd had been cohesive and territorial. Shouting 'Clear out' and 'Stay off our ground,' the Irish-Catholics had rebuffed the authorities only when they had attempted to remove the arch. No general rioting had ensued, and the contingent had been allowed to leave York Point. Many of the Irish, being recent immigrants, had not recognized the mayor.[23] As in the morning, when the crowd had remained to protect York Point and had not pursued the Orangemen to Portland, the incident at the bough had illustrated a defensive unanimity of purpose amongst the Irish-Catholics.

Upon withdrawing from the abortive effort to disperse the Catholics, Wilmot decided to appeal to the Orangemen. As his emissary he dispatched Jacob Allan, Portland's police magistrate. Allan intercepted the procession near the foot of Fort Howe Hill in Portland. Corum and Anderson consented to listen to his arguments, and the three retired to nearby St Luke's Church for a brief meeting. Allan asked the Orange leaders to bypass the Catholic district by using the longer Valley Road on their approach to Saint John. Allan would later testify that Coram had vacillated, but the fateful decision rested on the entire Orange contingent. When Coram and Anderson presented the proposal to their brethren, they were shouted down by a chant of 'Death or Victory.' The Orangemen had suffered humiliation by marching under the green arch in the morning; now they were reinforced and better armed. Squire Manks, Portland's veteran of several confrontations, summed up the sentiments of his brethren when he cockily claimed, 'We have not come to go back again.' Coram calmly informed the dejected police magistrate that the Orangemen would keep to their original route. Remounting his white steed and giving the motion for advance, he led his force of six hundred on the last leg of the journey to York Point and an almost assured battle.[24]

Mayor Wilmot had not remained idle after dispatching Allan to Portland. His failure to persuade the Orangemen the previous evening gave him little hope of altering the procession's path. Therefore, he went to the barracks of the Royal Regiment of British Regulars in Saint John and convinced Lieutenant Colonel Deane of the impending danger. Deane sent sixty men and officers to Market Square. The choice of location illustrated the attitudes of the authorities towards the Irish district. The square lay at the foot of York Point; but more germane to the issue, it was not in the vicinity of the green bough. Although the desire to prevent a clash between civilians and soldiers partially accounted for placing the troops out of harm's way, the gesture effectively ensured that the riot, if it came, would be contained to York Point. The detachment had plenty of time to station itself at the end of the Portland Bridge on Mill Street between the advancing Orangemen and the offensive arch.[25] With their weapons aimed up Dock Street, the soldiers awaited further orders. Mayor Wilmot arrived shortly after the troops and read the Riot Act to the Irish-Catholic crowd in two locations at York Point. It proved a futile effort: the Orangemen were closing quickly on the bridge and the authorities could not act on the terms of the Riot Act until an hour's grace period had passed. Minutes – not an hour – separated the belligerents.[26]

General rioting broke out along Mill Street before the procession arrived at the bough. The Catholic crowd had doubled since the earlier incident; like their enemy, many of its members had used the interim to gather firearms. Reports of who fired the first shots varied, but roofers working on a Mill Street building agreed that Orangemen shot into the crowd after being met with a volley of stones and brickbats.[27] Several Catholics lay wounded or dying after the barrage, and then their guns answered the Orangemen's. A heated battle ensued. Men and women along Mill Street threw anything within reach at the better-armed Orange contingent. Some engaged in fist fights with individuals they were able to pull from the ranks. Coram struggled to free himself after a handful of Irish grabbed his horse's tether. A dozen Catholics captured the wagon filled with arms and gave Alexander Boone a sound thrashing. In all, Orangemen and Catholics traded hundreds of shots that took the lives of at least twelve combatants. After several minutes of furious fighting, the Orangemen emerged from York Point. As they headed for the safety of the troops, their procession appeared intact.[28]

The British garrison, after remaining stationary in Market Square throughout the heat of the battle, leaped into action as soon as the Orangemen had left the Irish-Catholic ghetto. Without firing a shot the soldiers marched past the procession and positioned themselves on Dock Street to seal off the crowd. This manoeuvre effectively doused what remained of the conflict.[29] It also gave the Orangemen the opportunity to continue their procession unmolested, for any Catholics wishing to leave York Point in pursuit would have to contend first with the soldiers. The Orangemen, heady with their successful assault on the enemy's territory and unrestrained by the authorities because they had never received the Riot Act, proceeded through Market and King squares and made a circle through the city's centre. Only when they had re-entered Market Square, with the intention of parading through York Point for the third time, were the troops commanded to impede their progress. Satisfied with their efforts, they cheerfully agreed to disband.[30]

The Orange procession dispersed in the same manner that it had assembled. The Portland and northern New Brunswick contingents broke off and, detouring York Point, returned to their lodges or the steamer at Indiantown. Brethren gave the Carleton group a rousing farewell at the steam ferry, where only hours earlier it had disembarked. The Saint John Orangemen retired to Nethery's Hotel to dine and celebrate their victory. Five in the afternoon – a scant eight hours after the martial forces had begun to mobilize – found the city's streets hushed with an eerie silence. The York Point riot was over.[31]

Despite the quiet, the British soldiers wheeled an artillery piece into Market Square at nightfall. Symbolically, they placed it at the foot of Dock Street pointing up the hill at York Point. Mayor Wilmot also swore in several special constables. Given the circumstances of the conflict, both gestures were unnecessary.[32] The riot had never become general; violence erupted only when Orangemen had marched with arms through Irish-Catholic York Point. The precautions of the nervous mayor, magistrates, and military were understandable, but the recurrence of a fracas was doubtful after the Orangemen had dispersed.

The day following the riot brought a flurry of official activity. Magistrates examined witnesses and participants and contemplated the maintenance of public order, constables scoured York Point for suspects, and the coroner held several inquests. After being informed of the severity of the battle, Lieutenant-Governor Head left Fredericton on the evening of the thirteenth with his chief law advisers, Attorney General Lemuel A. Wilmot and Solicitor General William B. Kinnear. They arrived early the next morning on the same steamer that had transported the upcountry Orangemen.[33] Although the city's placidity astounded Head, he authorized arming the Saint John and Portland police forces with weapons and ammunition from the militia's ordnance office. In addition, Attorney General Wilmot recommended the addition of twenty special constables to the Saint John force, and a majority of magistrates promptly agreed. At least one justice, however, protested this procedure. Hugh Sharkie pointed out that the names of at least five known Orangemen graced the appointment list. His colleagues quickly snuffed the challenge, for the excesses and possible containment of the Orange Order clearly did not trouble Saint John's magistracy in the days following the riot. Their pre-eminent fear concerned a possible rebellion among the 'lower class of Irish.' The strategy of keeping the masses enclosed in York Point, which had proved its effectiveness during the riot, continued to be the official policy. Heavily armed constables – many of them Orangemen – patrolled York Point and its perimeter in the weeks following the disturbance.[34]

The coroner's inquests and magistrates' examinations, besides collecting scores of valuable eyewitness reports, quickly provided enough evidence to confirm what New Brunswickers had suspected since the evening of the Twelfth: the Orange-Green riot of 1849 had been the province's bloodiest. Heavy armament on both sides, particularly among the Orangemen, and the confined battle zone of the city's streets accounted for a casualty rate that far outstripped New Brunswick's other costly riot at Woodstock, where two years earlier the fighting transpired on an open hillside. Circumstances made an accurate count of dead and wounded virtually impossible. Irish-Catholics dragged their fallen comrades into York Point homes even as the rioting peaked in its intensity. Burial parties had already completed their dreary chores by the time Head had arrived on the morning of 13 July.[35]

Similarly, Orangemen carried their wounded to the friendlier quarters of Saint John and Carleton. Conservative estimates by the coroner and local physicians listed twelve killed, including an Irish-Catholic woman. At least one hundred had been injured by gunshots and flying debris such as stones and bricks. Catholics had suffered the majority of the casualties, but Orangemen had paid a higher price than in any previous clash. Brethren from Kings County, Golden Grove, Carleton, Portland, and Saint John had received injuries serious enough to warrant treatment.[36] Clearly, the disturbance had affected many New Brunswickers: it had even touched the lieutenant-governor. Head returned to Fredericton to find that a construction worker at Government House – an Orangeman – had received a leg wound during the riot.[37]

Considering the magnitude of the disturbance and its containment to several streets in York Point, authorities arrested few participants in its wake. Yet the litigation brought a new wrinkle to the pattern established early in the 1840s. For the first time officials served warrants to Orange participants and grilled them more rigorously in examinations. This new policy reflected Head's insistence that known offenders on both sides, especially the leaders, be prosecuted. While his predecessor had routinely pre-established the guilt of Irish-Catholics, Head saved his harshest condemnation for the Orangemen whom he believed had provoked the disturbance. Head and his judicial lieutenants specifically outlined their instructions for equitable prosecution, but in practice the investigative teams concentrated their energies on bringing Irish-Catholics to trial. The discrepancy between agenda and execution held little mystery, for Justice William H. Needham, an Orange Grand Master who had been active in the provincial lodge throughout the 1840s, assumed the role as chief examiner.[38]

Despite the prejudice of the examining board of justices, at least part of the executive order's spirit survived intact. In the face of overwhelming evidence, authorities served warrants to Coram, Anderson, and another Orangeman named Thomas Knowles implicating them in the death of a Catholic participant. Thirteen Orangemen received warrants for carrying guns in public and fighting, while four others faced charges of the less-serious offence of illegal assembly. Squire Manks, who had been implicated in past disturbances but never convicted, was among the latter group.[39] Strikingly, Irish-Catholics were served with only four more warrants then their Orange foe. This equity resulted because authorities could easily identify the Orangemen, thanks to their cohesive procession, but had to struggle to find Catholic offenders who had melted into their surroundings at York Point. Three Irish-Catholics were arrested for the assault on Mayor Wilmot before the riot, three more for attacking Alexander Boone and his wagon, one for shooting into the Orange procession, one for murder, and sixteen for unlawful assembly. The latter charge included warrants for four rioters who had absconded.[40] Superficially, the twenty Orangemen and twenty-four Catholics officially implicated in the riot reflected an attempt to prosecute transgressors indiscriminately.

But the judicial proceedings swiftly destroyed the illusion of impartial treatment. Since all the rioters established recognizances to await arraignment, none spent time in jail before the trial.[41] Saint John's grand jury showed its reluctance to prosecute the arraigned Orangemen as soon as court had convened on 7 August. The jury pre-emptively dropped the bills against Coram and Anderson. The thirteen implicated for carrying weapons in public received the same favour, despite abundant testimony that most of the Orange procession had been illegally armed throughout the day. Only the four Orangemen accused of illegal assembly and Thomas Knowles were held over for trial.[42] Indeed, the plight of a witness who had the temerity to record evidence against three Orangemen for shooting at buildings at York Point epitomized the court's pro-Orange atmosphere. Not only did the grand jury ignore the charges, they quickly accepted a counter-suit by the Orangemen and issued a bill against the witness for perjury.[43] Even if the witness had lied, the grand jury would have no way of knowing until it had examined the evidence on both sides of the charge. By accepting the allegations of the Orangemen without question, the jury had betrayed its responsibility and exposed its partiality.

The grand jury successfully brought more bills against the Irish-Catholic defendants. It dropped the charges against the murder suspect, owing to insufficient evidence, and twelve of those arraigned for unlawful assembly. But it ordered six to face trial for assault, one for attempted murder and four for unlawful assembly.[44] Although the jury reduced the numbers of both the Orange and Catholic defendants, it showed a dramatic preference for bringing the latter to trial.

Once given the schedule of charges, the prosecution began to compile vigorously cases against the accused of both parties. William B. Kinnear, the solicitor general and chief prosecutor, built his argument around the fact that the defendants brought weapons to the procession and counter-demonstration. Empowered by recent legislation that explicitly defined various forms of public disturbances, he also sought advice on the legality of processions from the Home Office.[45] The lawyers for the Orangemen, however, maintained that their clients had acted entirely in self-defence. While this argument embodied the spirit of Orangeism, and was assuredly believed to be perfectly valid by the defendants, it drew considerable criticism.[46] Judge James Carter, veteran of the Woodstock and Fredericton riot trials, made an impassioned appeal for the conviction of both opponents. He reviewed the public-disturbance laws and informed the jury that if the accused were armed and intended to do harm then they were clearly guilty as charged. He saved his strongest condemnation for the Orangemen who deliberately returned to York Point with arms: 'No body of men can band together for purposes which must lead to a breach of the peace, even in the very act of what they call self-defence.'[47]

The jurors remained singularly unimpressed with either the prosecution's arguments or the considered opinions of Judge Carter; they found it easier to convict Catholics. On 15 August they established the guilt of two Irishmen, largely on the testimony of an Orange policeman named John Nixon: John Haggerty received one year in the provincial penitentiary for assaulting the mayor at the bough incident, and Daniel Haggerty landed in the county jail for six months for attacking the Orange teamster,

Alexander Boone. The jury acquitted the remaining four who faced similar charges. Finally, the authorities continued the warrants for three Irish-Catholics who had failed to appear for their trial.[48] Three days later, without leaving their seats for private discussion, the same jurors swiftly vindicated every Orange defendant. They debated at length about the fate of the remaining Irish-Catholic before dropping the murder charge because of insufficient evidence.[49] Thus, the York Point riot trial ended with only two convictions, the least of any similar inquest of the 1840s.

Several reasons explained the prosecution's failure to bring successful convictions against the defendants of both sides. Although the jury displayed overtly partisan sentiments, no evidence suggested that its members included Orangemen. Certainly none was Roman-Catholic. The Orange counsel's argument of self-defence had convinced the jury, despite the objections of the lieutenant-governor, the attorney and solicitor generals, and Judge Carter. The recent public-disturbances statute outlawed any group that formed 'with intent' to aggress, but the lack of a definitive law against public processions that were obnoxious to other parties undermined the prosecutor's case.[50] Ironically, Head received guidance on this issue from the Home Office several weeks after the trial's conclusion. Lord Howick enclosed a recent decision from a similar case in Britain, wherein the Queen's Counsel had successfully contended that even in the absence of explicit legislation, common law applied: 'Large processions, carrying arms, and under such circumstances as to inspire fear in the minds of the people ... are, beyond all question, illegal assemblages.'[51] However unambiguous the Home Office's advice, no documentary evidence indicated that it would have been taken had it arrived during the trial.

New Brunswick's officials in the 1840s displayed great reluctance to legislate against Orange processions even if they offended Catholics to the point of rioting. Tough talk by Head, the judiciary, and even members of the House of Assembly failed to convince loyal New Brunswickers that the Orange Order represented a disruptive impulse.[52] Finally, the York Point riot trial adhered to judicial patterns established earlier in the decade at Woodstock and Fredericton. Only two men received convictions – neither were Orangemen. This result illuminated the greatest underlying thread of the social violence of the 1840s: only Irish-Catholics would be found guilty of offences connected with riots.

The outcome brought immediate rebuke from all quarters of the province. Solicitor General Kinnear expressed outrage because the law clearly prohibited armed groups, and the jury ignored the admissions of Orangemen who carried weapons. Head added his voice to the chorus of lament, arguing that given the magnitude of the disturbance and its confined location, it was inexcusable that more offenders in both crowds had not been arrested and brought to conviction.[53] More severe condemnations flowed from the pens of local editors. Several newspapers characterized the trial a sham or at best a waste of taxpayers' money. George Fenety, editor of the *Saint John Morning News*, cynically reasoned that only the lawyers had benefited from the proceedings because at least they had received stipends.[54] Undoubtedly, many citizens interested in seeing the demise of armed confrontations between religious groups felt cheated by the trial's results.

Criticisms levelled at the constabulary and judiciary were justified. The commitment of Saint John's authorities to contain or prevent riots of a religious nature was negligible when the trial evidence was considered. The case of John Haggerty highlighted the judicial system's failure to apply the law to all, regardless of religious persuasion. Implicated as the Catholic 'ringleader' protecting the arch across Mill Street, he had received the only felony conviction at the trial. While serving his sentence he appealed to Head for a commutation, complaining that out of hundreds of participants, he was the only one arrested and convicted of a felony. His point had merit, but his vital statistics more sharply etched the dubious nature of justice. An immigrant widower and father of three, John Haggerty would spend his sixty-third birthday in the provincial penitentiary for allegedly masterminding the York Point riots.[55]

As New Brunswick's largest and bloodiest riot in the nineteenth century, the 1849 Saint John disturbance has achieved a measure of notoriety. (See appendix A.) Basing his assessments almost exclusively upon Colonial Office papers, New Brunswick's premier historian, W.S. MacNutt, addressed the riot and suggested that it might be understood as an epilogue to responsible government.[56] In another vein, an antiquarian account by Reverend J.W. Millidge attributed the disturbance entirely to a 'tribal spirit of antagonism' between Irish-Protestants and Catholic immigrants.[57] Though both of these assessments hold a kernel of truth, they do not adequately explain the event. The riot evolved from religious, ethnic, and economic issues, not political concerns. And while Irish-Protestant immigrants participated, many of the Orangemen were New Brunswickers of Loyalist stock or English and Scottish backgrounds.[58] The most recent assessment provided by Saint John historian T.W. Acheson has altered moderately the above interpretations. Interpreting the riot as primarily a clash between Irish-Catholic and Irish-Protestants, lamentably transferred to the city of Saint John, Acheson also assumed that the leaders of the march were the Orange Order's 'sergeants,' not its commanders.[59] Indeed the evidence submitted above suggests strongly that Orange leaders, including Coram, Manks, and Anderson, orchestrated the day's proceedings. The marchers, and subsequently the rioters, cut across both the Orange Order's and New Brunswick's class and socio-economic boundaries.

Finally, and most egregiously, one nineteenth-century account blatantly misled readers. In his essay on Saint John's history, D.R. Jack concluded his narrative of the event with the following comment: 'In the year 1849 one of the permanent ornaments on King Square was a gallows.' With only two rioters convicted and serving sentences of six and twelve months, Jack's apocryphal allusion to capital punishment served exclusively to embellish the city's tale of woe. Jack, who was undoubtedly influenced by contemporary assessments, also sustained the myth that religious antagonisms in New Brunswick represented a wholesale importation of Irish problems.[60]

A thorough examination of all relevant sources undermines, to varying degrees, earlier interpretations of this conflict. All the eyewitness accounts and testimonials, excluding those of the Orangemen, viewed the battle as a direct result of the Orange Order's decisions on two separate occasions to march through the Irish-Catholic district.[61] Moreover, observers heaped blame on the legislature and local officials for their failure to outlaw or prevent incendiary public displays.[62] The most convincing critics focused their attack on Mayor Wilmot and Saint John's magistrates who, despite forewarning of an Orange procession through York Point, failed to prevent bloodshed. For example, Wilmot did not attempt to buttress the constabulary until after the riot was over. Only a handful of justices responded to the mayor's summons on the morning of the Twelfth; the rest either stayed home or left town rather than become involved. Only one constable accompanied the mayor to York Point on the mission to dismantle the arch. Apparently he was the only law enforcer who could be located, for the other constables were either following the magistrates' example or marching in the Orange procession.[63] Some critics believed that a more professional police organization, such as Portland's, might have successfully defused the problem or controlled the crowds.[64] Still others questioned the failure of the British detachment, which was already posted to Market Square, to respond immediately to the affray.[65]

The troublesome questions raised by critics forced civic and provincial authorities to defend their actions. Lieutenant-Governor Head supported Mayor Wilmot's cautious and minimal attempts to defuse the confrontation. Wilmot's hands were tied by a dearth of effective statutory tools, Head argued, such as a mandate to cancel a public procession and the power to press magistrates and constables into service even against their wills. In addition, officials backed the military's decision to remain outside the field of conflict; Orangemen and Irish-Catholics alike found the prospects of a direct confrontation between professional soldiers and civilians anathema. The presence of troops primarily functioned as an emotional ploy to buttress the morale of civilian authorities on the scene, and served as a reminder that those who became too belligerent would have to deal with a well-armed professional force.[66]

The York Point riot had long-range ramifications as well. The most apparent legacy, similar to Woodstock's in 1847, was the boost it gave to Orangeism in the Saint John–Portland region. At the time of the riot, Orangemen already occupied civic and judicial positions. Marching in the procession were a city marshal, a Saint John constable who acted as a standard-bearer, and several stipendiary policemen and night watchmen. Throughout the 1850s, Portland's police force would remain entirely Protestant in composition, while Saint John's would add only a token handful of Catholic constables to the overwhelmingly Protestant force in numbers grossly disproportionate to the city's percentage of Catholic and Protestant inhabitants.[67] Thus, the police force reinforced both figuratively and literally the hegemony of Protestantism and Orangeism in New Brunswick.

Other linkages between the Orange Order and Saint John's governing élite appeared. In addition to the cases noted above, an influential Orangeman who would later become a leader of the Provincial Grand Lodge of New Brunswick served as a member of the riot's panel of examiners.[68] Indeed, in the riot's wake Orangeism achieved even a greater popularity among residents who perceived the Irish-Catholics as a threat to the established order. Protestants inundated Orange lodges after 12 July, seeking membership and wanting to know what they could do to support the anti-Catholic crusade.[69] Non-Orange newspapers inaugurated editorial campaigns that paralleled the propaganda from established Orange organs. Editors variously depicted Orangemen as defenders of the Protestant faith, protectors of liberty, misunderstood civil libertarians, or even peacemakers. The marches through York Point were trumpeted as heroic and selfless actions; containment of the unruly Irish-Catholics became a noble cause. Even non-Orangemen, including local authorities, began to view the organization in the light of a group whose rights of free expression were being unjustly infringed.[70]

As in the other communities under discussion, the riots tended in some cases to create and in others to reinforce linkages between Orangemen and public officials. Illustrations abound. Three of Saint John's most influential Common Council aldermen during mid-century were Thomas Hardy, George Bond, and Gregory Van Horne.[71] Significantly, the latter two also held a variety of leadership positions in the Orange Order throughout the period. Orangemen figured prominently in the ranks of aldermen from 1848 throughout the 1850s. For 1848 and 1849, *at least* three out of six claimed Orange membership; during the 1850s an average of two confirmed Orangemen sat on the Common Council each year. Most important, Mayor John R. Partelow wore another hat as the Orange provincial secretary from 1848 to 1854.[72] Outside of the political sphere Orangemen represented the ranks of the city's important businessmen and property holders, including the powerful merchant and importer Stephen Wiggins.[73] A high percentage of Orangemen appeared in the city's service sector, most notably in the various fire companies of the late 1840s and 1850s. In fact, Orangemen headed two of the three companies listed in 1849.[74]

Yet despite these powerful linkages, Orangemen were not without their critics who found the group a perennial obstacle to peace. For example the Saint John grand jury recorded the following condemnation after the riot: 'This county does not require the aid of public processions, of Secret Societies, composed of men dressed in fantastic uniforms or badges, in order to preserve the Protestant Religion; but that on the contrary ... such a procession as took place in this City on the 12th of July, is *unnecessary, and the results are calculated to scandalize and injure any good cause.*'[75] Many involved in the trials, including Judge Carter, Attorney General Wilmot and Solicitor General Kinnear, concluded that the proliferation of riots during the 1840s was cause enough to stifle Orangeism.[76] A few contemporaries even began to understand that the organization represented far more than the simple transfer of Irish grievances to New Brunswick. Head grasped the fact that natives were supplanting the traditional Irish-Protestant membership, and noted that Orangemen were 'generally speaking men in a better station in society, and better educated than the misguided persons whom they provoke to break the peace.'[77] While Orange detractors ultimately failed in their efforts to curtail the organization's growth, they knew that

Irish cultural transfer served as an inadequate explanation of the phenomenon.

Effective organization and the manipulation of Protestants through propaganda and scare tactics explained the spread of Orangeism in the late 1840s. Saint John Orangemen burned in effigy L.A. Wilmot and William Kinnear because they had supported the prosecution of riotous Orangemen for the first time in New Brunswick's history.[78] The *Saint John Morning News* received dozens of threats from 'Protestants' who disapproved of its editorials calling for the conviction of both Catholic and Orange defendants.[79] Non-Orange Protestants apparently paid attention to the anti-Catholic rhetoric. Nowhere was this tendency more evident than in the petition campaign kindled in 1850 to incorporate the Orange Order. Over the years hundreds of signatures flooded into Fredericton from Portland and Saint John residents; the numbers far surpassed Orange membership in the region, for the petition's wording made it possible for any Protestant to sign.[80] Indeed, the Orange Order had become so firmly entrenched that two months after the riot Head expressed his doubts that it could ever be expunged by legislation.[81] Thanks to the York Point disturbance and a fervent and industrious membership, Orangeism had become an institutional fixture in the Saint John region by mid-century.

Finally, the 1849 disturbance marked the end of large-scale social violence in Saint John, although skirmishes between Orangemen and Irish-Catholics would continue for years. The Orange Order's abstention from processions until the incorporation bill passed in 1875 probably contributed most significantly to the abeyance of violence. The perennial debate over the legitimacy of public marches and the hesitancy of the New Brunswick legislature to condone Orangeism accounted for the quarter-century hiatus. Orange leaders sagaciously decided not to risk any negative publicity that might accompany another riot with Irish-Catholics. Yet even without grand processions in Saint John and Portland, violence occasionally erupted. In 1851 city Orangemen travelled to Golden Grove in the neighbouring Parish of Simonds to celebrate the Twelfth. The festivities passed without incident, but an Orangeman sustained a gunshot wound on his return to Saint John. A small Irish-Catholic crowd had gathered to harass the Orangemen, but apparently the wound had been self-inflicted.[82]

Two years later, after a similar festival at the Saint John suburb of Pisarinco, a fight erupted on the new suspension bridge in Portland. A party of Orangemen assaulted two Irish-Catholic males and a female after trading insults, leaving one of the men with serious knife wounds. The incident brought a chorus of indignation from city residents because it had raised the spectre of collective violence between Orange and Green. The judiciary quickly buried the issue; in a trial reminiscent of 1849s, the jury, without leaving their seats for deliberation, found all four Orange defendants not guilty.[83] The next two decades brought a reduction in the reported cases of social violence in the Saint John region.[84] But the fundamental tensions underlying religious conflict had not disappeared.

The passage of the Orange Order Incorporation Bill in 1875 brought the dawn of respectability to the organization and ushered in an age of ritualized 12 July processions that lasted well into the twentieth century. Saint John Orangemen, eager to utilize their new 'civil rights,' invited brethren from across the province to celebrate with them the following year.[85] Approximately one thousand converged on Saint John for a procession and banquet, including a contingent from the United States. The day passed with only one minor incident, despite the provocative parade that wound its way through York Point and Portland on a route strikingly evocative of 1849's.[86] Two hundred militiamen stood ready to prevent a riot, but the Irish-Catholics had decided not to mount a counter-demonstration. Given the similarities between the celebrations of 1849 and 1876, time had obviously changed the social dynamics of Saint John and Portland. Both Orange and Green displayed greater reluctance to engage in collective warfare.[87] The mutual rancor, however, remained:

Every one of common sense ridiculed the idea of an organized opposition being offered to the procession. The Orangemen did not depend on the sufferance of any power, on that of either the mob or the authorities, but entered on the exercise of their legal rights with numbers, courage and weapons that rendered opposition useless. There was not the ghost of a chance that any attempt would be made to deter them from marching over the route they had chosen. It was foreseen, of course, that individual quarrels might arise during the day; that it might become necessary to arrest, kick or shoot some misguided disturber of the peace; that an individual in the procession might be injured by accident or shot by a concealed murderer, but what of that? Are men to listen to the voice of cowardice, to give up their cherished rights (and abstaining, under menace, from exercising a right is giving it up) because a head may be broken?[88]

Rather than serving as a cathartic experience, the 1849 York Point riot deepened socio-religious antipathies. The methods of confrontation, however, would evolve from collective violence to less injurious forms of ritualized celebrations. The propagandists and politicians of the late nineteenth century would supplant the 'soldiers' of the 1840s.

# PART FOUR:
# THE PERSPECTIVE

# 9

# Aftermath:
# The pacific fifties

The dramatic decrease in collective social violence after the York Point riot of 1849 begs a brief analysis. For one thing, the colony's improved economy after mid-century assuaged some of the antagonisms between immigrants and New Brunswickers. With a healthier economy and more jobs to go around, Orangemen lost a vital component of their nativistic argument. Yet there were equally important factors that help to explain the demise of Orange-Green disturbances: the ascendancy of Orangeism, a reduction in Irish-Catholic immigration, and changes in the patterns of group rivalry. The social tranquillity that settled over New Brunswick after a decade of intensive rioting might be attributed to a combination of these ingredients.

One plausible reason for the disappearance of riots was the hegemony established by Orangemen in every community that experienced social violence. Judged by the frequency of collective activity after mid-century, Orangemen won the battle of the 1840s. After the riots of 1847, they clearly 'owned' the streets of Woodstock and Fredericton. In both communities, Orangemen proclaimed their victories by staging massive demonstrations and processions the following year. Conversely, Irish-Catholics essentially abandoned their collective efforts. No doubt they grudgingly accepted their adversary's show of strength; their attempts to check the growth of Orangeism with counter-demonstrations had indeed yielded the opposite results. Moreover, they suffered the most casualties on the day of the riots and stood alone in the docket to pay the judicial price.

Saint John and Portland exhibited similar dynamics, with one important exception: Orangemen in these communities waited until the passage of the Orange incorporation bill to take possession of the streets. The lavish procession of 12 July 1876 was a testament to the legitimacy of Orangeism in New Brunswick; it might also be interpreted as a reaffirmation of Protestant dominance over Irish-Catholics. Indeed the enemies of Orangeism received a strong signal from the riots of the 1840s: a fusion between all levels of authority and the Orange Order had taken place. The Orange soldiers had realized two of their most cherished dreams – they had relegated Irish-Catholics to social and cultural subservience and simultaneously had strengthened the bonds of Protestantism and loyalty in the province.

Yet as colony became province, and the effusive marches of the 1840s atrophied owing to the search for legitimacy and declining Irish-Catholic immigration, the New Brunswick Orange Order changed. Political linkages, tertiary at best before mid-century, became critical in the aftermath of the riots. Orange politicians in the 1850s, in all the communities under consideration, signalled the change by currying favour with their brethren through the use of circulars and delivering political addresses at lodge meetings.[1] Within a decade, leaked news that an Orangeman had purchased votes from his brethren reached members of the House of Assembly.[2] The Fenian threat of the 1860s, the separate-schools issue of the following decade, the growing influence of the Acadian community, and the swelling numbers of Orange members in positions of provincial power all led to structural and ideological changes in New Brunswick's Orange lodges. The emotive and vigilante Orangemen of the 1840s in a sense became 'legitimized' along with the organization.

As the end of the century approached, the Orange Order would seek and gain both political and economic entrenchment. Bloc voting, particularly in urban areas, became ubiquitous. The organization would also become synonymous with patronage, a critical means of gaining access to the corridors of community and provincial power. The Orange Order, which a New Brunswicker might have joined in 1847 because he feared the encroachment of indigent Catholics, would attract an aggressive businessman in Saint John in the 1880s for different reasons. It had become a socio-political club of sorts, potentially a ticket to economic and political prosperity. The Orange Order served as a clearing-house where the enterprising could associate with the 'right' people, where connections could be made and bargains could be struck. A typical Orange member of the 1880s sought fraternal comforts, as did his mid-century predecessor, but increasingly he used the organization for its salubrious powers of patronage.[3]

Equally important, the cross-fertilization between the Orange Order and community élites, in the form of magistrates, councillors, petty bureaucrats, mayors, sheriffs, policemen, constables, judges, juries, and even members of New Brunswick's House of Assembly, proved the successes of vigilante behaviour and institutionalized nativism. The tumultuous events of the 1840s served to reinforce principles grown in New Brunswick's initial seedbeds. The creation and growth of professionalized police forces in all three communities under scrutiny yielded the most compelling proof of this point. One of the earliest manifestations of a coherent police force, the Saint John Mutual Protection Association, consisted of several hundred loyal Protestants, virtually all of them freeholders and established members of the community.[4] Contemporaries tended to view episodic bouts of crime and collective violence as by-products of Irish-Catholic immigration. While the validity of this argument deserves a serious challenge, shifting immigration patterns acted as a catalyst for both the rise of the Orange Order and more legitimate forms of social repression, including professional police forces. As T.W. Acheson carefully pointed out in his Saint John study, the emphasis shifted from protecting property to individuals during the 1820s and 1830s.[5] Acheson's observation proved insightful, yet the impulse to secure and protect the hegemony of a certain 'correct' ideology did more to spur the growth of institutionalized forces of order. These faculties, often with potent and repressive legislative measures at their disposal, laid part of the groundwork for the quiescent 1850s.

The drastic reduction of the number of Irish-Catholic immigrants provided an equally important factor for the demise of collective conflict after mid-century. A discriminatory immigration policy, instituted at the behest of Lieutenant-Governors Colebrooke and Head, curtailed Catholic immigration while it increased the number of more desirable Protestant settlers from the British Isles. The policy generated striking results: between 1851 and 1861 the percentage of Irish as compared with the total immigrant population dropped dramatically in every community that had experienced ethno-religious riots. Moreover, in every region except for Carleton County the total Irish population decreased. By 1861 the Irish – particularly the Catholics – constituted a smaller percentage of the total populations of Saint John, Fredericton, and Portland than they had a decade earlier (see table 1, chapter 3). This decrease also reflected the continuing out-migration of transient Catholics to the 'Boston States' and other British North American provinces. Finally, it indicated the beginnings of a process of acculturation; the sons and daughters of famine immigrants would be listed as New Brunswickers in the 1861 census. The tide of Irish-Catholic immigration dropped as precipitously as it had risen. The soldiers of the 1840s, both Orange and Green, would be supplanted by generations of New Brunswickers to whom the violent experiences of the decade would be historical anecdotes.

Finally, New Brunswick's crowd activity in mid-century did not die so much as it changed. The early patterns of expressive, apolitical crowd behaviour may have diminished, much as they had in America's post-Jacksonian period, but they were superseded by more organized and sophisticated forms of issue-oriented collectives. Like those found in other developed regions of the industrial world, New Brunswick's crowds began to grow in direct response to political or economic issues. Expressive crowds, with their propensity to engage in warfare, lost both their utility and acceptability after mid-century. For example, a potentially violent conflict concerning Fenianism in the 1860s did not materialize largely because attitudes towards crowds and riots had shifted.[6] When collective violence erupted after mid-century, as it did at Caraquet in 1875, it focused on political issues such as the separate-schools question. Although Caraquet mirrored the 1840s in several ways, particularly in the discord between Protestants and Catholics, it did not experience the expressive and symbolic riots of the earlier period.[7] In retrospect, crowd behaviour and riots evolved after 1849 because of altered societal conditions and changes in individual attitudes.[8]

# 10

# A tumultuous decade

Why did the riots break out, and why did they seem rooted to the 1840s? While contemporaries tended to interpret the disturbances as the transatlantic implantation of Irish 'party spirits' and feuds, their diagnosis uncovered only one element in the pathology of social violence.[1] Local exigencies moulded the riots; they fostered the symbiotic relationship between a nativistic ideology and a vigilante methodology, typified by the Orange Order's role in this period. While on one hand they appeared quite analogous, especially in that they tended to occur on symbolic holidays and involved similar protagonists, the riots in Saint John, Portland, Fredericton, and Woodstock grew out of local issues. The distinctive actors who participated in the riots, Orangemen and Irish-Catholics alike, the local luminaries who represented the forces of social control, the community economies, and the geographical boundaries between cultural groups all contributed to give each riot – even in areas with several outbreaks such as Saint John and Portland – unique characteristics.

For example, the 1847 Woodstock riot erupted because two organized crowds were prepared to do battle. Orangemen and Irish-Catholics came to town well armed; they clashed in an engagement on an open hillside that resembled an eighteenth-century military exercise. Conversely, the disturbance at Fredericton on the same day reflected a looser affiliation of combatants, particularly among the Irish-Catholics. No Orange procession materialized, therefore small skirmishes fought with fists and sticks became the mode of battle. Fredericton's 'riot' in fact might be most appropriately characterized as a series of scattered incidents, bound together by the common agendas of Orangemen and Irish-Catholics.

Portland and Saint John also suffered from multiple episodes of collective violence that were different from one another as well as from the clashes in Woodstock and Fredericton. The disturbances of 1842 and 1844–5 reflected little organization among Orangemen and Irish-Catholics alike. The 12 July riots of 1847 and 1849, however, mushroomed into large-scale confrontations in the Woodstock tradition. Yet, unlike the hinterland battle, territoriality shaped their nature. Orangemen deliberately provoked the riots by marching through the Irish-Catholic ghettos in York Point and Portland. Irish-Catholics acted offensively at Woodstock and defensively in Saint John and Portland. As the decade progressed, both sides honed their martial skills, most notably their preparedness and cohesiveness in battle. A chasm separated the precipitating factors and mechanics of the 1842 and 1849 hostilities.

Yet the riots' dissimilarities pale in the overpowering light of evidence that binds them together. Like many episodes of collective violence in the Western experience, all the disturbances occurred on symbolic holidays.[2] Most erupted on 12 July, the anniversary of the Battle of the Boyne that all Orangemen pledged to celebrate annually. Indeed, it was the date of all the major Orange-Green confrontations: Woodstock, Fredericton, Saint John, and Portland in 1847, and Saint John and Portland in 1842, 1849, and 1853. Another clash occurred on St Patrick's Day in 1845, the Irish-Catholic holiday, in the port communities. Finally, the same region staggered through a series of riots from Christmas in 1844 until after New Year's Day. Violence between Orangemen and Irish-Catholics irrevocably shaped these holidays. Both sides prepared well in advance, either for a celebration or a counter-demonstration. Propaganda, regalia, and symbols encouraged group solidarity. Riots easily ensued when Orangemen and Irish-Catholics awoke expecting trouble on the mornings of 17 March and 12 July.[3]

Both sides used symbolic tactics to provoke and torment their opponents. The orange lilies on the lapels of men in Fredericton incited fist fights with Irish-Catholics; rousing tunes, such as 'Croppies Lie Down,' played by Orange band members as they marched through York Point essentially ensured a bloody confrontation. Conversely, a cleverly designed green arch bridging the path of a procession of Orangemen brought a symbolic victory to the Irish-Catholics. Thus, symbolism played an important role in kindling collective violence in New Brunswick, much as it did in other British North American colonies during the same period.[4]

In another striking similarity between the riots, Orange opponents routinely provoked Irish-Catholics into throwing the first stone or firing the opening salvo. At a superficial glance, the Irish-Catholics appeared the aggressor. In Woodstock they attacked an Orange procession after several tactical manoeuvres. Fredericton in the same year saw angry Irish-Catholics gather in front of a lodge and engage with Orangemen in individual fights. The smaller Saint John and Portland disturbances of 1842 and 1845 lacked a clear definition, but in both of the massive 1847 and 1849 riots Irish-Catholics assaulted Orange processions when they entered their territory. Irish-Catholics undeniably allowed themselves to be drawn into conflict by the presence of Orangemen in their midst, manifested either in flagrant processions or lodge meetings.

But why did the Irish-Catholics – indisputably a minority in all the localities discussed above – so eagerly battle with Orangemen who enjoyed superior weaponry and the support of authorities and many Protestant residents?[5] The answer lies in historical patterns of violence between the Irish and the English, between the rulers and the subjugated. The Irish struggle against domination included a rejection of British laws; many Irish brought this pattern to North America as part of their 'cultural baggage.' The Irish-Catholics' willing participation in public disturbances could be interpreted as a form of protest. The Irish and English confronted one another as established 'conflict groups' whose patterns of interaction were rooted in authority and repression.[6]

The Irish propensity to engage in collective violence in hostile lands can also be explained by an inequitable distribution of power. Cultural or social groups become frustrated if they are barred from the decision-making process and positions of authority. Because the groups exercising power always dictate and enforce the laws – both social and statutory – at a concrete level they also determine where and how to confront their opponents.[7] The Orange Order, acting as an extra-legal arm of the forces of social control, defined the scenario for the riots by its processions and lodge meetings. The only viable alternatives open to Irish-Catholics if they wished to protest Orangeism were to attack the processions or stage counter-demonstrations. During the 1840s they did both; 12 July became an 'acceptable' day of conflict. If Irish-Catholics appeared to start the disturbances, they did so because they confronted limited options and they drew guidance from historical patterns of conflict with symbols of authority and repression.

New Brunswick's riots invite another level of comparison because of their purposeful nature. Orangemen and Irish-Catholics prepared carefully for each confrontation, particularly at Woodstock in 1847 and at Saint John and Portland in 1847 and 1849. Even when the combatants displayed less cohesive behaviour, such as at Fredericton in 1847 and in the port communities during the Christmas and New Year's disturbances of 1844–5, they conscientiously targeted their quarry. In the heat of battle rioters sometimes made mistakes, but Catholics and Orangemen were always the intended victims.[8] Moreover, the disturbances never became general or spilled over into neutral territory. Neither Orangemen nor Irish-Catholics looted or destroyed the property of disinterested residents. The enemy's bastions, however, temptingly loomed as fair game: Nethery's Hotel in Saint John, the Fredericton Orange Hall, and the Irish-Catholic enclaves in York Point and Portland. Even the smallest engagement demonstrated a measure of planning and intelligible execution.[9]

The Irish-Catholics also refrained from attacking either the political or social structures of New Brunswick. Orangemen and Protestant alarmists would often accuse them of assaulting the foundations of British liberty, but this argument is totally unsubstantiated by the evidence. New Brunswick's Irish-Catholic immigrants exhibited neither revolutionary not fundamentally destructive tendencies. They collided only with Orangemen, despite the fact that they often shared a common socio-economic status. This phenomenon, labelled a 'paradox' by one historian, compared favourably to the Irish immigrant experience in nineteenth-century America. Members of similar social or economic groups often grappled with one another for ethnic or religious reasons, leaving unscathed the capitalistic or political structures that profoundly shaped their plight.[10] Irish-Catholics in New Brunswick engaged in collective violence only with the most provocative and willing of adversaries – the Orangemen.

Another similarity of the collective disturbances during the 1840s emerged in the fact that the Irish-Catholics consistently suffered tactical defeats or at best drew stalemates. In Woodstock Orangemen joined the authorities to rout an organized crowd of Catholics. Similarly, Fredericton's Irish-Catholics dispersed without mounting an attack on the Orange hall. The pattern was most striking in the Saint John region, where Orangemen, the constabulary, and the military combined their resources to contain every major battle to the Irish-Catholic ghettos of York Point and Portland.

The casualty records of the various conflicts yielded further evidence of the Irish-Catholics' failure to gain even a nominal 'victory.' In spite of the proclivity of both sides to minister privately to the wounded and secretly bury the dead, a lopsided casualty pattern emerged. In all the localities under analysis, and in every disturbance, Irish-Catholics suffered the greatest losses. They accounted for the only deaths in Woodstock and Fredericton, as well as a majority of the wounded. The same point held true in Saint John and Portland throughout the decade, until the 1849 York Point riot claimed the first official Orange fatality. Superior Orange numbers, organization, and arms explained this inequality. They marched in military ranks behind mounted leaders; their favourite weapons were muskets, pistols, and sabres. The Irish-Catholics, by contrast, gathered in looser coalitions, often without leadership, and preferred to fight with fists, sticks, stones, brickbats, and occasionally firearms. Given the differences between the resources available to each side, the preponderance of Orange victories made sense from a tactical standpoint.

Factors other than arms and numbers virtually assured Irish-Catholic losses. During the 1840s, Orangemen and British military units in all three localities forged a strong linkage to suppress and contain the Irish-Catholics. The attending troops in Woodstock watched while the Orangemen crushed their opponents, despite the fact that both contingents had been read the Riot Act and thus clearly broke the law. The fusion in Saint John and Portland was even more apparent. Soldiers aided the authorities on five separate occasions during the decade; in each they curtailed the movements of Irish-Catholics while allowing Orangemen to continue their processions unmolested. Even at Fredericton, the only community where authorities failed to summon the military, individual soldiers assisted Orangemen in street fights. Two elements accounted for the linkage. Most fundamentally, British troops claimed a great deal of responsibility for the transferral of Orangeism to New Brunswick early in the nineteenth century. Soldiers still belonged to the organization; for example, an Orange flag flew over the British barracks in Fredericton during the 12 July 1847 disturbances.[11] In addition, the Orange Order represented an acceptable accomplice for social control. Although they often engaged in illegal activity, Orangemen offered their unflagging support to authorities and British institutions. A double standard clearly emerged: the military found Orange infractions preferable to 'mob rule' by the Irish-Catholic 'lower orders.'[12]

The riots also illuminated a growing fusion between Orangeism and elements of social control. In every community experiencing collective violence, Orangemen served as constables, justices, and even legislative representatives. Excepting one active magistrate in Saint John, a combination of legislative measures and social mores virtually excluded Irish-Catholics from positions of power. This inequity irrevocably moulded law enforcement during the disturbances as well as the judicial aftermaths. No Roman Catholic would be allowed to sit on juries in Woodstock,

Fredericton, or Saint John. Moreover, only Irish-Catholics would be found guilty of rioting offences. Even in the rare cases when Orangemen stood in the docket, such as after the York Point riot of 1849, partisan juries expeditiously exonerated them.[13] Ethnicity and religion targeted the Irish-Catholics for suppression during the 1840s; the challenge that they represented to New Brunswick's economic and social order helped Orangeism to develop into an unofficial arm of social control.

New Brunswick's executive, ostensibly the vanguard of social control, either overtly or tacitly favoured the Orangemen over the Irish-Catholics throughout the period. Lieutenant-Governor Colebrooke failed to support a law against Orange processions, although both imperial and colonial advisers suggested he do so on several occasions. Instead, he responded to the blossoming social violence by attempting to shut off Irish-Catholic immigration, which he perceived to be the fundamental irritant.[14] His successor, Sir Edmund Head, acted more judiciously but continued to sanction Orangeism. He insisted that the judiciary prosecute Orangemen after collective disturbances, yet refused to eradicate obvious inequities in the system. Like his predecessor, he ignored strong directives from the Home Office to curtail Orangeism and outlaw armed processions.[15] Both Colebrooke and Head insisted that local authorities shoulder the burden of dealing with the riots. In essence, this attitude allowed the prejudicial behaviour of magistrates, sheriffs, constables, and juries to continue unchecked. The lieutenant-governors were aware of the strong connections between the Orangemen and élites in every riot-torn community, and their reluctance to intervene on behalf of the Irish-Catholics indicated their approval of the Orangemen's extra-legal efforts to suppress the undesirable immigrants.[16]

New Brunswick's House of Assembly also consistently favoured Orangemen over Irish-Catholic immigrants. Rather than legislating against armed processions, as directed by the Home Office, it buttressed statutes against riot and civil disorder. As they focused on culture rather than socio-economic conditions, legislators clearly targeted Irish-Catholics because they considered them the prime offenders in collective disturbances as well as the criminal element in Saint John, Portland, and Fredericton.[17] The armed, premeditated processions that Orangemen preferred remained unaddressed in the new statutes, whereas assemblymen explicitly outlawed the more typical Irish-Catholic manifestation of spontaneous gatherings. In addition, the legislature in 1849 officially defined for the first time the Riot Act, a popular weapon against Irish-Catholic crowds.[18]

A brief analysis of membership patterns in the House of Assembly from the late 1840s through the 1860s helps to explain the motivational underpinning of this legislative behaviour. Carleton County, entitled to two members throughout this period, returned zealous Orange member Charles Connell on several occasions (1846–51, 1853–8, 1864–7). Horace A. Beardsley, another Orangeman, served from 1850–4, while his fraternity colleague Leonard R. Harding filled the seat of a deceased member in 1856. Thus, in the elections following the 1847 riot Carleton County electors returned at least three Orangemen to the House of Assembly, two of them for extended terms. In York County, entitled to four seats, Orangemen Thomas Pickard served from 1850–4 and William H. Needham sat from 1865–6 and 1868–70.

Saint John County voters, also permitted four members, elected at least five confirmed Orangemen in the same period. John R. Partelow, introduced above in his role as Saint John's mayor, represented the county for an extended term (1827–50, 1854–5). Other Orange legislators included John Gray (1850–61), John F. Goddard (1851–4, 1855–7), John W. Cudlip (1857–66), and the notable riot veteran Joseph Coram (1865–6, 1867–75). Voters in the city of Saint John, laying claim to two assemblymen, replaced Barzilla Ansley, one of the legislature's more moderate voices concerning Irish-Catholic immigration, with William H. Needham in the year following the 1849 York Point riot.

Finally, two of the counties compressed between York and Saint John exhibited a strong proclivity to elect Orangemen. Queens County returned two men who also served as Orange Grand Masters in the late 1840s and 1850s, including the Loyalist descendant John Earle (1842–6, 1847–54, 1856–7) and Samuel H. Gilbert (1852–6, 1857–65). Kings County, entitled to three members, sent two confirmed Orangemen to Fredericton: William McLeod (1834–42, 1844–50) and Loyalist descendant Dr Sylvester Z. Earle (1842–50, 1856–7). Thus, during the 1840s at least two of Kings County's three House of Assembly members claimed Orange affiliation.[19] Orangemen may not have dominated the House of Assembly in the years around mid-century, but they enjoyed an overwhelming edge over their counterparts, who found themselves contending with a plethora of legislative and social obstacles that effectively barred them from representative service.[20]

The social disturbances of the 1840s also prompted lawmakers to fortify the constabulary. Two factors contributed to this effort. Most immediately, New Brunswick's militia had deteriorated because Colebrooke and Head had feared clashes between trained soldiers and civilians. Moreover, England began to phase out its military units in the colony because of improving relations with the United States and budgetary constraints.[21] The rash of civil disorders from 1845 to 1849 forced legislators to augment their means of social control.[22] They codified and improved the police forces in Portland (1847–8) and Saint John (1848–50).[23] Each of the statutes tightened security, yet none addressed fundamental problems. In fact, the police acts drove the wedge between Catholics and Protestants even deeper. Every community that suffered from riots either explicitly or unofficially excluded Catholics from law-enforcement service, whereas they clearly welcomed Orangemen to join.[24] Thus, New Brunswick's legislators strengthened the bonds between Orangemen and local authorities in mid-century.

The New Brunswick disturbances of the 1840s also displayed remarkable similarities in the composition of the crowds – both Orange and Green.[25] From various examinations, testimonials, trial transcripts, arrest records, and reports, a fairly sharp cross-section of crowd participants emerges.[26] The most striking conclusion that can be gleaned from the evidence is that homogeneity characterized neither group; Orangemen and Irish-Catholics who engaged in social violence represented various social classes and economic ranks. Orangemen showed the greatest divergence;

their processions included community leaders, such as magistrates and proprietors, as well as constables, merchants, artisans, and unskilled labourers.[27] This crowd analysis confirmed Orangeism's attraction to Protestants from all levels of society.

The Irish-Catholic crowds probably reflected a higher proportion of working-class members, although they also transcended social and economic class lines. Arrest records from Woodstock included Irish-Catholic farmers, proprietors, innkeepers, tailors, masons, blacksmiths, shoemakers, merchants, lumbermen, and even a former deputy sheriff.[28] Similar documents from Fredericton revealed the same type of cross-section; however, artisans and labourers constituted a proportionately larger group. Most of the arrested Irish-Catholics, employed at the time of the disturbances, lived in the community.[29] Saint John's and Portland's Irish-Catholic rioters came predominantly from the working classes, a fact that mirrored the communities' roles as important ports and shipbuilding centres. Yet attempts to characterize these rioters as destitute has obscured the truth: they laboured as cartmen, clerks, mechanics, shoemakers, butchers, and stevedores. Almost every identified crowd member lived in York Point or Portland's wharf district. When the Irish-Catholics attacked the Orange processions in 1847 and 1849, they unquestionably defended their own territory.[30]

Overall the Irish-Catholic crowds weighted the scales towards the working classes while the Orangemen represented a broader spectrum of social and economic levels. Neither group could be justifiably labelled a 'rabble' or the wretched 'lower orders,' as contemporaries were wont to describe them.[31] The difference in crowd structure suggests a class conflict that lay embedded in the more explicit ethno-religious struggle. Protestants from the middle and upper classes joined the Orange Order to exercise control over the Irish-Catholics and to ensure their positions in society. Keeping undesirables from moving up the social ladder constituted one the nativists' most important goals. Orangemen of all classes engaged in social violence to remind Irish-Catholics of their inferior status in New Brunswick's society.

Every Orange-Green disturbance of the 1840s shared the same

underlying causes, a fact that far overshadows the similarities of the precipitating causes and the details of the riots and their aftermaths. Social violence erupted during the decade because of the Orange Order's nativist response to Irish-Catholic immigration. A profound, traceable correlation emerged between the appearance of Orange lodges and processions and the outbreak of riots in each community. In Woodstock Orangemen established the first lodge in August 1846; within a year the town suffered its most tragic riot in history. Orangeism rooted in Fredericton in 1844; 12 July in 1846 and 1847 brought major collective disturbances with Irish-Catholic residents. Saint John and Portland traced their Orange origins to the early decades of the nineteenth century, yet the organization languished as a small, homogeneous, and essentially indiscernible fraternity. With the appearance of the Provincial Orange Lodge in Saint John in 1844, and as a result of minor skirmishes with Irish-Catholics from 1842 to 1845, Orangeism grew dramatically. The first official procession in 1847 brought a bloody conflict with Irish-Catholics. Two years later Saint John reeled from the colony's worst riot of the century. Thus, in all four localities, the establishment and visibility of the Orange Order directly preceded social violence.

The Orange Order's role in Canada needs to be carefully reconsidered in light of this study. Local factors and ideological agendas made the New Brunswick Orange Order a distinctive organization during this period. It probably only loosely resembled other British North American lodges, especially those in the other Orange bastion of Ontario. New Brunswick's fraternity certainly fulfilled social and sometimes economic functions for its members, yet it drew its doctrinal strength from nativism and instrumentally shaped the province's vigilante response during mid-century. While some New Brunswickers, including newspaper editors, legislators, and local officials, deplored and attempted to counteract the Orange impulse, probably most Protestants overtly or philosophically supported the organization's tenets and agenda. Hundreds, then thousands, added their signatures to petitions calling for the organization's incorporation during the two decades after mid-century.[32]

While historians typically focus their energies on tracing the Orange Order's Irish-Protestant roots, socio-economic contributions, and then political linkages, the possibility that the organization played nativist and vigilante roles in other British North American colonies remains to be explored.[33] A virulent extralegal impulse explained the Orange Order's meteoric rise in the 1840s. Implicitly racist in its orientation, the organization attracted the support of only certain kinds of New Brunswickers and immigrants.[34] Orangemen became the defenders of the Old World, the spear carriers of Protestant, loyal, and British ideals. They temporarily filled an extra-legal void in mid-century when Irish-Catholic immigration reached its zenith and authorities found themselves overwhelmed by potentially cataclysmic changes.[35] Allowed to bask only briefly in the glow of its successes, the Orange Order discovered that institutional forces of control and repression rapidly made its extra-legal duties redundant and then obsolete. The political or occupational characterizations of the Orange Order later in the nineteenth century, as presented by other historians, need not erode the arguments advanced in this study.[36] During the 1840s the Orange Order espoused nativist ideals and performed a vigilante role; its raison d'être, along with its membership, adapted to the times.[37]

Orangeism grew in Woodstock, Fredericton, Portland, and Saint John for the same reasons. The Irish-Catholic immigrant population reached a 'critical mass' in each community during the 1840s. The Catholics threatened Protestant hegemony and, as the nativists argued, they disturbed the social order. Yet Irish-Catholics filtered into other regions of the province, so the question arises as to why collective social violence erupted where it did, leaving some areas with relatively high immigrant populations unscathed.

The answer lies in the make-up of the communities and Irish-Catholic settlement patterns. Superficially, the regions that experienced social violence appeared dissimilar. Saint John and Portland functioned as bustling port cities and the reception points for most of New Brunswick's Irish-Catholic immigrants. Fredericton, by contrast, drew its sustenance as a government town that also serviced the province's central region. Finally, Woodstock relied upon agriculture and lumbering for its livelihood. These communities shared three important traits, however, that made them the focal points of social violence. First, Loyalists settled all of them and over time they retained a strong identity with their British and Protestant heritages. Moreover, they all housed permanent detachments of British troops, visible reminders of New Brunswick's colonial status.

The third factor, the dynamic that Irish-Catholic immigrants settled in the midst of these bastions of loyalism and Protestantism, proved critical for the eruption of social violence. In Saint John and Portland they clustered in conspicuous squalor in the hovels at York Point and along the wharves, where they competed with natives and Protestants for limited jobs as stevedores and sawyers. In Fredericton they filled the rooming houses that bordered the major thoroughfares and laboured as cartmen and shoemakers, often for substandard wages. They developed farms in the Woodstock region amongst their neighbours, and toiled in the forests of the hinterland alongside timber cutters of different cultural and religious backgrounds. Unlike immigrants in other regions of New Brunswick, such as the Miramichi where they set up farms and small communities on lands passed over by earlier Protestant settlers, the Irish-Catholics in the riot-torn communities were numerous, visible, competitive, and aggressive.[38] They introduced a foreign culture and a misunderstood religion to some of New Brunswick's most Protestant and loyal citizens.

Both the North American demography of Irish-Catholic immigration and the experiences of immigrants need to be re-evaluated. Contrary to traditional notions that they represented the most indigent of all mid-nineteenth-century immigrants, for example, the Irish-Catholics in fact consisted of a varied, and in many cases stable, population grouping before the famine years.[39] And while Donald Akenson convincingly argued that the differences between Irish-Catholics and Irish-Protestants had limited impact in governing occupational and social standing in Ontario, the religious factor held the key to shaping New Brunswick's nativist response. Akenson's attempts to extrapolate the findings from his

Ontario 'lab' to make sweeping conclusions about the 'Canadian' experience are ill advised.[40] Religious differences *were* profoundly important in New Brunswick in the mid-nineteenth century, and undoubtedly long after. A socio-economic chasm separated Irish-Catholics from the host society.[41]

Furthermore, the tendency of historians to paint the British North American Irish-Catholic experience with one brush obfuscates important subtleties. For example, Kerby Miller, in his massive study of the Irish, assumed that the Quebec City embarkation saga automatically telescoped to characterize the experiences of all Irish-Catholics in British North America. Miller's conclusion that Irish-Catholics in Quebec did not find themselves 'isolated or besieged' has failed to withstand the New Brunswick evidence.[42] Protestants forcibly and systematically excluded Irish-Catholics from virtually any meaningful form of governance or representation in New Brunswick at least through the third quarter of the nineteenth century.[43] Even as late as 1879 the provincial legislature voted to expel Roman Catholic children from the Saint John Protestant Orphan asylum, an institution originally created to minister to the needy without regard to religious sect or colour.[44] Thus, in concrete terms Irish-Catholics found themselves relegated to a class with severely limited occupational and social horizons. New Brunswick's Irish-Catholics were proportionately over-represented in labouring and semi-skilled occupations and under-represented in farming and the professions.[45] The corpus of evidence relating to Irish Catholics during the mid-nineteenth-century years, partially related in this work, should be submitted with warts fully exposed.

An important caveat accompanies the above distillation of historical factors that attempt to explain the riots in their settings. As Charles Tilly eloquently reminded us, we continue to suffer from the nineteenth-century idea that rapid socio-economic change leads unerringly to social conflict. To the contrary, the historian more easily plucks exceptions to that rule from the fields of history than she or he is able to ferret out cases to prove it. Moreover, social behaviours, even of collective groupings, do not emerge from the impact of society on individual minds;

rather they spring from relationships among individuals and groups.[46] Therefore, New Brunswick's riots can only be understood by appreciating the sensibilities, ideologies, and experiences of the protagonists, and by placing the conflicts squarely into local and chronological frameworks.[47] With multiple clues, no single key emerges to unlock the mystery of collective, spontaneous violence.

New Brunswick's riots, steeped in ethnic and religious differences and hinting at deeper class divisions, were the manifestations of a larger native-immigrant confrontation in North America. While the literature remains relatively small in the Canadian context, less so in the American, ultimately they will best be comprehended by a systematic comparison with other tumultuous events. As one historian has suggested, 'impressionistic' and nationally oriented surveys yield less understanding than 'systematic comparisons of different kinds of communities having different experiences with riots.'[48] The nexus between community and riot remains central, yet a richer appreciation emerges when the riots are subjected to national and international comparisons. It is hoped this analysis will provide useful fodder for future comparative studies, for these riots reach well beyond the anecdotal or parochial. They gain greater significance when exposed to the Canadian, North American, and Western European contexts of the nineteenth century.

Finally, hidden structural factors also provided a foundation for New Brunswick's social violence before mid-century. In order to analyse the riots and place them in their proper perspective, both the individual beliefs of the participants and New Brunswick's societal conditions must be taken into account. Indeed, the examination of both the individual and societal conditions that underscored New Brunswick's Orange-Green disturbances places them squarely into contemporary patterns of European and North American social conflict. Like their neighbours to the south, New Brunswickers found themselves in the midst of a 'turbulent era' in the decade before mid-century.[49]

Individual attitudes and beliefs contributed to the emergence of social violence in New Brunswick. At the most basic level, many colonists displayed a 'willingness' to use collective action to display cultural and religious sentiments or to achieve a desired goal. Each crowd participant was, as historian Charles Tilly has asserted, a 'repertoire' of collective behaviour.[50] Perhaps descendants of the Loyalists retained the bitter lessons of successful crowd activity during the American Revolutionary War. British immigrants, both Protestants and Catholics, may have participated in or witnessed a collective disturbance before they settled in New Brunswick. For whatever reasons, enough people believed in the utility of crowds to make collective violence a common phenomenon in the 1840s.

A measure of social legitimacy that crowds and even riots enjoyed in the eighteenth and nineteenth centuries reinforced this propensity to participate in collective action. To many people in Western Europe and North America, a worthy cause might provide justification enough for collective violence. For example, Britain and France experienced ubiquitous and popularly supported food riots to lower bread prices during this period.[51] Riots became a social or moral weapon, a tool to ensure the rights of the common folk. New Brunswickers inherited this concept. Orangemen used processions and risked conflict because of their 'preservatist' attitudes.[52] Their response was an essentially conservative attempt to maintain social, religious, and economic hegemony. Undoubtedly many Irish-Catholic immigrants perceived crowds and riots as the only viable defence against a hostile reception in a foreign land. Both groups clearly employed crowds to express solidarity and to achieve goals.

A belief in the justification of extra-legal movements, especially among Orangemen, provided yet another factor that contributed to social violence. Vigilantism, a tradition long assumed to be a unique aspect of the American frontier experience, evolved when individuals banded together, usually in the absence of an effective peacekeeping force, to protect their traditional rights and self-interests against real or perceived lawlessness by outsiders.[53] New Brunswick's Orangemen displayed classic vigilante behaviour against Irish-Catholic immigrants. They marched in armed processions to 'preserve' their rights, to 'defend' the Crown and to 'ensure' the ascendancy of British law in the colony. The Saint John region, where Orangemen habitually marched through the Irish-Catholic ghettos in York Point and Portland, exhibited the most virulent vigilante impulse. Fervent Protestants found the violence that erupted as a result of these processions both rational and justifiable. Indeed, the campaign to crush lawlessness among the Irish-Catholics, with the explicit or tacit approval of local and provincial authorities, represented to these Protestants a noble endeavour.[54]

In fact, New Brunswick's Orangemen invoked vigilantism, an effective tactic in a complex nativist campaign, *to suppress* the Catholics. Orangemen targeted all Irish-Catholics as ruffians and villains. This might best be interpreted as a scapegoat ploy, one mirrored by American vigilante groups who attacked newer, weaker, and competitive peoples in times of economic and social distress.[55] Annual marches did not prove an effective weapon against lawlessness. While many Orangemen may have earnestly believed in the potency of their campaign against civil disorder, the vigilante response functioned as but a skirmish in a larger war shaped by religion, race, and class. Xenophobia – not illegality – provided the impulse for Orange vigilantism.

New Brunswick had a willing pool of crowd members and rioters because of the fundamental role religion played in its social and cultural life. In an over-arching sense, religious fervour marked the nineteenth century in North America and Europe. Religion often proved a more compelling determinant of an individual's social, economic, and political status than did secular considerations. In Canada religion cannot be understated as an important cultural and social backdrop for the Victorian age.[56] Religious beliefs, significant enough for all of British North America, became intensified in the areas suffering from the harshest environments. The evangelical revivalism of denominations such as Methodists and Baptists found fertile soil for converts in the frontier regions of North America. In a hard-scrabble environment, such as New Brunswick's, religion provided a comforting refuge.[57] Religious orientation served as a keystone for both self and community identification; for the Catholic and Protestant immigrants to North America it constituted the most conspicuous piece of 'cultural baggage' that they transported to the new world.[58]

Long and deplorable, the history of religious conflict underscores virtually all human experience. In the Western world religious riots, steeped in ritualism and usually occurring on symbolic holidays, evolved into perennial events in many regions.[59] Some historians believe religious violence to be one of the most primitive forms of combat between opposing groups.[60] Thus, the history of Western Europe is fraught with examples of group conflict defined by religious affiliation. In Great Britain this problem was manifest in a centuries-old struggle between Protestants and Catholics.[61] New Brunswick's patterns of social violence in the mid-nineteenth century mirrored this feud. Fervent Protestant Orangemen, defending their religion against 'encroachment,' combated Irish immigrants who clung tenaciously to Catholicism in a hostile environment. Religious conflict – violence with a tradition – was an important element in the province's riots.

Underlying factors for the outbreak of collective social violence also existed on a societal level. Less visible than the human ones discussed above, such as personal beliefs, religion, and vigilantism, these reasons none the less provided the essential cornerstones for a turbulent decade. In a concrete sense, the colony's immersion in a wrenching transition that touched the lives of virtually every inhabitant created the milieu for social violence in the mid-nineteenth century. New Brunswick confronted dramatic changes: economically it foundered through the sharpest and longest depression in its history; politically it made tentative steps towards a viable form of responsible government; and socially it absorbed the first significant immigration of non-Anglo-Saxon Protestants. These factors created a societal tension, a structural underpinning for crowd conflict.

Economic and political stresses caused by rapid change, though insufficient antecedents in themselves, have been clearly linked to collective violence. Many historians have traced the nexus between change and violence, especially in the United States and

England. The Jacksonian period lent particular credence to the pattern; a relentless transition to industrialism, coupled with Irish immigration and the economic and social dislocation of native Americans, provided the structural factors conducive to collective violence.[62] Similarly, Great Britain experienced a dramatic increase in crowd activity as it shifted to industrialism in the late eighteenth and early nineteenth centuries.[63]

The transition from pre-industrialism to industrial capitalism is a pivotal phenomenon for theoreticians of crowd behaviour. The pre-industrial crowd, Eric Hobsbawm's 'primitive rebels,' dispensed a sort of rough justice through collective activity. These crowds tended to be apolitical and loosely organized; conversely, a measure of coordination and political rhetoric characterized the crowds in industrial societies. Over time the relatively sophisticated gatherings of labour and political organizations supplanted the pre-industrial crowd, with its emphasis on traditional justice. Industrialism, decidedly a revolutionary event in the Western world, altered the traditional patterns of collective expression.[64]

New Brunswick's crowd activity reflected changes associated with the penetration of a capitalist market economy into New Brunswick during the 1840s. Faced with the decline of its staple timber economy, the colony wallowed in a purgatorial world between mercantilism and capitalism. The increasing concentration of economic and political power in the hands of a small number of entrepreneurs who exercised paternal control over their workers signified this transition.[65] The phrase 'hungry forties' indeed represented more than a historical cliché to many colonists. A sustained depression brought scarcities of goods, food, and services. Natives competed with Irish-Catholic immigrants for limited jobs, a factor that contributed to the growth of Orangeism. Significantly, the re-emergence of a favourable economic climate in 1850 ushered in a new age, made conspicuous by its absence of collective social upheaval.[66] Economic variables did not cause the Orange-Green riots, but they undeniably contributed to the foundation of social tension.

Perhaps most fundamentally, this work suggests a closer inspection of the 'Peaceable Kingdom' myth, a nationalistic legacy growing out of nineteenth-century convictions as Canadians sought to draw important distinctions between themselves and their behemoth neighbour. The idea, given life perhaps as early as the late eighteenth century, still flourishes and infuses the interpretations of Canada's most esteemed scholars. The Irish in Canada, the argument goes, faced less discrimination than their hapless counterparts in the supposedly egalitarian United States. In its extreme form, the 'Peaceable Kingdom' ideal relegates the malignancies of cultural, ethnic, or racial discrimination – racism – to mere aberrations in Canadian history.[67] When the ugly visage of racism does make its appearance, outside forces inevitably bear the blame for co-opting or duping Canadians, or sometimes for tapping the thin, racist veins that course just below the surface of Canada's society.[68] Even non-nationalistic scholars, indeed foreigners, have perpetuated this idea. Miller, for example, concluded that Canadian nativism represented but a 'pale reflection' of the United States version.[69] Perhaps Miller made a valid point, but we cannot possibly know that now. The phenomenon has barely been recognized in the Canadian context, much less studied in a systematic fashion.[70]

Racism and social violence in the historical record need to be directly confronted. Orange scholars such as Houston and Smyth continue to gloss over the deep divides that separated groups in Canada's past; for example, they argue that 'the unending tensions between the two communities and the rare bouts of violence that disrupted a usually peaceful coexistence were expected by both Orangeman and Catholic.'[71] This study points to a different conclusion. Canada experienced social violence that easily matched the virulence of episodes in England, Wales, France, Ireland, and the United States in the same period. In fact, given the relative sizes of population, Saint John's and Woodstock's riots caused perhaps even more trauma than other contemporary North American disturbances. Determining either quantitatively or qualitatively the relative impact of riots is virtually impossible, especially for comparative purposes. Still, the angry gatherings at the arch in Saint John in 1849 probably unleashed forces as tumultuous as those found in New York City's anti-abolition riots and Philadelphia's anti-black episodes.[72] If living in most large American cities in the nineteenth century was a dangerous proposition, as one historian has observed, then certainly the same held true for British North America's larger communities.[73]

Racism, including its stepchild nativism, charted a tortuous and complex path, one that will not be fully understood as long as scholars cling to the image that they were tragically imported to Canada. Some authors have perhaps overstated the argument by suggesting that racism underscored virtually all Canadian historical writing; others have maintained that Canada has always been, and continues to be, essentially devoid of racial animosity. The current impulse to embrace and cherish multiculturalism, a noble idea, should not obscure or suppress the study of structural inequities in Canada's past and present.[74] Applying the labels 'nativism,' 'vigilantism,' and 'racism' to Canada's historical landscape is not to imply that the country lacks distinctive qualities or exhibits at best only subtle variations on the grander theme of the human saga. It is to suggest instead that an enriched sense of Canada's past would emerge by exposing even its most traumatic, reprehensible, or lamentable moments. In Woodstock, Fredericton, Portland, and Saint John Irish-Catholics found themselves rebuffed, isolated, and repressed in a systematic fashion by both legal and extra-legal forces. Ultimately, New Brunswick's experience fits into patterns of conflict in the Western world during the nineteenth century – it also tells us much about the nature of social violence and nativism in British North America.

# APPENDIX A

# 'The Battle of York Point, 1849, St. John N.B.'
## (by John Knox, eyewitness)

It was on the 12th day of July, in the year of '49,
Six hundred of us Orange boys together all did join
To celebrate the Glorious Twelfth, in memory of our King.
Who from popish chains and idol gods he did us all redeem.

(*Chorus*)

*Then we will sing, our Orange boys, of courage bold and free,*
*Resolved to die before you fly from the popish enemy*

Then we marched down to Water Street, linked by heart and hand
    did go;
You would think it was a Paradise assembled here below;
Our freedom badge shone like the sun that lurks in the sky
And our music would delight you, whilst our Orange flags did fly.

(*Chorus*)

Then we reached their green arch, the stones they flew like hail;
Our Orange balls caused some to fall, and some to turn their tail.
They ran like hunted horses, their hair stood up on end,
Whilst our Orange boys undaunted stood, their freedom to defend.

(*Chorus*)

Then we marched through the papist crowd, their stones we did defy,
For to meet our Orange Brethren on the Twelfth day of July,

And to let those popish rebels for them to think that we
Were some of the highest branches on King William's Orange tree.

(*Chorus*)

Then we marched over to Indiantown, to meet our Brethren there,
The steamboat it saluted us with Orange voices so clear,
And everyone that passed us by would seem to make a pause,
But in their countenance you could read 'Your welcome, Orange
    Boys.'

(*Chorus*)

Now we all returned safe back again, our number to increase;
We thought to go through York Point, they would all be in peace;
But when we came to York Point the stones and bullets flew,
There were so many papists there as French at Waterloo.

(*Chorus*)

Then we marched through York Point again, with guns and bullets
    all,
The papists, like pigeons off the housetops they did fall;
When they stopped at their stone heap, the brickbats for to throw,
Our Orange guns were leveled straight, and brought them all quite
    low.

(*Chorus*)

Here is a health to our worshipful; all Protestants come join,
And celebrate the Glorious Twelfth, King William and the Boyne.
Come, join with us, all Protestants, these papists we defy,
And have your guns well primed, Orange boys, for the next 12th of
    July.

(*Chorus*)

Source: *The Sentinel Orange and Patriotic Song Book* (Toronto: Sentinel
Publishing 1935) 36

# APPENDIX B

# New Brunswick Immigration and Primary Orange Lodges, 1831–55

Total
immigration
(in thousands)

Sources:
Immigration Returns,
New Brunswick Blue
Books, 1832–55, NAC;
'Report on Trade and
Navigation,' *Journal
of the House of
Assembly*, 1866

Number of
primary
Orange
lodges

Sources:
*Minutes of the Grand
Orange Lodge of New
Brunswick*, 1846–55;
Steele, *History of
Orange Lodges of
New Brunswick*

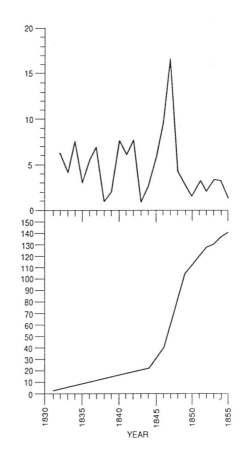

# Abbreviations

| | |
|---|---|
| CHR | *Canadian Historical Review* |
| CO | Colonial Office |
| CP | Campbell Papers |
| GS | General Sessions |
| NAC | National Archives of Canada |
| NB | New Brunswick |
| NBEC | New Brunswick Executive Council |
| NBM | New Brunswick Museum |
| NBSC | New Brunswick Supreme Court |
| PANB | Public Archives of New Brunswick |
| R&D | Riots and Disasters |
| RGA | Records of the General Assembly |
| SJCC | Saint John Common Council |

NEWSPAPERS

| | |
|---|---|
| *Carleton Sentinel* | *Carleton Sentinel and Family Journal* |
| *Courier* | *New Brunswick Courier* |
| *Loyalist* | *Loyalist and Conservative Advocate* |
| *Morning News* | *Saint John Morning News* |
| *Reporter* | *New Brunswick Reporter and Fredericton Advertiser* |

# Notes

INTRODUCTION

1 See W.S. MacNutt's *New Brunswick, a History: 1784–1867* (Toronto: Macmillan 1963) 347–9 and 'The Coming of Responsible Government to New Brunswick,' *CHR* 33 (1952): 127; T.W. Acheson, *Saint John: The Making of a Colonial Urban Community* (Toronto: U of Toronto P 1985) 110–12.
2 See appendix A for an example of a ballad that commemorates the York Point riot.
3 'Violence in Canadian History,' in *Character and Circumstance: Essays in Honour of Donald Grant Creighton*, ed. John S. Moir (Toronto: Macmillan 1970) 66–84
4 For a strident example of this defence see one of Canada's most prolific authors of popular history, Peter C. Newman, 'Bold & Cautious,' *Maclean's* 3 July 1989.
5 Canadian historians in the last four decades have subjected episodes of collective violence to rigorous analysis and placed them squarely in the context of the Canadian experience. For the most important studies, see Michael Cross, 'The Shiners' War: Social Violence in the Ottawa Valley in the 1830s,' *CHR* 54 (1973): 1–26; Michael Cross, 'Stony Monday, 1849: The Rebellion Losses Riots in Bytown,' *Ontario History* 63 (1971): 177–90; Gregory S. Kealey, *Toronto Workers Respond to Industrial Capitalism 1867–1892* (Toronto: U of Toronto P 1980); Allan Greer, 'From Folklore to Revolution: Charivaris and the Lower Canadian Rebellion of 1837,' *Social History* 15 (1990): 25–43; Terence Crowley, ' "Thunder Gusts": Popular Disturbances in Early French Canada,' Canadian Historical Association *Papers* (1979): 11–32. For crowd studies that focus on the narrative, see George F.G. Stanley, 'The Caraquet Riots of 1875,' *Acadiensis* 2 (1972): 21–38; Martin A. Galvin, 'The Jubilee Riots in Toronto,' Canadian Catholic Historical Association *Annual Report* (1959): 93–107; A. Jeffrey Wright, 'The Halifax Riot of April, 1863,'

*Nova Scotia Historical Quarterly* 4 (1974): 299–310; E.C. Moulton, 'Constitutional Crisis and Civil Strife in Newfoundland, February to November 1861,' *CHR* 48 (1967): 251–72; G.R.C. Keep, 'The Irish Adjustment in Montreal,' *CHR* 31 (1950): 39–46; J.K. Johnson, 'Colonel James Fitzgibbon and the Suppression of Irish Riots in Upper Canada,' *Ontario History* 58 (1966): 139–55; Ruth Bleasdale, 'Class Conflict on the Canals of Upper Canada in the 1840s,' *Labour / Le Travail* 7 (1981): 9–39.

6 See E.J. Hobsbawm's argument in 'From Social History to the History of Society,' *Daedalus* 100 (1971): 39–40.

7 For a representative sample of studies of these riots, consult Natalie Zemon Davis, 'The Rites of Violence: Religious Riot in Sixteenth-Century France,' *Past and Present* 59 (1973): 51–91; George Rudé, 'The Gordon Riots: A Study of the Rioters and Their Victims,' *Transactions of the Royal Historical Society* (1956): 93–114; John Stevenson, *Popular Disturbances in England, 1700–1870* (London: Longman 1979); John Bohstedt, *Riots and Community Politics in England and Wales 1790–1810* (Cambridge: Harvard UP 1983); Michael Feldberg, *The Turbulent Era: Riot and Disorder in Jacksonian America* (New York: Oxford UP 1980).

8 For key proponents of the purposeful-crowd theory, see George Rudé's *The Crowd in History: A Study of Popular Disturbances in France and England 1730–1848* (New York: John Wiley 1964) and *Ideology and Popular Protest* (New York: Pantheon 1980); E.J. Hobsbawm, *Primitive Rebels: Studies in Archaic Forms of Social Movement in the Nineteenth and Twentieth Centuries* (New York: W.W. Norton 1959); Charles Tilly, 'Collective Violence in European Perspective,' in *The History of Violence in America: Historical and Comparative Perspectives*, ed. Hugh Davis Graham and Ted Robert Gurr (New York: Frederick A. Praeger 1969) 4–45.

9 'The Revival of Narrative: Reflections on a New Old History,' *Past and Present* 85 (1979): 23

10 See Charles Tilly's useful distinction between 'legitimate' and 'illegitimate' crowds in their contemporary settings in *Big Structures, Little Processes, Huge Comparisons* (New York: Russell Sage Foundation 1984) 3–4, 56–9.

11 Rudé, *Crowd in History* 7–10, 195

12 12 Victoria, c. 29, 1849, in *New Brunswick Statutes* (Fredericton: Queen's Printer); Sir William Blackstone, *Commentaries on the Laws of England*, ed. Thomas M. Cooley, 4th ed. (Chicago: Callaghan 1899) 2:142–55

13 The term is borrowed from J.K. Johnson, *Becoming Prominent: Regional Leadership in Upper Canada, 1791–1841* (Kingston: McGill-Queen's UP 1989).

14 Kerby Miller's exhaustive work on the Irish underscores this idea. See *Emigrants and Exiles: Ireland and the Irish Exodus to North America* (New York: Oxford UP 1985).

15 One historian provides a useful definition of culture: 'a pattern of interpretation for organizing the unstructured data of life. Every individual seeks understanding and adopts a complex language of words and symbols

to order the world; every social system contains such patterns of interpretation.' William Westfall, *Two Worlds: The Protestant Culture of Nineteenth-Century Ontario* (Kingston: McGill-Queen's UP 1989) 13. See also Sidney W. Mintz, foreword, *Afro-American Anthropology: Contemporary Perspectives*, Norman Whitten and John F. Szwed, eds (New York: Free P 1970) 1–16.

16 For an insightful discussion of the various interpretations – some of them fallacious – that historians traditionally rely upon to make sense of social change and disorder, see Charles Tilly, 'Retrieving European Lives,' in *Reliving the Past: The Worlds of Social History*, ed. Olivier Zunz (Chapel Hill: U of North Carolina P 1985) 17–19, 37.

17 The Miramichi experienced ethnic conflict in the 1820s and election disturbances during the early 1840s. For a brief description of the former, see MacNutt, *New Brunswick* 180. Scott W. See explored the latter in 'Polling Crowds and Patronage: New Brunswick's "Fighting Elections" of 1842–3,' *CHR* 72 (1991): 127–56.

18 For an example of this type of predictive modelling, see W.W. Rostow, *British Economy of the Nineteenth Century* (Oxford: Clarendon P 1948).

19 See Stanley's description of this disturbance in 'Caraquet Riots.'

20 Consult John Higham's now classic study of nativism, *Strangers in the Land: Patterns of American Nativism 1860–1925* (New Brunswick, NJ: Rutgers UP 1955).

21 Various historians have applied the nativist model to Canada. Virtually all of them have concentrated on western immigration patterns in the late nineteenth and twentieth centuries and anti-Semitism. For an overview of these studies, consult Howard Palmer's 'Canadian Immigration and Ethnic History in the 1970s and 1980s,' *Journal of Canadian Studies* 17 (1982): 40–2 and 'Strangers in the Land: A Canadian Perspective,' *American Jewish History* 76 (1986): 117–24. For some of the most important studies of western nativism, see Howard Palmer, *Patterns of Prejudice: A History of Nativism in Alberta* (Toronto: McClelland & Stewart 1982); Peter Ward, *White Canada Forever: Popular Attitudes and Public Policy Toward Orientals in British Columbia* (Montreal: McGill-Queen's UP 1978); Ann Sunahara, *The Politics of Racism: The Uprooting of Japanese Canadians during the Second World War* (Toronto: Lorimer 1981); and Patricia Roy, *A White Man's Province: British Columbia Politicians and Chinese and Japanese Immigrants, 1858–1914* (Vancouver: U of British Columbia P 1989). Twentieth-century studies of nativism and anti-Semitism include David Rome, *Clouds in the Thirties: On Antisemitism in Canada 1929–1939*, 3 vols (Montreal: Canadian Jewish Archives 1977); Irving Abella and Harold Troper, *None Is Too Many: Canada and the Jews of Europe 1933–1948* (Toronto: Lester & Orpen Dennys 1982); and Martin Robin, *Shades of Right: Nativist and Fascist Policies in Canada* (Toronto: U of Toronto P 1992). For a thoughtful criticism of the use of nativism in Canadian history, see Lovell Clark, 'Nativism – Or Just Plain Prejudice?' *Acadiensis* 10 (1980): 163–71.

22 For a comparative assessment of vigilantism, see H. Jon Rosenbaum and Peter C. Sederberg, eds, *Vigilante Politics* (Philadelphia: U of Pennsylvania P 1976). For vigilante traditions in the United States, see Richard M. Brown, *Strain of Violence: Historical Studies of American Violence and Vigilantism* (New York: Oxford UP 1975) and William E. Burrows, *Vigilante!* (New York: Harcourt Brace Jovanovich 1976).

23 For a cogent analysis of the intersections between culture and class see Gerald M. Sider, *Culture and Class in Anthropology and History: A Newfoundland Illustration* (Cambridge: Cambridge UP 1986) esp. 6–9.

24 *Small Differences: Irish Catholics and Irish Protestants, 1815–1922: An International Perspective* (Kingston: McGill-Queen's UP 1988)

CHAPTER 1

1 For general histories of New Brunswick, see W.S. MacNutt, *New Brunswick, a History: 1784–1867* (Toronto: Macmillan 1963) and James Hannay, *History of New Brunswick*, 2 vols (Saint John: John A. Bowes 1909).

2 Graeme Wynn, *Timber Colony: A Historical Geography of Early Nineteenth Century New Brunswick* (Toronto: U of Toronto P 1981) 3–9, 53

3 Ibid. 10–33

4 Ibid. 43–51

5 P.D. McClelland, 'The New Brunswick Economy in the Nineteenth Century,' *Journal of Economic History* 25 (1965): 686–90

6 Wynn, *Timber Colony* 130–49

7 W.S. MacNutt, 'New Brunswick's Age of Harmony: The Administration of Sir John Harvey,' *CHR* 32 (1951): 123–4; Wynn, *Timber Colony* 43–51

8 W.C. Milner, *Saint John in the Forties* (Saint John: New Brunswick Natural History Society 1923) 3–5; W.S. MacNutt, 'The Coming of Responsible Government to New Brunswick,' *CHR* 33 (1952): 112; MacNutt, 'Age of Harmony' 123–4; MacNutt, *New Brunswick* 283–4; Wynn, *Timber Colony* 43–4

9 For an example of free trade's optimistic supporters, see Rev. William T. Wishart, *Extracts of Lectures on Political Economy, Delivered During the Session of 1844–45, in the Hall of the Mechanics' Institute of Saint John, N.B.* (Saint John: Henry Chubb 1845).

10 *Colonial Advocate* 14 July 1845; MacNutt, *New Brunswick* 285; MacNutt, 'Responsible Government' 116; Wynn, *Timber Colony* 51–3

11 Wynn, *Timber Colony* 51–3; MacNutt, *New Brunswick* 296; D.G.G. Kerr, *Sir Edmund Head: The Scholarly Governor* (Toronto: U of Toronto P 1954) 39–54; Terrence M.F. Kilbride, 'The Process of Growth and Change in Carleton County 1783–1867,' MA thesis, U of New Brunswick, 1969, 130

12 *Reporter* 13 Oct. 1848, 24 Aug. 1849; *Morning News* 28 May 1849; Milner, *Saint John* 18; Wynn, *Timber Colony* 150–5; MacNutt, *New Brunswick* 320

13 Rev. W.C. Atkinson, *A Historical and Statistical Account of New Brunswick, B.N.A. with Advice to Emigrants* (Edinburgh: Anderson & Bryce 1844) 76–7; James S. Buckingham, *Canada, Nova Scotia, New Brunswick, and the Other British Provinces in North America* (London: Fischer & Sons 1843) 433–64

14 James Richard Rice, 'A History of Organized Labour in Saint John, New Brunswick 1813–1890,' MA thesis, U of New Brunswick, 1968; Kathryn Y. Johnston, 'The History of St. John, 1837–1867: Civic and Economic,' Honours thesis, Mt Allison U, 1953, 22–4

15 *Weekly Chronicle* 20 May 1842

16 *Courier* 7 Apr. 1849

17 *Morning News* 28 May 1849

18 MacNutt, *New Brunswick* 322–4; Kerr, *Head* 53–4

19 *Morning News* 2 June 1848; *Courier* 3 June 1848

20 MacNutt, *New Brunswick* 323–4, 329–34. For an analysis of the effects of the Reciprocity Treaty of 1854 on the Maritimes, see Stanley A. Saunders, 'The Maritime Provinces and Reciprocity,' *Dalhousie Review* 14 (1934): 355–71.

21 See Martin Hewitt's useful assessment of Saint John's Mechanics Institutes in 'Science as Spectacle: Popular Scientific Culture in Saint John, New Brunswick, 1830–1850,' *Acadiensis* 18 (1988): 91–119.

22 *Morning News* 30 July, 1 Aug. 1849; *Courier* 4 Aug. 1849; *Headquarters* 15, 22 Aug. 1849

23 MacNutt, *New Brunswick* 320–30

24 Wynn, *Timber Colony* 84–6, 166–7; MacNutt, *New Brunswick* 329

25 *Royal Gazette* 22 Nov. 1785; Ganong MSS, NBM; MacNutt, *New Brunswick* 59–61

26 S.W. See, 'Polling Crowds and Patronage,' *CHR* 72 (1991); MacNutt, *New Brunswick* 285; MacNutt, 'Responsible Government' 115

27 Peters to Colebrooke, 24 Jan. 1846; John O'Grady petition, 27 Mar. 1847; Justices of the Peace to Saunders, 13 May 1847; R&D, NBEC, PANB. See also MacNutt, *New Brunswick* 275–6; 'Age of Harmony' 123.

28 Justices of the Peace to Chipman, 15 Aug. 1823, Chipman Papers, NBM; *Gleaner* 1 Nov. 1842; *Reporter* 10 May 1850; Price to Smyth, 6 Dec. 1821, R&D, NBEC, PANB; MacNutt, *New Brunswick* 179–80, 216; Joseph W. Lawrence, *The Judges of New Brunswick and Their Times* (Saint John: Jack 1907) 109–10; Rev. W.O. Raymond, 'New Brunswick: General History, 1758–1867,' in *Canada and Its Provinces*, ed. Adam Shortt and Arthur G. Doughty, 22 vols (Edinburgh: Edinburgh UP 1914) 13:194–5; John S. Springer, *Forest Life and Forest Trees* (New York: Harper 1851) 252

29 Judge Parker, 11 Sept. 1841, RGA, PANB

30 Parker to Colebrooke, 11 Sept. 1841; Restigouche Magistrates to Colebrooke, July 1841; Restigouche Grand Jury to Colebrooke, July 1841; Restigouche Clerk of the Peace to Odell, 18 July, 9 and 21 Aug. 1841; Documents, NBEC, PANB. Also *Morning News* 9 Aug. 1841

CHAPTER 2

1 Its mid-century population stood at 23,000, making one in every 8.5 New Brunswickers a Saint John resident; 1851 NB census. See also T.W. Acheson, *Saint John* (Toronto: U of Toronto P 1985).
2 Acheson, *Saint John* 5, 21
3 Abraham Gesner, *New Brunswick; with Notes for Emigrants* (London: Simmons & Ward 1847) 122–4; Alexander Monro, *New Brunswick, with a Brief Outline of Nova Scotia, and Prince Edward Island* (Halifax: Richard Nugent 1855) 125–6
4 Acheson, *Saint John* 249
5 1840, 1851 NB census; *Morning News* 8 Sept. 1843; Gesner, *New Brunswick* 122–6; W.C. Atkinson, *A Historical and Statistical Account of New Brunswick* (Edinburgh: Anderson & Bryce 1844) 28–9
6 Acheson, *Saint John* 40–1
7 Presentment of the Grand Jury, 27 Oct. 1847, in Minutes, Saint John GS, PANB
8 1851 NB census; *Morning News* 11 Sept. 1843; Atkinson, *Historical Account* 36–7; Gesner, *New Brunswick* 124
9 Minutes, 1840s, SJCC, PANB; Acheson, *Saint John* 27–30
10 Acheson, *Saint John* 33–4, 41–2; Minutes, 1840s, SJCC, PANB
11 See the excellent description of the role of New Brunswick's justices of the peace in Raymond G. Watson, 'Local Government in a New Brunswick County: Kings County, 1784–1850,' MA thesis, U of New Brunswick, 1969.
12 See J.K. Johnson, *Becoming Prominent* (Kingston: McGill-Queen's UP 1989) 61–8.
13 Gail G. Campbell made some interesting observations on this subject, although her focus was Albert County: 'The Most Restrictive Franchise in British North America? A Case Study,' *CHR* 71 (1990): 159–88.
14 Acheson, *Saint John* 31–2
15 *Morning News* 8 Sept. 1843; Gesner, *New Brunswick* 122–4; Atkinson, *Historical Account* 28–9
16 Acheson, *Saint John* 10–19, 22–6
17 Ibid. 48–9
18 S.A. Saunders, 'The Maritime Provinces and Reciprocity,' *Dalhousie Review* 14 (1934); Acheson, *Saint John* 20–1, 26
19 Acheson, *Saint John* 54–5, 66, 91
20 J.R. Rice, 'A History of Organized Labour in Saint John,' MA thesis, U of New Brunswick, 1968, 18–20
21 Ibid. 23
22 Ibid. 20–1
23 New Brunswick, *Journal of the House of Assembly*, 1849 (Fredericton: John Simpson); Colebrooke correspondence, in *Royal Gazette* 7 July 1847; *Weekly Chronicle* 28 May 1847

24 *Morning News* 8 Sept. 1843; Peter M. Toner, 'The Irish of New Brunswick at Mid Century: The 1851 Census,' in *New Ireland Remembered*, ed. Peter M. Toner (Fredericton: New Ireland P 1988) 122–3; Acheson, *Saint John* 231–3

25 J.W. Lawrence, *Foot-Prints; or, Incidents in Early History of New Brunswick* (Saint John: J. & A. McMillan 1883); Acheson, *Saint John* 97

26 Saint John's Roman Catholics numbered 10,697 out of a total population of 27,317, while Portland's Catholics accounted for 4,764 out of 11,500: 1861 NB census; *Morning News* 11 Sept. 1843; Monro, *New Brunswick* 125; Buckingham, *Canada* 409–10; Peter Fisher, *Notitia of New Brunswick for 1836, and Extending into 1837* (Saint John: Henry Chubb 1838) 45.

27 Kings Ward, which encompassed York Point and was roughly equal in size to other wards, had twice the population of any ward in 1851. See 1851 NB census. For descriptions of York Point, see Grand Jury Report, 16 Dec. 1848, Minutes, Saint John GS, PANB; and D.H. Waterbury, 'Retrospective Ramble over Historic St. John,' *New Brunswick Historical Society Collections* 4 (1919): 86–8.

28 1851 NB census; Colebrooke to Grey [Lord Howick], 28 Jan. 1848, CO 188; Gesner, *New Brunswick* 124

29 For an example of this fusion of concepts, see the editorial in the *Morning News* 11 Aug. 1847.

30 Grey to Colebrooke, 19 Jan. 1848, CO 189; Presentment of the Grand Jury, 18 Sept. 1847, Minutes, Saint John GS, PANB; *Morning News* 11 Oct. 1844, 11 Aug. 1847; Gesner, *New Brunswick* 124–6

31 Alexander McHarg Diary, NBM; Queen v. David Nice, 1847, Records, NBSC, PANB; *Morning News* 8 Jan., 8 Dec. 1841, 6 Jan., 14 June 1843; *Weekly Chronicle* 5 Jan., 28 June 1844, 26 Nov. 1847; *Reporter* 9 July 1847

32 Queen v. William Walsh and Queen v. William McGagley, 1847, 1848, Records, NBSC, PANB; Minutes, 9 Sept. 1847, Saint John GS, PANB; *Weekly Chronicle* 30 Jan., 15 May 1846; *Morning News* 29 Jan., 19 Feb. 1841

33 *The Story of Fredericton 1848–1948* (Fredericton: T. Amos Wilson 1948) 11–21; Lilian M.B. Maxwell, *The History of Central New Brunswick* (Sackville: Tribune P 1937) 162–4; Gesner, *New Brunswick* 159–62

34 W.G. MacFarland, *Fredericton History: Two Centuries of Romance, War, Privation and Struggle* (Fredericton: The Sun 1893); *Story of Fredericton* 33–9

35 MacFarland, *Fredericton*; Maxwell, *Central New Brunswick* 162–4

36 Atkinson, *Historical Account* 69–78; Gesner, *New Brunswick* 159–62; *Story of Fredericton* 81

37 Terrence M.F. Kilbride, 'The Process of Growth and Change in Carleton County,' MA thesis, U of New Brunswick, 1969, 92

38 1851 NB census; *Story of Fredericton* 81–94

39 MacFarland, *Fredericton* 54–5

40 Minutes, 1840s, York County GS, PANB

41 1824, 1834, 1840, and 1851 NB censuses; Monro, *New Brunswick* 163–5; *Story of Fredericton* 54–5

42 Atkinson, *Historical Account* 69–78; Gesner, *New Brunswick* 159–62; Monro, *New Brunswick* 163–5; Lilian M.B. Maxwell, 'A History of Fredericton's Gaols,' *The Maritime Advocate and Busy East* 34 (1943): 6–7; NB Blue Books, 1837, NAC

43 Peter M. Toner, 'The Foundations of the Catholic Church in English-Speaking New Brunswick,' in *New Ireland*, ed. Toner, 65

44 Maxwell, *Central New Brunswick* 158; Atkinson, *Historical Account* 70; *Story of Fredericton* 110. Roman Catholic sees were later established in Saint John and Chatham.

45 1861 NB census. Roman Catholics numbered 1811 out of a total population of 5652.

46 Kilbride, 'Growth and Change' 103–6

47 William T. Baird, *Seventy Years of New Brunswick Life* (Saint John: George E. Day 1890) 153–6

48 1851 NB census

49 Fisher, *Notitia* 101; Atkinson, *Historical Account* 79, 108–9, 168–9; Gesner, *New Brunswick* 172; Esther Clark Wright, *The Saint John River* (Toronto: McClelland & Stewart 1949) 201–3

50 'Woodstock' will denote Woodstock Parish throughout this book, except for descriptions of the riot.

51 1851 NB census; Monro, *New Brunswick* 172; Kilbride, 'Growth and Change' 66–7. Peter Toner's compelling argument about Irish immigration to the province offers a major revision to the notion that most Irish–Catholics arrived during the famine years of the late 1840s. See 'Irish of New Brunswick' 106–32; and 'The Origins of the New Brunswick Irish, 1851,' *Journal of Canadian Studies* 23 (1988): 104–19.

52 Kilbride, 'Growth and Change' 58–67

53 *Carleton Sentinel* 30 Oct. 1852; *A Woodstock Album*, L.P. Fisher Library, Woodstock

54 *Two Months on the Tobique, New Brunswick: An Emigrant's Journal, 1851* (London: Smith, Elder & Co. 1866) 87–8; Baird, *Seventy Years* 153–6

55 Winslow to Colebrooke, 17 Mar. 1842, Documents, NBEC, PANB

56 Records, Carleton County, PANB; Kilbride, 'Growth and Change' 100, 141–3

57 Records, Carleton County, PANB

58 Kilbride, 'Growth and Change' 66–7

CHAPTER 3

1 Virtually all of North America shared this pattern. Consult Kerby Miller, *Emigrants and Exiles* (New York: Oxford UP 1985). For a useful study of the Canadian experience, see Cecil J. Houston and William J. Smyth, *Irish Emigration and Canadian Settlement: Patterns, Links, and Letters* (Toronto: U of Toronto P 1990).

2 William A. Spray, 'Reception of the Irish in New Brunswick,' in *New Ireland*

*Remembered*, ed. Peter Toner (Fredericton: New Ireland P 1988) 234–7; Miller, *Emigrants and Exiles* 256–7

3 Peter Fisher, *History of New Brunswick* (Saint John: Chubb & Sears 1825; New Brunswick Historical Society 1921) 43–8; L.M.B. Maxwell, *The History of Central New Brunswick* (Sackville: Tribune P 1937) 151

4 T.W. Acheson, *Saint John* (Toronto: U of Toronto P 1985) 98–9

5 See, for example, John McGregor, *Historical and Descriptive Sketches of the Maritime Colonies of British America* (London: Longman, Rees, Orme, Brown & Green 1828; New York: S.R. Publishers 1968); Robert Cooney, *A Compendious History of the Northern Part of New Brunswick, and of the District of Gaspe, in Lower Canada* (Halifax: Joseph Howe 1832; Chatham, NB: D.G. Smith 1896); Peter Fisher, *Notitia of New Brunswick for 1836* (Saint John: Henry Chubb 1838); Hugh Murray, *Historical and Descriptive Account of British America*, 3 vols (Edinburgh: Oliver & Boyd 1839); M.H. Perley, *A Hand Book of Information for Emigrants to New Brunswick* (Saint John: Chubb 1854); Alexander Monro, *New Brunswick* (Halifax: Richard Nugent 1855).

6 Spray, 'Reception' 234–9

7 1840 Survey, Immigration Papers, PANB

8 Two historical geographers estimated that 60 per cent of all arrivals to British North America from 1825 to 1845 were from Ireland, and that Ulster served as the major point of embarkation. See Cecil J. Houston and William J. Smyth, 'Irish Emigrants to Canada: Whence They Came,' in *The Untold Story: The Irish in Canada*, 2 vols, ed. Robert O'Driscoll and Lorna Reynolds (Toronto: Celtic Arts of Canada 1988) 1:27–35.

9 Donald H. Akenson, *The Irish in Ontario: A Study in Rural History* (Kingston: McGills-Queen's UP 1984) 20–6

10 Toner, 'Irish of New Brunswick,' in *New Ireland*, ed. Toner, 106–32

11 Miller, *Emigrants and Exiles* 131–68

12 William F. Adams, *Ireland and Irish Emigration to the New World* (New York: Russell & Russell 1932) 152–3, 422; Maxwell, *Central New Brunswick* 151

13 Spray, 'Reception' 234–5

14 NB Blue Books, 1832–55, NAC; 'Report of Trade and Navigation,' New Brunswick, *Journal of the House of Assembly*, 1866 (Fredericton: John Simpson)

15 Accounts and Assistance Documents, 1840s, Immigration Papers, PANB

16 Spray, 'Reception' 228

17 In the 1851 census, only one county – Restigouche – was an exception to the rule that Irish-born constituted the largest immigrant group. See 1851 NB census; and William F. Ganong, *A Monograph of the Origins of Settlements in the Province of New Brunswick* (Ottawa: Royal Society of Canada 1904) 90–120; Murray, *Account of British America* 3:176–9; Harold A. Davis, *An International Community of the St. Croix* (Orono: U of Maine P 1950) 127; H.C. Pentland, 'Labour and the Development of Industrial Capitalism in Canada,' Ph.D. diss., U of Toronto, 1960, 215–17; H.C. Pentland, *Labour and*

*Capital in Canada, 1650–1860* (Toronto: Lorimer 1981); Donald H. Akenson, 'Ontario: Whatever Happened to the Irish?' *Canadian Papers in Rural History*, ed. Donald H. Akenson (Gananoque, Ont.: Longdale 1981) 204–56; Helen I. Cowan, *British Emigration to British North America: The First One Hundred Years* (Toronto: U of Toronto P 1961).

18 See Toner, 'Irish of New Brunswick' 110–11; 'Another "New Ireland" Lost: The Irish of New Brunswick,' in *Untold Story*, ed. O'Driscoll and Reynolds, 1:291 3; 'The Origins of the New Brunswick Irish, 1851,' *Journal of Canadian Studies* 23 (1988): 104–19.

19 Cecil Woodham-Smith, *The Great Hunger: Ireland 1845–9* (London: Hamish Hamilton 1962) 206–9; Lawrence J. McCaffrey, *The Irish Diaspora in America* (Bloomington: Indiana UP 1976) 59–62; Adams, *Irish Emigration*; Akenson, 'Whatever Happened?' 219–21; Pentland, 'Labour and Capitalism' 215–19

20 Miller, *Emigrants and Exiles* 196–201

21 McCaffrey, *Irish Diaspora* 59–62; Woodham-Smith, *Great Hunger* 210–13; Davis, *International Community* 127; John I. Cooper, 'Irish Immigration and the Canadian Church Before the Middle of the 19th Century,' *Journal of the Canadian Church Historical Society* 2 (1955): 13–14; Pentland, 'Labour and Capitalism' 217–19

22 Toner's incomplete study, admittedly biased in favour of Catholic sources, suggested that no clear pattern emerged in the counties of origin for the Irish before 1851; however, Cork clearly sent the most immigrants. See 'Irish of New Brunswick' 106–32.

23 Miller, *Emigrants and Exiles* 193–6; Toner, 'Irish of New Brunswick' 111–12

24 For an excellent treatment of the Irish famine, see Woodham-Smith, *Great Hunger*. See also McCaffrey, *Irish Diaspora* 59–62.

25 Miller argued that the Catholic-Irish tended to be 'protocapitalistic' in the early nineteenth century, meaning that as a group they were less business-minded than their Protestant counterparts who were more conditioned by capitalism and exhibited an entrepreneurial spirit. See *Emigrants and Exiles* 131–5, 268–9, 274.

26 Resolutions of the Saint John Common Council, in *Reporter* 10 Sept. 1847; Woodham-Smith, *Great Hunger* 226–8; Oliver MacDonagh, 'Irish Emigration to the United States of America and the British Colonies During the Famine,' in *The Great Famine: Studies in Irish History 1845–52*, ed. R. Dudley Edwards and T. Desmond Williams (Dublin: Browne & Nolan 1956) 332–40

27 Matthews to Odell, 25 June 1842, Correspondence, Immigration Papers, PANB

28 NB Blue Books, 1832–55, NAC; Cowan, *British Emigration* 191

29 Ganong, *Settlements* 90–120; Cowan, *British Emigration* 199–200; MacDonagh, 'Irish Emigration' 332–9; Woodham-Smith, *Great Hunger* 370–1

30 This closely follows patterns across North America. See Miller, *Emigrants and Exiles* 297.

31 Perley's Report on 1846 Emigration, in Colebrooke to Grey, 29 Dec. 1846, CO 188; *Royal Gazette* 17 Mar., 7 July 1847

32 Perley to Colebrooke, 20 Sept. 1847, Records, NBEC, PANB. Miller estimated that 30 per cent of all the destitute passengers heading to British North America in 1847 died in passage or in quarantine: *Emigrants and Exiles* 292.

33 Prosecution Papers, 1840s, Immigration Papers, PANB

34 Woodham-Smith, *Great Hunger* 213–21, 238; MacDonagh, 'Irish Emigration' 319–29

35 Perley's Report on 1846 Emigration, in Colebrooke to Grey, 29 Dec. 1846, CO 188; Perley's Report on 1847 Emigration, Abstracts and Reports, Immigration Papers, PANB; *New Brunswick Almanac and Register* (Saint John: Henry Chubb 1848); MacDonagh, 'Irish Emigration' 374–6; Cowan, *British Emigration* 193

36 Perley to Colebrooke, 2 Aug. 1847, Records, NBEC, PANB

37 Quebec City relied upon its Grosse Ile, while the Miramichi used Middle Island. For a history of the former, see Marianna O'Gallagher, *Grosse Ile: Gateway to Canada 1832–1937* (St Foy: Carraig 1984).

38 Partelow to Special Commissioners, 9 Oct. 1847, Records, NBEC, PANB

39 Partelow to Colebrooke, 9 Oct. 1847, Records, NBEC, PANB

40 James M. Whalen provided a useful description in '"Allmost as Bad as Ireland": The Experience of the Irish Famine Immigrant in Canada, Saint John, 1847,' in *Untold Story*, ed. O'Driscoll and Reynolds, 1:155–6. See also his 'New Brunswick Poor Law Policy in the Nineteenth Century,' MA thesis, U of New Brunswick, 1966, 29–30.

41 Various doctors to Colebrooke, 7 July 1847, Correspondence, Immigration Papers, PANB. Note also Whalen's description in '"Allmost as Bad"' 160–1.

42 Various doctors to Colebrooke, 14 Sept. 1847, Records, NBEC, PANB; Whalen, 'Poor Law' 29–30

43 Wolhaupter to Colebrooke, 28 July 1847, Records, NBEC, PANB

44 Minutes, 3 Sept., 10 Nov. 1847, SJCC, PANB

45 Audit Office Report, 13 Oct. 1847, Records, NBEC, PANB

46 Immigration Papers, in Colebrooke Records, PANB

47 Minutes, 10 Nov. 1847, SJCC, PANB

48 Whalen, '"Allmost as Bad"' 161

49 Saint John Emigrant Hospital Records, Immigration Papers, PANB

50 *Weekly Chronicle* 27 Aug. 1847; MacDonagh, 'Irish Emigration' 368–76; Rev. John A. Gallagher, 'The Irish Emigration of 1847 and Its Canadian Consequences,' *Report of the Canadian Catholic Historical Association* (1935–6): 43–57

51 Woodham-Smith, *Great Hunger* 228–9, 239–40

52 *Royal Gazette* 7 July 1847; *Saint John Herald* 12 Nov. 1845; Perley's Report on 1846 Emigration, in Colebrooke to Grey, 29 Dec. 1846, CO 188; Adams, *Irish Emigration* 234; MacDonagh, 'Irish Emigration' 368–73; James Hannay, *History of New Brunswick*, 2 vols (Saint Johm: John A. Bowes 1909) 2:70; Woodham-Smith, *Great Hunger* 209–10

53 Perley to Head, n.d., Head Correspondence, PANB
54 Although Akenson has argued that Upper Canada's Irish – both Protestant and Roman Catholic – were predominantly rural, the evidence from New Brunswick does not suggest such a sharply defined pattern of settlement. See *Irish in Ontario* 42–5.
55 A debate continues over the Irish immigrants' experience in North America. Much of the argument concentrates on rural and urban settlement patterns. For a sampling, see Akenson, 'Whatever Happened?' 231–41; Kenneth Duncan, 'Irish Famine Immigration and the Social Structure of Canada West,' *Canadian Review of Sociology and Anthropology* 2 (1965): 37–8; Pentland, 'Labour and Capitalism' 220–3; Woodham-Smith, *Great Hunger* 265–9.
56 Perley to Saunders, 22 Apr. 1846, Correspondence, Immigration Papers, PANB
57 Spray, 'Reception' 231
58 John J. Mannion, *Irish Settlements in Eastern Canada: A Study of Cultural Transfer and Adaptation* (Toronto: U of Toronto P 1974) 17–27; Ganong, *Settlements* 73–9; Kilbride, 'Growth and Change' 66–7; Cooper, 'Irish Immigration' 1–20
59 Oscar Handlin, *The Uprooted* (Boston: Little, Brown & Co. 1951); McCaffrey, *Irish Diaspora* 62–9; Mannion, *Irish Settlements* 165–74
60 For example, Toner estimated that approximately half of Saint John's Irish in 1851 were Gaelic speakers, a point that further exacerbated tensions between Irish-Catholic immigrants and Protestants. See 'Irish of New Brunswick' 114–18.
61 Conrad M. Arensberg, *The Irish Countryman* (Gloucester, Mass.: Peter Smith 1959) 185–90, 206–7; G.R.C. Keep, 'The Irish Adjustment in Montreal,' *CHR* 31 (1950): 39–44
62 Miller, *Emigrants and Exiles* 300–44
63 James S. Olson, *Catholic Immigrants in America* (Chicago: Nelson-Hall 1987) 21–6
64 Handlin, *Uprooted* 117–43; Thomas D'Arcy McGee, *The Catholic History of North America* (Boston: Patrick Donahoe 1855) 149–50
65 Akenson argued that religious fervour for both Protestants and Catholics intensified after the famine years as both groups sought to retain their cultural identity on the strife-torn island. See *Small Differences* (Kingston: McGill-Queen's UP 1988) 129–33, 138–40.
66 Rowland Berthoff, *An Unsettled People: Social Order and Disorder in American History* (New York: Harper & Row 1971) 251–2; Adams, *Irish Emigration* 364–6; Carl Wittke, *The Irish in America* (Baton Rouge: Louisiana State UP 1956) 187–9; Handlin *Uprooted* 130–8
67 Donald H. Akenson, *Being Had: Historians, Evidence, and the Irish in North America* (Port Credit, Ont.: Meany 1984) 194–7; *Irish in Ontario* 350–1
68 Acheson, *Saint John* 101–3

69 1851, 1861 NB censuses; *Gleaner*, 18 July 1853; Fisher, *History of New Brunswick* 22; W.C. Milner, *Saint John in the Forties* (Saint John: New Brunswick Natural History Society 1923) 8–10; W.P. Kilfoil, *Johnville: The Centennial Story of an Irish Settlement* (Fredericton: Unipress 1962) 17–18; William M. Baker, *Timothy Warren Anglin 1822–96: Irish Catholic Canadian* (Toronto: U of Toronto P 1977) 11–14; MacNutt, *New Brunswick* 280; Arthur T. Doyle, *Front Benches and Back Rooms* (Toronto: Green Tree 1976) 14–15

70 Ecclesiastical returns, NB Blue Books, 1842–57, NAC; 1861 NB census; John Medley, *Notes of a Visitation Tour Through Parts of the Diocese of Fredericton, New Brunswick in 1846* (London: Society for the Propagation of the Gospel 1846) 24–6; Abraham Gesner, *New Brunswick* (London: Simmons & Ward 1847) 319–20

71 1851 NB census. This census included no religious data.

72 1861 NB census

73 For a religious history of the Acadians, see Léon Thériault, 'The Acadianisation of the Catholic Church in Acadia, 1763–1953,' *The Acadians of the Maritimes*, ed. Jean Daigle (Moncton: Centre d'études acadiennes 1982) 271–339.

74 John Garner, 'The Enfranchisement of Roman Catholics in the Maritimes,' *CHR* 34 (1953): 203–18. Note also Garner's discussion of Roman Catholic disqualification in *The Franchise and Politics in British North America* (Toronto: U of Toronto P 1969) 131–45.

75 50 George III, c. 36, 1810, in *New Brunswick Statutes* (Fredericton: Queen's Printer)

76 10 George IV, c. 7, 1829, in *Statutes of Great Britain*; 11 George IV, c. 33, 1830, in *New Brunswick Statutes* (Fredericton: Queen's Printer)

77 John Saunder's protest, in J.W. Lawrence, *The Judges of New Brunswick and Their Times* (Saint John: Jack 1907) 112–13

78 *Morning News* 18 Nov. 1842; Lawrence, *Judges* 118

79 J.K. Johnson found the same phenomenon in Upper Canada. See *Becoming Prominent* (Kingston: McGill-Queen's UP 1989) 33, 105–8, 164.

80 Acheson, *Saint John* 52–3

81 9 Victoria, c. 72, 1846, in *New Brunswick Statutes* (Fredericton: Queen's Printer); Petition of Roman Catholics in Saint John, in Colebrooke to Grey, 11 June 1846, CO 188; *Reporter* 3, 6 Mar. 1846

82 Adams, *Irish Emigration* 326–8; *Morning News* 30 May 1845

83 Richard C. Harris and John Warkentin, *Canada Before Confederation: A Study in Historical Geography* (New York: Oxford UP 1974) 173–6

84 Minutes, Sept. to Nov. 1847, SJCC, PANB; Resolutions of Saint John Common Council, in *Reporter* 10 Sept. 1847

85 Colebrooke to Grey, 30 July 1847, CO 188; Colebrooke Correspondence, 1847, PANB; Grey to Colebrooke, 2 Dec. 1847, in Minutes, 14 Jan. 1848, SJCC, PANB

86 Perley to Head, 31 Dec. 1848, Head Records, PANB

87 Perley's report, 1850, Abstracts and Reports, Migration Papers, PANB
88 Reports, 1854, Immigration Papers, PANB
89 See Perley's various reports and letters from 1851, 1852, 1853, and 1855, Correspondence, Immigration Papers, PANB
90 For important studies of Canadian anti-Catholicism, see James T. Watt, 'Anti-Catholic Nativism in Canada: The Protestant Protective Association,' *CHR* 48 (1967): 45–58; A.J.B. Johnston, 'Popery and Progress: Anti-Catholicism in Mid-Nineteenth-Century Nova Scotia,' *Dalhousie Review* 64 (1984): 146–63. J.K. Johnson suggested that in Upper Canada a combination of being culturally disadvantaged and the general prejudice of the host society meant that 'being Irish ... regardless of denomination, does not seem to have been a good thing.' See *Becoming Prominent* 113–118, quote on 114.
91 Higham, *Strangers in the Land* (New Brunswick, NJ: Rutgers UP 1955) 3–4; 'Another Look at Nativism,' *Catholic Historical Review* 44 (1958): 148–50. For another history of nativism in the United States, see Ray Allen Billingham, *The Protestant Crusade, 1800–1860: A Study of the Origins of American Nativism* (New York: Macmillan 1938).
92 Many of New Brunswick's Scots and Northern Irish settlers had Celtic origins; however, their Protestant affiliations strengthened their ties with the Loyalists and English of Anglo-Saxon ancestry.
93 McCaffrey, *Irish Diaspora* 85–106; Howard Palmer, 'Nativism in Alberta, 1925–1930,' Canadian Historical Association *Papers* (1974): 192–5
94 *Weekly Chronicle* 15 July 1842, 4 Feb. 1848; *Christian Visitor* 8 Mar. 1848
95 For superb discussions of the conspiracy theory, see Seymour Martin Lipset and Earl Raab, *The Politics of Unreason* (New York: Harper & Row 1970) 47–59; and David Brion Davis, 'Some Themes of Counter–Subversion: An Analysis of Anti-Masonic, Anti-Catholic, and Anti-Mormon Literature,' *Mississippi Valley Historical Review* 47 (1960): 205–7.
96 Higham, *Strangers in the Land* 5–6
97 Robert F. Hueston, *The Catholic Press and Nativism 1840–1860* (New York: Arno P 1976) 33
98 Documents, Northumberland County, PANB; Manny Collection, NBM
99 Chief Justice Saunders's Protest to the Roman Catholic Emancipation Bill, 27 Feb. 1830, in Lawrence, *Judges* 112–13
100 *Loyalist* 23 Mar. 1848; *Colonial Watchman* 8 July 1850
101 *Church Witness* 21 Sept. 1853
102 *Reporter* 1 Oct. 1847; *Weekly Chronicle* 31 Aug. 1849; *Carleton Sentinel* 15 June 1850
103 *Weekly Chronicle* 18 July 1851
104 *Church Witness* 16 July, 13 Aug. 1851; Fisher, *History of New Brunswick* 94
105 *Loyalist* 24 Sept. 1847; *Church Witness* 6 July 1853
106 The theme of competition between immigrant labourers and natives in North America has been explored in the following: Oscar Handlin, *Boston's*

*Immigrants* (Cambridge: Belknap Press 1959) 180–7; Higham, *Strangers in the Land* 57; Adams, *Irish Emigration* 353.

107 The following argument makes a profound contrast to Akenson's assertion that, thanks to a lack of restrictive laws, both Protestant- and Catholic-Irish enjoyed 'fair competition' in Upper Canada. See *Irish in Ontario* 351.

108 Rice, 'Organized Labour' 1–8

109 Saint John Common Council Report, 13 May 1840, in *Courier* 16 May 1840; *Morning News* 8 Nov. 1839, 9 Apr. 1841; *Courier* 18 July 1840; Rice, 'Organized Labour' 8–11

110 Thomas W. Acheson, 'Denominationalism in a Loyalist Country: A Social History of Charlotte, 1783–1940,' MA thesis, U of New Brunswick, 1964, 115; W.T. Baird, *Seventy Years of New Brunswick Life* (Saint John: George E. Day 1890) 157

111 Perley's Report on 1846 Emigration, in Colebrooke to Grey, 29 Dec. 1846, CO 188; *Royal Gazette* 17 Mar., 7 July 1847; Davis, *International Community* 290; Graeme Wynn, *Timber Colony* (Toronto: U of Toronto P 1981) 155–6; K.Y. Johnston, 'The History of St. John, 1837–1867,' Honours thesis, Mt Allison U, 1953, 24–8

112 *Loyalist* 28 Oct., 4 Nov., 23 Dec. 1847

113 See Tom Garvin, 'Defenders, Ribbonmen and Others: Underground Political Networks in Pre-Famine Ireland,' *Past and Present* 96 (1982): 133–55; Joseph Lee, 'The Ribbonmen,' *Secret Societies in Ireland*, ed. T. Desmond Williams (Dublin: Gill & Macmillan 1973) 26–35; Woodham-Smith, *Great Hunger* 27–8.

114 Sectarian tensions between Catholic- and Protestant-Irish gave credence to this perception; competition for land and employment, as well as cultural and ritualistic disputes, underscored the past and set the tone for the struggles described here. See Miller, *Emigrants and Exiles* 26–9, 40–2, 247–8, 258.

115 John MacTaggart, *Three Years in Canada: An Account of the Actual State of the Country in 1826-7-8*, 2 vols (London: Henry Colburn 1829) 1:240–8; J.K. Johnson, 'Colonel James Fitzgibbon and the Suppression of Irish Riots in Upper Canada' *Ontario History* 58 (1966): 154–5; Higham, *Strangers in the Land* 26

116 A useful collection of essays that focuses on Irish collective action is *Irish Peasants: Violence and Political Unrest*, ed. Samuel Clark and James S. Donnelly, Jr (Madison: U of Wisconsin P 1983).

117 Adams, *Irish Emigration* 363–4; Wittke, *Irish in America* 46–7; Duncan, 'Famine Immigration' 33, 39. For analyses of disturbances involving Irish-Catholic immigrants in North America, see the following: Feldberg, *Turbulent Era*; Michael Feldberg, *The Philadelphia Riots of 1844: A Study of Ethnic Conflict* (Westport, Ct.: Greenwood 1975); Michael Cross, 'The Shiners' War,' *CHR* 54 (1973); Johnson, 'Irish Riots in Upper Canada'; Martin A. Galvin, 'The Jubilee Riots in Toronto,' Canadian Catholic Historical

Association *Annual Report*, 1959; Keep, 'Irish Adjustment'; Ruth Bleasdale, 'Class Conflict on the Canals of Upper Canada,' *Labour / Le Travail* 7 (1981).
118 *Loyalist* 6 Apr. 1848
119 James Boyd's Address, House of Assembly, in *Loyalist* 30 Mar. 1848; *Morning News* 11 Aug. 1847
120 *Loyalist* 4 Nov. 1847
121 *Reporter* 30 July 1847; *Loyalist* 4, 23 Nov., 16 Dec. 1847
122 Charles Connell's Address, House of Assembly, 11 Mar. 1848, in *Reporter* 17 Mar. 1848; editorials and letters, *Loyalist* 13, 20, 27 Aug., 15 Oct. 1847
123 George F.G. Stanley, 'The Caraquet Riots of 1875,' *Acadiensis* 2 (1972)
124 Nicholas P. Canny, *The Elizabethan Conquest of Ireland: A Pattern Established 1565–76* (New York: Barnes & Noble 1976); Woodham-Smith, *Great Hunger* 18
125 Akenson argued that over time the Celtic-Irish embraced the differences. They essentially captured the term 'Irish' in the nineteenth century, making 'Irish' and 'nation' virtually synonymous and decidedly Catholic terms. See *Small Differences* 133–4.
126 For excellent studies of racism against the Celtic-Irish in the British Isles, see L.P. Curtis, Jr, *Anglo-Saxons and Celts: A Study of Anti-Irish Prejudice in Victorian England* (Bridgeport, Ct.: Conference of British Studies, U of Bridgeport 1968) 8–9, 24–6; *Apes and Angels: The Irishman in Victorian Caricature* (Devon, Eng.: David & Charles 1971).
127 Higham, *Strangers in the Land* 9–11
128 For a contemporary British view of the Irishman in Canada, see MacTaggart, *Three Years in Canada* 242–60. See also Johnson, 'Irish Riots in Upper Canada' 155; Donald Power, 'The Paddy Image: The Stereotype of the Irishman in Cartoon and Comic,' in *Untold Story*, ed. O'Driscoll and Reynolds, 1:36–57.
129 *Weekly Chronicle* 31 Aug., 28 Sept. 1849; *Loyalist* 24 Sept. 1847; H. Dibblee to G. Dibblee, 5 Aug., 8, 30 Sept. 1847; D. Dibblee to G. Dibblee, 7 Aug., 20 Sept. 1847: New Brunswick Historical Society Papers, NBM
130 *Loyalist* 1 Oct. 1847
131 The *Loyalist*, for example, regularly ran an 'Odd Fellow's Corner' in 1847. The column often mocked Irish-Catholics through the use of poems, jokes, and folk stories.
132 *Carleton Sentinel* 7 Jan. 1854
133 Ibid. 12 Nov. 1850
134 Ibid. 23 July 1853; *Loyalist* 11 Nov. 1847
135 *Loyalist* 13, 20, 27 Aug. 1847

CHAPTER 4

1 For the standard treatment of the roots of the Orange Order, see Hereward Senior, *Orangeism in Ireland and Britain 1795–1836* (London: Routledge &

Kegan Paul 1966) esp. 4–21. See also Peter Gibbon, 'The Origins of the Orange Order and the United Irishmen,' *Economy and Society* 1 (1972): 134–59; Kerby Miller, *Emigrants and Exiles* (New York: Oxford UP ₋985) 231.

2 Hereward Senior, 'The Early Orange Order 1795–1870,' in *Secret Societies in Ireland*, ed. T. Desmond Williams (Dublin: Gill & Macmillan 1973) 36–9; Senior, *Orangeism* 16–19

3 Gibbon, 'Origins of the Orange Order' 134–5, 159–60

4 Senior, 'Early Orange Order' 39–40; Gibbon, 'Origins of the Orange Order' 142–3

5 Senior, *Orangeism* 194–206 and 'Early Orange Order' 41–2

6 Great Britain, Parliament, *Hansard's Parliamentary Debates* (Commons), 3rd ser., 31 (1836): House of Commons Resolution, 23 Feb. 1836; King William IV's reply, 25 Feb. 1836; Duke of Cumberland's address, 26 Feb. 1836. Also Documents, CP, PANB; Senior, *Orangeism* 243–4 and 'Early Orange Order' 41–3

7 Great Britain, Parliament, *Hansard's Parliamentary Debates* (Commons), 3rd ser., 31 (1835): 8 Feb. 1835

8 *Sentinel* 27 July 1899; Hereward Senior, *Orangeism: The Canadian Phase* (Toronto: McGraw-Hill Ryerson 1972) 5–7

9 Cecil J. Houston and William J. Smyth, *The Sash Canada Wore: A Historical Geography of the Orange Order in Canada* (Toronto: U of Toronto P 1980) 15–20; Nicholas F. Davin, *The Irishman in Canada* (Toronto: Maclear & Co. 1877) 323; Hereward Senior, 'The Genesis of Canadian Orangeism,' *Ontario History* 60 (1968): 13–14

10 Houston and Smyth, *Sash* 21–4; Senior, 'Genesis' 18–27. The reader might also want to consult the semi-fictitious work by Donald H. Akenson, *The Orangeman: The Life and Times of Ogle Gowan* (Toronto: James Lorimer 1986).

11 Cecil J. Houston and William J. Smyth, 'The Orange Order in Nineteenth-Century Ontario: A Study in Institutional Cultural Transfer,' paper, Department of Geography, U of Toronto, 1977, 4, 11–12; Houston and Smyth, *Sash* 3–7, 15–16, 20, 26–69

12 William J.S. Mood, 'The Orange Order in Canadian Politics, 1841–1867,' MA thesis, U of Toronto, 1950, 11; Daniel C. Lyne, 'The Irish in the Province of Canada in the Decade Leading to Confederation,' MA thesis, McGill U, 1960, 154–5; Houston and Smyth, 'Orange Order in Nineteenth-Century Ontario' 20; Senior, 'Genesis' 18–19

13 Lyne, 'Irish in Canada' 150–66; Mood, 'Orange Order in Canadian Politics' 16–18, 26–32; Houston and Smyth, *Sash* 146–52; Senior, *Orangeism: The Canadian Phase* 29–45, 67–81

14 Eldon Lodge even bailed a member out of debtor's prison, providing a dramatic example of fraternal bondage. See Minutes Book, Wellington Orange Lodge, NBM; Minutes Books, Eldon, Long's Creek, and Prince William lodges, CP, PANB.

15 Houston and Smyth, *Sash* 112–41; Senior, *Orangeism: The Canadian Phase* 71–81

16 *Laws and Ordinances of the Orange Association of British North America* (Toronto: Rogers & Thompson 1840) 9; *The Orange Question Treated by Sir Francis Hincks and the London 'Times'* (Montreal: True Witness 1877)

17 For a history of this struggle, consult Scott W. See, 'The Fortunes of the Orange Order in 19th Century New Brunswick,' in *New Ireland Remembered*, ed. Peter Toner (Fredericton: New Ireland P 1988) 90–105.

18 James McNichol's Report, in *Annual Report of the Proceeding of the Grand Lodge of the Loyal Orange Association of Canada* (Toronto: The Church 1886); *Sentinel* 3 July 1930; J. Edward Steele, comp., *History and Directory of the Provincial Grand Orange Lodge and Primary Lodges of New Brunswick, 1690–1934* (Saint John: J.E. Steele 1934) 11

19 James McNichol's Report, *Proceedings of Orange Association of Canada*; Steele, *History and Directory* 11–21; Houston and Smyth, *Sash* 69–70

20 There may have been seventeen by 1837, though this is not clear from available documents. See CP, PANB; Steele, *History and Directory* 17–21. James McNichol later exaggerated the number of lodges, saying that 'forty or fifty' had been officially established by 1838. This was clearly incorrect; no. 18 originated on 18 Mar. 1844. See James McNichol's Report, *Proceedings of Orange Association of Canada.*

21 For details of the New Brunswick–British North America union in the 1840s, consult See, 'Fortunes' 103–4.

22 James McNichol's Report, *Proceedings of Orange Association of Canada*; Houston and Smyth, *Sash* 69–70; Steele, *History and Directory* 11; Minutes Book, 1844–67, Wellington Orange Lodge, NBM

23 *Loyalist* 18 July 1844; *Weekly Chronicle* 19 July 1844

24 *The Story of Fredericton* (Fredericton: T. Amos Wilson 1948) 190–2; Steele, *History and Directory* 37–9

25 *Carleton Sentinel* 15 July 1854; Steele, *History and Directory* 53–9

26 *Laws and Ordinances of the Orange Association of British North America*; *Loyalist* 15 Oct. 1847, 30 Mar. 1848; Steele, *History and Directory* 15, 21

27 Minutes Book, Eldon Lodge, CP, PANB; see also Bowes Correspondence, CP, PANB

28 Minutes Books, Rules and Regulations, Eldon, Long's Creek, and Prince William lodges, CP, PANB

29 Minutes Book, Wellington Lodge, NBM; Minutes Books, Eldon, Long's Creek, and Prince William lodges, CP, PANB

30 As in all organizations, members clashed regularly over issues ranging from the profound to the absurd. One Orangeman complained that a particularly malicious colleague threatened to 'knock [his] brains out with a sled stake' during a minor dispute. See Letter, n.a., 30 Dec. 1854, CP, PANB.

31 Bowes Correspondence and Minutes Book, Eldon Lodge, CP, PANB

32 Comprehensive rules governed each level; for example, the Scarlet Chapter rules included directions for appropriate dress, key rituals, and proper

forms to address leaders. The master received the honour of being called 'Worshipful companion in command.' See Correspondence, CP, PANB.

33 *Constitution and Laws of the Loyal Orange Association of British America* (Truro, NS: Isaac Baird 1869) 8; *Loyalist* 8 June 1848

34 Lodge returns, in *Minutes of the Annual Meeting of the Grand Orange Lodge of the Province of New Brunswick, 1846–53; Annual Report of the Proceedings of the Grand Lodge of the Loyal Orange Association of BNA, 1846–50;* John Earle's address, House of Assembly, 13 Apr. 1850, in *Reporter* 10 May 1850; *Sentinel* 3 July 1930; Steele, *History and Directory* 11–13

35 *Sentinel* 29 Oct. 1891; *Loyalist* 15 Oct. 1847

36 Minutes Book, Wellington Orange Lodge, NBM

37 Petition, 6 Sept. 1848, CP, PANB

38 Judge Robert Parker's address to convicted rioters, in *Reporter* 4 Aug. 1848

39 Minutes of the Grand Orange Lodge of New Brunswick and Nova Scotia, in *Weekly Chronicle* 6 July 1849; *Sentinel* 3 July 1930; Correspondence, CP, PANB

40 *Minutes of the Annual Meeting of the Grand Orange Lodge of the Province of New Brunswick, 1846–50*

41 Donald H. Akenson, *Being Had* (Port Credit, Ont.: Meany 1984) 139–40. For problems encountered when attempting to define ethnicity, see Akenson, *The Irish in Ontario* (Kinston: McGill-Queen's UP 1984) 6–7.

42 John Earle's address, House of Assembly, in *Loyalist* 30 Mar., 6 Apr. 1848

43 Houston and Smyth found essentially the same anti-Catholic and colonial dynamic as Newfoundland's Orange Order grew: 'Orangemen in Canada,' *Untold Story*, ed. O'Driscoll and Reynolds, 2:746–7.

44 Orange Order Address to Head, Jan. 1849, in *Morning News* 24 Jan. 1849; *Headquarters* 24 Jan. 1849

45 While Acheson asserted that Saint John's Protestants and 'bluenoses' were somehow co-opted into joining the organization, the following argument suggests that Protestants flocked to the order precisely because of its anti-Catholic and paramilitary nature. See T.W. Acheson, *Saint John* (Toronto: U of Toronto P 1985) 106–14.

46 Rev. Gilbert Spurr's speech, in *Loyalist* 15 Oct. 1847

47 *Minutes of the Annual Meeting of the Grand Orange Lodge of the Province of New Brunswick*, 1852; Head to Grey, 26 July 1848, CO 188; Rev. Gilbert Spurr's speech, in *Loyalist* 15 Oct. 1847; *Reporter* 26 Oct. 1849; *Carleton Sentinel* 2 July 1850; Steele, *History and Directory* 13–15, 21

48 George Anderson testimony, Fredericton Riot Trials, in *Reporter* 19 Nov. 1847; *Loyalist* 16 July, 15 Oct. 1847

49 *Sentinel* 29 Oct. 1891. For an excellent example of the heroic theme in Orangeism, see 'The Battle of York Point' in appendix A.

50 *Loyalist* 1, 15 Oct. 1847

51 Barzilla Ansley's address, House of Assembly, 4 Apr. 1850, in *Reporter* 20

Apr. 1850; Daniel Hannington's address, House of Assembly, 1 Mar. 1850, in *Reporter* 8 Mar. 1850

52 Orange Order Address to Head, Jan. 1849, in *Morning News* 24 Jan. 1849; *Royal Gazette* 17 Jan. 1849; *Headquarters* 24 Jan. 1849

53 *Loyalist* 28 Oct. 1847; *Reporter* 15 Mar. 1850

54 Charles Connell's address, 8 Mar. 1850, Debates, RGA, PANB; *Carleton Sentinel* 19 Mar. 1850

55 J. Dibblee to Lt. Col. Shore, 19 July 1847, R&D, NBEC, PANB; *Woodstock Telegraph* 17 July 1847, repr. in *Gleaner* 27 July 1847; Barzilla Ansley's and Daniel Hannington's address, House of Assembly, in *Reporter* 8 Mar., 26 Apr. 1850

56 *Minutes of the Annual Meeting of the Grand Orange Lodge of the Province of New Brunswick*, 1846–53; 1851, 1861 NB censuses; Charles McPherson's testimony, Fredericton Riot Trials, in *Reporter* 19 Nov. 1847; Major E.T. Sturdee, *Historical Records of the 62nd St. John Fusiliers* (Saint John: J. & A. McMillan 1888) 3–5. These points will be pursued in more detail in the chapters on the riots.

57 *Laws and Ordinances of the Orange Association* 12; *The Orange Question Treated by Sir Francis Hincks*

58 *Minutes of the Annual Meeting of the Grand Orange Lodge of the Province of New Brunswick*, 1853–5; *Annual Report of the Proceedings of the Grand Lodge of the Loyal Orange Association of BNA*, 1853, 1856. See also 'Up, Orangemen, Up!' in *The Sentinel Orange and Patriotic Song Book* (Toronto: Sentinel 1935) 31.

59 S.H. Gilbert's sermon, in *Minutes of the Annual Meeting of the Grand Orange Lodge of the Province of New Brunswick*, 1854, 1855

60 Grand Orange Lodge of New Brunswick's Address to Queen Victoria, Apr. 1851, in Head to Grey, 28 Apr. 1851, CO 188; Grey to Head, 7 June 1851, CO 189

61 James Boyd's address, House of Assembly, 4 Apr. 1850, in *Reporter* 9 Apr. 1850

62 Circulars, 1853–4, CP, PANB

63 L.P. Fisher's speech, Orange Order meeting, 12 July 1850, in *Carleton Sentinel* 16 July 1850; S.H. Gilbert's sermon, in *Minutes of the Annual Meeting of the Grand Orange Lodge of the Province of New Brunswick*, 1854

64 *Minutes of the Annual Meeting of the Grand Orange Lodge of the Province of New Brunswick*, 1846–52

65 William McKenzie's address to Richmond Lodge no. 51, in *Carleton Sentinel* 23 July 1850

66 Joseph A. Allan, *Orangeism, Catholicism, and Sir Francis Hincks* (Toronto: Hart & Rawlinson 1877)

67 For example, 'Croppies Lie Down' was a popular song played by New Brunswick's Orangemen during processions. Its lyrics evoked negative images of the Celtic-Irish, such as racial inferiority, ignorance, cowardice, and duplicity. See *Sentinel Song Book* 48.

68 John Earle's address, House of Assembly, 13 Apr. 1850, in *Reporter* 10 May 1850; editorials, *Loyalist* 16 July, 17 Sept., 15 Oct. 1847; *Weekly Chronicle* 29 July 1842

69 *Reporter* 10 Sept. 1847

70 *Loyalist* 24 Mar. 1845, 9, 23 Dec. 1847

71 William Carrick testimony, Fredericton Riot Trials, in *Reporter* 19 Nov. 1847; *Loyalist* 17 Sept. 1847

72 John Earle correspondence, in *Annual Report of the Proceedings of the Grand Lodge of the Loyal Orange Association of BNA*, 1851; Houston and Smyth, *Sash* 70–2, 100–1

73 Barzilla Ansley's address, House of Assembly, 4 Apr. 1850, in *Reporter* 26 Apr. 1850; *Courier* 25 July 1840

74 1851 NB census; Minutes of the 1844 organizational meeting, in Steele, *History and Directory* 11

75 In fact some of the earliest civilian lodges in Saint John were staffed entirely by Loyalists from New England and southern states. See Houston and Smyth, *Sash* 70–2; Steele, *History and Directory* 115–18

76 William T. Baird, *Seventy Years of New Brunswick Life* (Saint John: George E. Day 1890) 158; *Sentinel* 3 July 1930

77 J. Dibblee to Lt. Col. Shore, 19 July 1847, and James McCann and other Roman Catholics to Head, 30 June 1848, R&D, NBEC, PANB; *Loyalist* 17 Sept., 15 Oct. 1847

78 John Earle correspondence, in *Annual Report of the Proceedings of the Grand Lodge of the Loyal Orange Association of BNA*, 1851; James Brown letters, *Reporter* 28 Apr., 5, 12 May 1848; *Morning News* 18 July 1849

79 Benjamin Wheeler's testimony, Fredericton Riot Trials, in *Reporter* 19 Nov. 1847. This phenomenon was not unique to New Brunswick. Ogle Gowan undertook a history of Canada's Orange Order because he was appalled by how ignorant Orange members were of the organization's history and symbolism. See Ogle R. Gowan, *Orangeism: Its Origin and History*, 3 vols (Toronto: Lovell & Gibson 1859–60).

80 J.A. Perley testimony, Fredericton Riot Trials, in *Reporter* 19 Nov. 1847

81 1851, 1861 NB censuses; Lodge returns, in *Minutes of the Grand Orange Lodge of the Province of New Brunswick*, 1846–55; *Annual Report of the Proceedings of the Grand Lodge of the Loyal Orange Association of BNA*, 1849–50; Minutes Books, Orange Order Documents, Petitions and Bowes Correspondence, CP, PANB; Minutes Book, Wellington Orange Lodge, NBM; Riot Trials, Saint John, Fredericton, Woodstock, R&D, NBEC, PANB; Trial Transcripts, 1845–50, NBSC, PANB. Newspapers included *Loyalist*, *Reporter*, *Weekly Chronicle*, *Carleton Sentinel*, and *Sentinel*. See also Steele, *History and Directory* and *Saint John Daily Sun* 13 July 1897.

82 NBSC, PANB; SJCC, PANB; Papers, 1840s, CO; NB Blue Books, 1840s, NAC; *Loyalist*, *Courier*

83 Thus, the total number will vary depending upon the valid, or census-

confirmed information available for each variable, i.e., birthplace, immigration date, and occupation.

84 The counties include Saint John, York, Carleton, Kings, Queens, Sunbury, and Victoria. All border the Saint John River; the former three experienced the social violence analysed in this study. Victoria County was included because during most of the 1840s it was part of Carleton County. Unfortunately, Saint John census material for 1851 is incomplete. Only four wards of the city are extant: Kings, Sydney, Queens, and Dukes. Carleton's wards and Portland's records are missing; however St Martins Parish is included. In addition, the manuscript census was consulted for the relatively few Orangemen identified in other counties, including Queens, Kings, and Sunbury. The author found the following census guides published by the Public Archives of New Brunswick at Fredericton quite useful: *The New Brunswick Census of 1851: York County* (1979), compiled by Elizabeth Sewell and Elizabeth Saunders; *The New Brunswick Census of 1851: Carleton County* (1980), edited by Robert F. Fellows; and *The New Brunswick Census of 1851: Saint John County* (1982), complied by the Saint John Branch of the New Brunswick Genealogical Society.

85 Cliometricians will immediately note that literally hundreds of discrete occupations have been identified in social histories of the workplace and ethnicity in nineteenth-century North America. For the purposes of this study, however, the author is confident that the basic categories are more than adequate for making general assumptions about the Orange Order's multidimensional nature.

86 Two ground-breaking works explored these ideas: Michael B. Katz, *The People of Hamilton, Canada West: Family and Class in a Mid-Nineteenth-Century City* (Cambridge: Harvard UP 1975); and Stephan Thernstrom, *Poverty and Progress: Social Mobility in a Nineteenth Century City* (Cambridge: Harvard UP 1964). For examples of more recent scholarship that explores these themes in nineteenth-century Canada, consult Gregory S. Kealey, *Toronto Workers Respond to Industrial Capitalism* (Toronto: U of Toronto P 1980) and Bryan D. Palmer, *Working-Class Experience: The Rise and Reconstitution of Canadian Labour, 1800–1980* (Toronto: Butterworth 1983).

87 Minutes Book, Wellington Orange Lodge, NBM; CP, PANB

88 Houston and Smyth traced similar Ontario patterns in *Sash*.

89 See, for example, Acheson's cogent study *Saint John*.

90 Ibid. 112–14

91 Judge Carter's address to Grand Jury, Fredericton Riot Trials, Oct. 1847, in *Loyalist* 11 Nov. 1847; Attorney General L.A. Wilmot's address, 8 Mar. 1850, *Debates*, RGA, PANB

92 Special Presentment, Grand Jury Report, 21 Aug. 1849, in *Courier* 25 Aug. 1849; Attorney General L.A. Wilmot's addresses, House of Assembly, in *Morning News* 22 Feb. 1850, *Courier* 23 Feb. 1850, and *Debates*, 8 Mar. 1850, RGA, PANB; Judge John A. Street's address to Grand Jury, 27 Oct. 1846, in

*Reporter* 30 Oct. 1846; Judge Street's address, in *Loyalist* 29 June 1848; Judge Street's address to Grand Jury, *Reporter* 7 July 1848; Judge James Carter's address to Supreme Court, in *Royal Gazette* 3 Nov. 1847; *Reporter* 26 July 1850; Grey to Head, 24 Aug. 1848, CO 188

93 *Reporter* 23 Nov. 1844

94 *Morning News* 11 Oct. 1844, 22 Nov. 1847

95 *True Liberator* 25 Sept. 1847, and miscellaneous issues from 1847 to 1850

96 *Freeman*; William M. Baker, *Timothy Warren Anglin* (Toronto: U of Toronto P 1977) 193–6

97 The same years witnessed a parallel struggle with the powerful Grand Orange Lodge of British North America over the right to maintain a degree of independence in deciding local issues and to keep the fundamental privilege of issuing warrants for new primary lodges. Arguably the Grand Orange Lodge of New Brunswick emerged triumphant by the 1870s. It had been granted a degree of legitimacy, thanks to incorporation, and it appeared that it would retain indefinitely its warrant-granting powers. Consult See, 'Fortunes,' *New Ireland*, ed. Toner, 102–4.

98 House of Assembly Debates, 11 Mar. 1848, in *Reporter* 17, 28 Mar. 1848; *Christian Visitor* 22 Mar. 1848; *Morning News* 14 Feb. 1848; New Brunswick, *Journal of the House of Assembly*, 1848 (Fredericton: John Simpson)

99 Bill no. 55, 'A Bill to Incorporate the Grand Lodges and Subordinate Lodges in New Brunswick,' Documents, 1850, RGA, PANB

100 New Brunswick, *Journal of the House of Assembly*, 1850 (Fredericton: John Simpson) 86, 100; Petitions, 1850, RGA, PANB; *Headquarters* 20, 23 Feb. 1850; *Reporter* 1 Mar. 1850

101 *Morning News* 13 Mar. 1850; *Headquarters* 9 Mar. 1850

102 9 Victoria, c. 72, 1846, in *New Brunswick Statutes* (Fredericton: Queen's Printer); Bill no. 59, 'A Bill to Incorporate the Albion Lodge of Free Masons,' Documents, 1850, RGA, PANB; *Headquarters* 23 Feb. 1850

103 Addresses by Charles Connell, John Earle, and others, 8 Mar., 4, 13 Apr. 1850, Debates, RGA, PANB; *Reporter* 11, 15, 22, 19 Mar., 12, 19, 26 Apr., 3, 10 May 1850; *Headquarters* 9 Mar. 1850; *Morning News* 13 Mar., 8 Apr. 1850

104 Addresses by Attorney General Wilmot, James Brown, and others, 8 Mar., 4, 13 Apr. 1850, Debates, RGA, PANB; *Journal of the House of Assembly*, 1850: 120, 124, 136–7; *Reporter* 11, 15, 22, 29 Mar., 12, 19, 26 Apr., 3, 10 May 1850; *Headquarters* 9 Mar. 1850; *Morning News* 27 Feb., 13 Mar., 8 Apr. 1850; *Christian Visitor* 15 Mar. 1850; *Courier* 9, 16 Mar. 1850

105 *Reporter* 10 May 1850; *Journal of the House of Assembly*, 1850: 291–2

106 New Brunswick, *Journal of the House of Assembly*, 1851–74

107 38 Victoria, c. 54, 1875, in *New Brunswick Statutes* (Fredericton: Queen's Printer); *Journal of the House of Assembly*, 1875; *Journal of the Legislative Council*, 1875: 84. This bill was amended twice, both times to address financial inadequacies. See 56 Victoria, c. 67, 1893, and 5 George V, c. 63, 1915, in *New Brunswick Statutes* (Fredericton: Queen's Printer). The New Brunswick bill, the first

of its kind in British North America, served as a model for the national legislation passed in 1890. See 53 Victoria, c. 105, 1890, *Statutes of Canada*.

CHAPTER 5

1 Resolution of Justices of the Peace, 23 Nov. 1846, RGA, PANB
2 Terrence M.F. Kilbride, 'The Process of Growth and Change in Carleton County 1783–1867,' MA thesis, U of New Brunswick, 1969, 66–7
3 William T. Baird, *Seventy Years of New Brunswick Life* (Saint John: George E. Day 1890) 158; Scott W. See, 'The Fortunes of the Orange Order in 19th Century New Brunswick,' *New Ireland Remembered*, ed. Peter Toner (Fredericton: New Ireland P 1988) 98–103
4 Connell and others to Saunders, 1 May 1847, CO 188; J. Dibblee to G. Dibblee, 18 May 1847, New Brunswick Historical Society Papers, NBM
5 Winslow to Saunders, 3 May 1847, Documents, NBEC, PANB; Saunders to Winslow, 8 May 1847; Winslow to Saunders, 14, 17 May 1847; Wetmore to Winslow, 14 May 1847; Saunders to Winslow, 18 May 1847: CO 188
6 The attorney general, Charles Peters, advised Colebrooke that only special constables should be used locally, and then only if a riot or tumult was 'reasonably apprehended.' Colebrooke obviously took his advice. See Peters to Saunders, 2 June 1847, R&D, NBEC, PANB.
7 Winslow to Saunders, 25 June 1847, Documents, NBEC, PANB
8 *Woodstock Telegraph* 14 July 1847, repr. in *Gleaner* 17 July 1847; Colebrooke to Grey, 30 July 1847, Colebrooke Correspondence, PANB; D. Dibblee to G. Dibblee, 13 July 1847, New Brunswick Historical Society Papers, NBM; Baird, *Seventy Years* 158–9
9 Judge Robert Parker's sentencing of rioters, in *Reporter* 4 Aug. 1848
10 *Woodstock Telegraph* 14 July 1847, repr. in *Gleaner* 17 July 1847; Baird, *Seventy Years* 158–9
11 Jacksontown, a farming community at a crossroads north of Woodstock, included two Baptist meeting-houses and an Anglican church. See Kilbride, 'Growth and Change' 145–6.
12 Winslow to Saunders, 14 July 1847, CO 188; *Woodstock Telegraph* 14 July 1847, repr. in *Gleaner* 17 July 1847; D. Dibblee to G. Dibblee, 13 July 1847, New Brunswick Historical Society Papers, NBM; *Loyalist* 16 July 1847; *Morning News* 16 July 1847; Baird, *Seventy Years* 158–9
13 D. Dibblee to G. Dibblee, 13 July 1847, New Brunswick Historical Society Papers, NBM; John Connell's address, House of Assembly, in *Reporter* 17 Mar. 1848; *Woodstock Telegraph* 14 July 1847, repr. in *Gleaner* 17 July 1847; Baird, *Seventy Years* 158–9; *Loyalist* 6 Apr. 1848
14 *Woodstock Telegraph* 14 July 1847, repr. in *Gleaner* 17 July 1847
15 Winslow to Saunders, 14 July 1847, CO 188; *Woodstock Telegraph* 14 July 1847, repr. in *Gleaner* 17 July 1847; John Connell's address, House of Assembly, in *Reporter* 17 Mar. 1848

16 *Loyalist* 23 July 1847; *Morning News* 16 July 1847; *Woodstock Telegraph* 14 July 1847, repr. in *Gleaner* 17 July 1847; John Connell's address, House of Assembly, in *Reporter* 17 Mar. 1848

17 Baird, *Seventy Years* 158–9; *Woodstock Telegraph* 14 July 1847, repr. in *Gleaner* 17 July 1847

18 Charles Connell later claimed that the Orangemen defied the orders of authorities in order 'to protect' villagers from Roman Catholics, a good example of the vigilante response of Orangemen to Irish immigration. See his address to the House of Assembly, in *Reporter* 15 Mar. 1850. See also *Woodstock Telegraph* 14 July 1847, repr. in *Gleaner* 17 July 1847; Baird, *Seventy Years* 158–9.

19 Winslow to Saunders, 14 July 1847, CO 188; *Woodstock Telegraph* 14 July 1847, repr. in *Gleaner* 17 July 1847; John Connell's address, House of Assembly, in *Reporter* 17 Mar. 1848; Baird, *Seventy Years* 158–9

20 John Dibblee and others to Saunders, 12 July 1847, Documents, NBEC, PANB; Baird, *Seventy Years* 158–9; *Woodstock Telegraph* 14 July 1847, repr. in *Gleaner* 17 July 1847

21 One account reported that a badly wounded Catholic was secreted across the American border at Houlton in women's clothing. See Baird, *Seventy Years* 158–9.

22 John Dibblee and others to Saunders, 20 July 1847, CO 188

23 Colebrooke to Grey, 30 July 1847, Colebrooke Correspondence, PANB; John Dibblee and others to Saunders, 12 July 1847, Documents, NBEC, PANB; John Dibblee and others to Saunders, 20 July 1847, CO 188; *Woodstock Telegraph* 14 July 1847, repr. in *Gleaner* 17 July 1847; *Loyalist* 16 July 1847; *Morning News* 16 July 1847; J. Dibblee to G. Dibblee, 13 July 1847, New Brunswick Historical Society Papers, NBM; John Connell's address, House of Assembly, in *Reporter* 17 Mar. 1848

24 See Baird, *Seventy Years*; J. Dibblee to G. Dibblee, 13 July 1847, New Brunswick Historical Society Papers, NBM; and Winslow to Saunders, 14 July 1847, CO 188.

25 See Woodstock Riot Papers, R&D, NBEC, PANB; and Woodstock Riot File, CO 188.

26 Baird, *Seventy Years* 159

27 One legislator, sympathetic to the Woodstock Irish-Catholics, claimed that the Orangemen were issued militia weapons for the 12 July procession. This was probably true; militia arms would likely have bayonets attached, and several Catholics were apparently bayoneted. See Martin Cranney's address, House of Assembly, in *Reporter* 17 Mar. 1848. See also Baird, *Seventy Years* 158–9.

28 *Weekly Observer* 20 July 1847; *Reporter* 16 July 1847

29 J. Dibblee to Lt. Col. Shore, 14 July 1847, CO 188; J. Dibblee to Colebrooke, 6 Sept. 1848, Documents, NBEC, PANB

30 Colebrooke to Saunders, 14 July 1847, Colebrooke Correspondence, PANB;

Lt. Col. Shore to Major Dibblee, 15 July 1847, CO 188; Saunders to Wood-stock Magistrates, 14 July 1847, Documents, NBEC, PANB; Saunders to Wins-low, 15 July 1847, CO 188; Minutes, 14 Oct. 1847, NBEC, PANB; *Reporter* 22 Oct. 1847; *Loyalist* 21 Oct. 1847

31 Although the sheriff and justices complained about the lack of an adequate jail from 1845–7, no action had been taken on the construction of a new one by July 1847. See Wetmore to Saunders, 24 Nov. 1846, RGA, PANB; Special Session Minutes, Carleton County, 23 Nov. 1846, RGA, PANB; Minutes, 10 Dec. 1846, NBEC, PANB; Winslow to Saunders, 27 Mar. 1847, Documents, NBEC, PANB.

32 J. Dibblee and other magistrates to Saunders, 14 July 1847, J. Dibblee to Lt. Col. Shore, 19 July 1847, R&D, NBEC, PANB; J. Dibblee and others to Saun-ders, 16 July 1847, CO 188

33 Saunders to Woodstock's magistrates, 15, 17 July 1847, CO 188; Colebrooke to Saunders, 16 July 1847, CO 188

34 Minutes, 18 July 1847, NBEC, PANB; Saunders to Wetmore, 19 July 1847, CO 188; Wetmore to Saunders, 21 July 1847, R&D, NBEC, PANB; Saunders to Wetmore, 22 July 1847, CO 188; Saunders to Peters and Kinnear, 22 July 1847, CO 188

35 *Loyalist* 17 Sept. 1847; *Woodstock Telegraph* 24 July 1847, repr. in *Gleaner* 3 Aug. 1847; *Woodstock Telegraph* 11 Sept. 1847, repr. in *Gleaner* 14 Sept. 1847

36 *Reporter* 24 Sept. 1847

37 *Loyalist* 17 Sept. 1847

38 See 31 George III, c. 6, 1791, in *New Brunswick Statutes* (Fredericton: Queen's Printer). The House of Assembly moved quickly to remove this rule so that it would not interfere with the upcoming trial: 11 Victoria, c. 15, 1848, in *New Brunswick Statutes* (Fredericton: Queen's Printer).

39 Kinnear to Colebrooke, 22 Sept. 1847; Colebrooke to Grey, 28 Sept. 1847; Parker to Colebrooke, 24 Sept. 1847: CO 188; *Woodstock Telegraph* 2 Oct. 1847, repr. in *Gleaner* 5 Oct. 1847; *Reporter* 24 Sept. 1847; *Courier* 25 Sept. 1847

40 Parker to Colebrooke, 24 Sept. 1847, CO 188; *Headquarters* 22 Sept. 1847

41 *Loyalist* 24 Sept. 1847

42 See *Loyalist* 1 Oct. 1847. The Grand Jury, however, publicly endorsed the Solicitor General's actions: *Reporter* 1 Oct. 1847; *Woodstock Telegraph* 22 Sept. 1847, repr. in *Loyalist* 1 Oct. 1847.

43 Kinnear to Colebrooke, 22 Sept. 1847; Parker to Colebrooke, 24 Sept. 1847: CO 188

44 *True Liberator* 25 Sept. 1847

45 *Loyalist* 1 Oct. 1847

46 Parker to Colebrooke, 24 Sept. 1847, CO 188; *Woodstock Telegraph* 2 Oct. 1847, repr. in *Gleaner* 5 Oct. 1847

47 Kinnear to Colebrooke, 22 Sept. 1847; Parker to Colebrooke, 24 Sept. 1847: CO 188

48 Colebrooke to Grey, 28 Sept. 1847, CO 188
49 Petition from freeholders of Carleton County, 9 Feb. 1848, RGA, PANB
50 Petition from Carleton County's Justices of the Peace, 3 Feb. 1848, Judicial Returns, RGA, PANB
51 Petitions, 1848, RGA, PANB
52 Colebrooke memorandum, Minutes, 17 Feb. 1848, NBEC, PANB
53 See petition from James McCann and others to Colebrooke, 30 June 1848, R&D, NBEC, PANB; Saunders to Cleary, Demill, and Baird, 5 July 1848; Demill to Partelow, 10 July 1848; Cleary to Partelow, 11 July 1848; Baird to Partelow, 13 July 1848: CO 188.
54 Partelow to Cleary, Demill, and Baird, 24 July 1848, CO 188
55 Petition from Carleton County's Justices of the Peace, 6 May 1848, R&D, NBEC, PANB
56 Saunders to Wetmore, 13 May 1848; Head to Grey, 15 May 1848: CO 188; Head to Lt. Col. Brown, 13 May 1848, Head Letterbook, PANB
57 James McCann and others to Colebrooke, 30 June 1848, R&D, NBEC, PANB
58 Petition from Roman Catholic freeholders to Head, 1 July 1848, R&D, NBEC, PANB
59 Head to Grey, 26 July 1848, CO 188. Grey approved of Colebrooke's decision not to meddle in county affairs: Grey to Head, 24 Aug. 1848, CO 189.
60 Kinnear to Partelow, 21 July 1848; Head to Grey, 26 July 1848: CO 188
61 The average immigration date was 1831; thus, the defendants averaged 16 years of residency at the time of the riot.
62 The mean age is useful, although it reflects the phenomenon that people often rounded off their birthdays to the nearest decade when the census was taken, either because of convenience, a faulty memory, or ignorance of their true year of birth. In this case, the disproportionately high number of 36-year-olds indicates the probability that many people rounded their birthdays off to 40 in the 1851 census; thus, the enumerator recorded 1811 as their birth year.
63 This assessment utilizes the various trial records and Executive Council reports cited above, in addition to the 1851 NB census.
64 Courier 22, 29 July 1848; Reporter 21 July 1848; Gleaner 1 Aug. 1848; Kinnear to Partelow, 21 July 1848, CO 188
65 Judge Parker's address, in Reporter 4 Aug. 1848; Head to Grey, 31 July 1848; Kinnear to Partelow, 21 July 1848: CO 188
66 A breakdown by decade follows: five were in their teens, six were in their twenties, eight were in their thirties, one was over forty, and the ages of eight were missing from the census.
67 Kinnear to Partelow, 21 July 1848, CO 188
68 Court of Oyer and Terminer, Carleton County, 29 June 1848, Documents, NBEC, PANB
69 Kinnear to Partelow, 21 July 1848, CO 188
70 Records, 1848, NBSC, PANB

71 Kinnear's report to Partelow, 23 Oct. 1848, Documents, NBEC, PANB. Many of these petitions were endorsed by the magistrates and the sheriff. See Petitions, R&D, NBEC, PANB; Minutes, 26 Oct. 1848, NBEC, PANB; Head Correspondence, PANB.

72 Minutes, 1 Dec. 1848, 24 Feb. 1849, NBEC, PANB; Petitions, R&D, NBEC, PANB; *Royal Gazette* 28 Feb. 1849; *Weekly Chronicle* 2 Mar. 1849

73 Petition from Saint John Catholics, Aug. 1848, Judicial Records, NBEC, PANB; *Weekly Chronicle* 18 Aug. 1848; *Gleaner* 29 Aug. 1848

74 For example, John Craven, who was arrested but not convicted, promptly lost his job as tidewaiter and special constable after the trial. See J Dibblee and others to Saunders, 12 Aug. 1847, R&D, NBEC, PANB; *Loyalist* 1 Oct. 1847.

75 Records, 1848, NBSC, PANB; Petitions, R&D, NBEC, PANB

76 *Loyalist* 1, 15 Oct. 1847

77 *Carleton Sentinel* 2, 10 July 1850, 15 July 1854; *Loyalist* 15 Oct. 1847

78 J. Dibblee to Lt. Col. Shore, 19 July 1847, R&D, NBEC, PANB

79 For evidence of this commitment to Orangeism, see the petitions from Carleton County in support of the Orange Incorporation Bill: Petitions, 1850–1, 1853–4, 1860, 1867, 1872, RGA, PANB.

## CHAPTER 6

1 Primary Lodge documents, CP, PANB

2 Lilian M.B. Maxwell, *The History of Central New Brunswick* (Sackville: Tribune P 1937) 166

3 George P. Wolhaupter Diary, PANB; *Headquarters* 15 July 1846

4 *Headquarters* 15, 17 July 1846

5 Grand Jury Report to General Sessions, Minutes, 4 June 1847, York County GS, PANB; *Reporter* 11 June 1847

6 Queen v. Jeremiah Hennessy, 1847, Records, NBSC, PANB

7 James Perley's testimony, Fredericton riot trials, in *Reporter* 19 Nov. 1847; *Reporter* 16 July 1847

8 See Charles McPherson's, James Perley's, and Sergeant Chalmer's testimonies, 1847, Records, NBSC, PANB; *Reporter* 19 Nov. 1847

9 *Courier* 17 July 1847; *Loyalist* 16 July 1847

10 Estimates varied from 200 to 400. See Nicholas Wheeler's testimony, 1847, Records, NBSC, PANB; Charles McPherson's testimony, Fredericton riot trials, in *Reporter* 19 Nov. 1847; *Loyalist* 16 July 1847.

11 Charles McPherson's testimony, Fredericton riot trials, in *Reporter* 19 Nov. 1847

12 George Anderson's and Nicholas Wheeler's testimonies, Fredericton riot trials, in *Reporter* 19 Nov. 1847. Both these men were in the Orange Hall during the riot.

13 Charles McPherson's, George Anderson's, and Nicholas Wheeler's testimonies, 1847, Records, NBSC, PANB; *Loyalist* 16 July 1847; *Reporter* 19 Nov.

1847. Anderson embellished his account. When the Irish-Catholics supposedly called him to come down to the street, taunting, 'We'll tear you from limb from limb, and pudding from pudding, and ate your heart,' Anderson claimed his reply was, 'Why don't you come up and have some lemonade and ginger beer.'

14 Charles McPherson's testimony, 1847, Records, NBSC, PANB
15 Anthony Stewart's testimony, 1847, Records, NBSC, PANB
16 Captain Walker's, William Shackleton's, Lambert White's, and Thomas Lamb's testimonies, 1847, Records, NBSC, PANB. All four were British soldiers in the 33rd Regiment. See also *Reporter* 19 Nov. 1847; and James Hogg's testimony, 1847, Records, NBSC, PANB.
17 Charles Bailey's and Thomas Pendergast's testimonies, 1847, Records, NBSC, PANB; *Loyalist* 16 July 1847
18 James Perley's testimony, 1847, Records, NBSC, PANB; *Reporter* 16 July 1847; *Courier* 17 July 1847
19 The pro-Orange *Loyalist* claimed that Armstrong was 'defending' his property although it was not clear that he was being attacked. See the issues of 16 and 23 July 1847.
20 Jeremiah Mahoney's and Christie Graham's testimonies, 1847, Records, NBSC, PANB; James Perley's testimony, Fredericton riot trials, in *Reporter* 19 Nov. 1847; *Loyalist* 16 July 1847
21 Sergeant Chalmer's testimony, 1847, Records, NBSC, PANB; *Reporter* 16 July 1847
22 L.A. Wilmont's speech for the defence, Fredericton riot trials, in *Reporter* 19 Nov. 1847; *Loyalist* 16 July 1847; *Reporter* 16 July 1847
23 *Reporter* 30 July 1847; *Loyalist* 16 July 1847
24 Fredericton Riot Trials, 1847, Records, NBSC, PANB; 1851 NB census
25 Queen v. John Clancy, Queen v. Jeremiah Mahoney, and Queen v. Patrick Gallagher, 1846, 1847, Records, NBSC, PANB; *Reporter* 19 Nov. 1847
26 L.A. Wilmont's speech for the defence, Fredericton riot trials, in *Reporter* 19 Nov. 1847; 1851 NB census
27 Charles Bailey's and Thomas Pendergast's testimonies, Fredericton riot trials, in *Reporter* 19 Nov. 1847
28 George Anderson's testimony, Fredericton riot trials, in *Reporter* 19 Nov. 1847
29 1851 NB census; Fredericton Riot Trials, 1847, Records, NBSC, PANB; *Reporter* 19 Nov. 1847
30 Fredericton Riot Trials, 1847, Records, NBSC, PANB; *Headquarters* 10 Nov. 1847; *Reporter* 19 Nov. 1847
31 Judge Carter's address to the Grand Jury, Fredericton riot trials, in *Reporter* 12 Nov. 1847; *Loyalist* 11 Nov. 1847
32 Fredericton Riot Trials, 1847, Records, NBSC, PANB; *Royal Gazette* 17 Nov. 1847; *Reporter* 19 Nov. 1847; *Loyalist* 18 Nov. 1847
33 Wilmont's final point could not be corroborated by available evidence. See

his speech for the defence, Fredericton riot trials, in *Reporter* 19 Nov. 1847.

34 William Watt's and John A. Street's addresses to the jury, Fredericton riot trials, in *Reporter* 19 Nov. 1847

35 Judge Carter's address to the Grand Jury, Fredericton riot trials, in *Royal Gazette* 3 Nov. 1847; *Reporter* 12 Nov. 1847; *Loyalist* 11 Nov. 1847; Judge Carter's charge to the rioters before sentencing, Fredericton riot trials, in *Reporter* 19 Nov. 1847

36 *Reporter* 16 July 1847; *Loyalist* 16, 23 July 1847

37 Judge Carter's charge to the rioters before sentencing, Fredericton riot trials, in *Reporter* 19 Nov. 1847

38 *Headquarters* 17 Nov. 1847; *Morning News* 22 Nov. 1847

39 A lodge that formed in nearby St Mary's Parish on 8 Sept. 1848 provided an admirable illustration of this growth. Of the fourteen charter members, all but two were born in New Brunswick. The two Irish-born members arrived in the province before 1827. Half were farmers, two were labourers, and three were sawyers. Their ages ranged from 18 to 59. See Petitions, CP, PANB.

40 John Earle's address to the House of Assembly, in *Reporter* 10 May 1850; *Weekly Chronicle* 14 July 1848; *Reporter* 13 Nov. 1849

41 For example, see James Perley's testimony, Fredericton riot trials, in *Reporter* 19 Nov. 1847.

42 George Anderson's testimony, Fredericton riot trials, in *Reporter* 19 Nov. 1847

43 See Grand Jury Report to General Sessions, in *Reporter* 11 June 1847

44 Documents, May 1848, Fredericton City Council Records, PANB

45 Constable Appointments, June 1848, Fredericton City Council Records, PANB

46 Petition from George Whittaker and others, 1850, Fredericton City Council Records, PANB

47 City Council Documents, 1851, Fredericton City Council Records, PANB

48 Resolutions, 1852, Fredericton City Council Records, PANB

49 34 Victoria, c. 1, 1871, in *New Brunswick Statues* (Fredericton: Queen's Printer); City Council Documents, 1857, 1858, Fredericton City Council Records, PANB

50 City Council Documents, May 1848, Fredericton City Council Records, PANB

51 Grand Jury Report, Minutes, June 1850, York County GS, PANB

52 'Confirmed' means clearly identified in the data set.

53 For a biographical sketch of Needham, see *Dictionary of Canadian Biography* 10:543–4.

54 *The Canadian Biographical Dictionary and Portrait Gallery of Eminent and Self-Made Men* (Toronto: American Biographical Publishing Co. 1881) 608–9

55 Documents, 1847–60, Fredericton City Council Records, PANB

56 For an example of this, see City Council Documents, 29 Mar. 1856, Fredericton City Council Records, PANB.

57 City Council Documents, Apr. 1858, Fredericton City Council Records, PANB
58 Of the 13, 11 were labourers, one was a tailor and the other was a shoemaker: Fredericton Riot Trials, 1847, Records, NBSC, PANB; 1851 NB census.
59 Fredericton Riot Trials, 1847, Records, NBSC, PANB; 1851 NB census
60 William Carrick's testimony, Fredericton riot trials, in *Reporter* 19 Nov. 1847
61 James Perley's testimony, Fredericton riot trials, in *Reporter* 19 Nov. 1847
62 See John Pendergast's testimony, Fredericton Riot Trials, 1847, Records, NBSC, PANB.
63 George Anderson's and Nicholas Wheeler's testimonies, Fredericton riot trials, in *Reporter* 19 Nov. 1847; Fredericton Riot Trials, 1847, Records, NBSC, PANB
64 *Loyalist* 16, 23 July 1847; *Reporter* 16 July 1847

CHAPTER 7

1 *Weekly Chronicle* 22 Mar. 1839
2 *Morning News* 24 Sept. 1847
3 *Weekly Chronicle* 11 June 1841; Clarence Ward, 'Old Times in St. John – 1847,' *Saint John Globe* 1 Apr. 1911
4 *Morning News* 4 Apr. 1845
5 *Weekly Chronicle* 17 Oct. 1845; W.S. MacNutt, *New Brunswick* (Toronto: Macmillan 1963) 302
6 Minutes, 6, 8, 9, 11, 12 Sept., 8, 12, Dec. 1843, 3–6, 14 Sept. 1844, Saint John GS, PANB; *Morning News* 26 Apr. 1841, 18 Aug., 1 Nov. 1843; *Weekly Chronicle* 3 Nov. 1843
7 Barzilla Ansley's and John Earle's addresses, House of Assembly, 4, 13 Apr. 1850, in *Reporter* 26 Apr., 10 May 1850; *Morning News* 11, 16 Oct. 1844, 16 July, 20 Sept. 1847; *Headquarters* 16 Oct. 1844
8 *Courier* 18 July 1840; *Weekly Chronicle* 14 July 1843, 18 July 1845
9 Brown to R. Hazen, 11 July 1837, Hazen papers, NBM; *Weekly Chronicle* 14 July 1837
10 John Earle's and Barzilla Ansley's addresses, House of Assembly, 4, 13 Apr. 1850, in *Reporter* 26 Apr., 10 May 1850
11 Minutes, 9, 10, 17 Dec. 1842, 25 Mar. 1843, Saint John GS, PANB; *Morning News* 13 July, 5 Aug. 1842; *Weekly Chronicle* 15 July, 12 Aug. 1842; *Courier* 16 July, 13, 27 Aug. 1842; *Sentinel* 29 Oct. 1891
12 *Courier* 16 July 1842; *Weekly Chronicle* 15 July 1842
13 *Weekly Chronicle* 15 July 1842
14 Barzilla Ansley's address, House of Assembly, 4 Apr. 1850, in *Reporter* 26 Apr. 1850
15 Donaldson to Reade, 8 Mar. 1844, R&D, NBEC, PANB; McHarg Diary, NBM, *Morning News* 5 Apr. 1844
16 *Weekly Chronicle* 3 Jan. 1845; *Morning News* 3 Jan. 1845; *Headquarters* 8 Jan. 1845; McHarg Diary, NBM

17 *Morning News* 30 Dec. 1844; *Weekly Chronicle* 3 Jan. 1845; *Loyalist* 24 Mar. 1845

18 Inquest papers, Yerxa murder trial, 1845, Records, NBSC, PANB; *Morning News* 17, 27, 31 Jan. 1845; *Weekly Chronicle* 17, 31 Jan. 1845

19 McHarg Diary, NBM

20 Donaldson to Reade, 29 Mar. 1845, R&D, NBEC, PANB

21 Saint John Grand Jury Report to Colebrooke, 27 Mar. 1845, R&D, NBEC, PANB; *Weekly Chronicle* 21 Mar. 1845

22 Gallagher to Donaldson, 22 Mar. 1845, R&D, NBEC, PANB

23 *Loyalist* 24 Mar. 1845

24 *Weekly Courier* 22 Mar. 1845; *Morning News* 19 Mar. 1845

25 Minutes, 7 Apr. 1845, NBEC, PANB; Report of Doctors Robert and William Bayard, 17 Mar. 1845, R&D, NBEC; McHarg Diary, NBM; *Weekly Chronicle* 21 Mar. 1845; *Morning News* 19 Mar. 1845; *Weekly Observer* 18 Mar. 1845; *Reporter* 21 Mar. 1845; *Courier* 22 Mar. 1845; *Loyalist* 24 Mar. 1845

26 Reade to Donaldson, 26 Mar. 1845, SJCC, PANB; Donaldson to Reade, 17 Mar. 1845; Whingate to Whannell, 20 Mar. 1845; Whannell to Colebrooke, 25 Mar. 1845: R&D, NBEC, PANB

27 Minutes, 20, 22, 26 Mar., 14 June 1845, Saint John GS, PANB; Donaldson to Reade, 22 Mar. 1845, R&D, NBEC, PANB; *Courier* 5 July 1845; *Saint John Herald* 2 July 1845

28 See 56 George III, c. 1, 1816; 4 William IV, c. 32, 1834; 7 William IV, c. 12, 1837; 6 Victoria, c. 39, 1843: all in *New Brunswick Statutes* (Fredericton: Queen's Printer). For deficiencies in the system, especially the night watch, see Minutes, 13, 17, 26, 28 Jan. 1842, 10, 17 Jan. 1845, SJCC, PANB.

29 Petition to Mayor Donaldson, 10 Jan. 1845, SJCC, PANB; Minutes, 18 Jan. 1845, SJCC, PANB; Saint John Grand Jury to Colebrooke, 22 Mar. 1845, R&D, NBEC, PANB; *Loyalist* 24 Mar. 1845; *Morning News* 22 Jan. 1845

30 *Minutes of the Annual Meeting of the Grand Orange Lodge of the Province of New Brunswick*, 1847; *Weekly Chronicle* 17 July 1846

31 *Morning News* 12 Apr. 1847

32 *Morning News* 14 July 1847

33 Orange supporters tried to disconnect the Orange Order, the Mechanics Institute Band, and the crowd that followed the procession. The *Loyalist* of 16 July 1847 claimed that the band had nothing to do with the Orange procession, while Clarence Ward made the dubious assertion that the Orange entourage consisted of 'children.' See 'Old Times.' Yet later an article in the Orange *Sentinel* proudly revealed that all the band members were Orangemen. See the issue of 29 Oct. 1891.

34 For a number of compelling examples, see R. McBride, ed., *The Canadian Orange Minstrel for 1860* (London: Free P 1860).

35 *Courier* 17 July 1847; *Morning News* 14 July 1847; *Loyalist* 16 July 1847; Ward, 'Old Times'; McHarg Diary, NBM

36 No account mentioned firearms until the Orangemen returned to York

Point, and then both sides appeared heavily armed. If Irish-Catholics carried weapons during the first confrontation, they failed to use them.

37 *Morning News* 14 July 1847; Colebrooke to Grey, 30 July 1847, NBEC, PANB; McHarg Diary, NBM; *Courier* 17 July 1847; *Loyalist* 16 July 1847; Ward, 'Old Times'

38 Judge Parker's opening address, Court of Oyer and Terminer, 3 Aug. 1847, in *Courier*, 7 Aug. 1847

39 Colebrooke to Grey, 30 July 1847, NBEC, PANB; *Morning News* 14 July 1847

40 *Loyalist* 16 July 1847; Ward, 'Old Times'

41 One newspaper referred to it as a 'civil war.' See *Morning News* 14 July 1847.

42 *Courier* 24 July 1847; *Morning News* 21, 23 July 1847; *Loyalist* 23 July 1847

43 *Weekly Chronicle* 30 July 1847; *Morning News* 28 July 1847; *Courier* 31 July 1847

44 *Courier* 24 July 1847; *Morning News* 23 July 1847

45 *Morning News* 23 July 1847

46 *Weekly Chronicle* 10 Sept. 1847; *Courier* 11 Sept. 1847; *Loyalist* 10 Sept. 1847; *Morning News* 8 Sept. 1847

47 Note particularly the testimonies of Thomas Clark, James Clark, Ezekiel Downey, and Edward McDermott, in Queen v. Dennis McGovern, 1847, Records, NBSC, PANB. See also James Clark's and Thomas Byrnes's testimonies, Trial of McGovern and McDermott, in *Morning News* 24 Jan. 1848.

48 Testimonies, Queen v. Dennis McGovern, 7–17 Sept. 1847, Records, NBSC, PANB; Testimonies, Trial of McGovern and McDermott, in *Morning News* 24 Jan. 1848

49 Minutes, 8 Dec. 1841 public meeting, in *Courier* 11 Dec. 1841; *Morning News* 3 Feb. 1841; Petition from Saint John's Common Council and Mayor to Colebrooke, 26, 28 Jan. 1842, SJCC, PANB; Petition from Stipendiary Constables, in *Morning News* 8 Jan. 1845; Petition for Police Force to Colebrooke, 10, 17 Jan. 1845, SJCC, PANB

50 Minutes, Saint John Common Council, 18 Jan. 1845, in *Morning News* 22 Jan. 1845; Colebrooke to Grey, 25 Nov. 1846, CO 188

51 Editorials and letters, *Morning News* 2, 16 Aug. 10, 13, 15 Sept. 1847

52 Allan to Reade, 12 Oct. 1847, in Minutes, 15 Oct. 1847, NBEC, PANB

53 Partelow to Saunders, 9 Nov. 1847, Allan to Saunders, 11 Nov. 1847, R&D, NBEC, PANB; *Weekly Chronicle* 12 Nov. 1847; *Morning News* 12 Dec. 1847

54 Simonds to Colebrooke, 14 Dec. 1847; Allan to Saunders, 24 Dec. 1847; Simonds to Saunders, 25 Dec. 1847; Colebrooke to Allan, 29 Dec. 1847; Colebrooke to Simonds, 29 Dec. 1847; Allan to Saunders, 3 Jan. 1848: R&D, NBEC, PANB

55 Thomas W. Smith's Petition, Dec. 1847, Moses Spragg's Petition, Dec. 1847, Documents, NBEC, PANB; *Morning News* 8 Dec. 1847; *Loyalist* 9 Dec. 1847

56 *Loyalist* 16, 23 Dec. 1847; *Morning News* 26 Jan. 1848; Judicial Records, NBEC, PANB

57 *New-Brunswicker* 7 Dec. 1847; Sharkey to Allan, 25 Jan. 1848, Allan to Saunders, 25 Jan. 1848, R&D, NBEC, PANB; Colebrooke to Grey, 28 Jan. 1848, CO 188
58 Allan to Executive Council, 19 Feb. 1848, in Minutes, 31 Mar. 1848, NBEC, PANB
59 11 Victoria, c. 12, 1848, in *New Brunswick Statutes* (Fredericton: Queen's Printer)
60 Minutes, 1 Apr. 1848, NBEC, PANB
61 Acheson argued that the creation of the Saint John police force took power away from the wards and placed it in the hands of city functionaries. See *Saint John* (Toronto: U of Toronto P 1985) 214–29.
62 Minutes, 27 Dec. 1847, SJCC, PANB; Presentment of Saint John Grand Jury, in Minutes, 18 Dec. 1847, Saint John GS, PANB; 11 Victoria, c. 13, 1848, in *New Brunswick Statutes*
63 Acheson, *Saint John* 214–29
64 12 Victoria, c. 68, 1849 and 13 Victoria, c. 1, 1850 (Local Acts), both in *New Brunswick Statutes*; Presentment of Saint John Grand Jury, in Minutes, 16 Dec. 1848, Saint John GS, PANB; Executive Council to Peters, 31 July 1849, in Minutes, 31 July 1849, NBEC, PANB; Grey to Head, 3 Aug. 1849, CO 189; Peters to Saint John Common Council, 15 Aug. 1849, and Head to Wilmot, 18 Sept. 1849, in Minutes, 17 Aug., 10 Oct. 1849, SJCC, PANB
65 Colebrooke to Grey, 30 July 1847, in Documents, NBEC, PANB; Colebrooke to Grey, 14 Dec. 1847, CO 188
66 *Weekly Chronicle* 22 Mar. 1839; *Morning News* 24 Sept. 1847

CHAPTER 8

1 *Weekly Chronicle* 14 July 1848
2 Testimony taken before Thomas Harding, 8 Mar. 1849, Records, Saint John Justice Court, PANB
3 *Morning News* 9 Mar. 1848; *Courier* 8 Mar. 1849; *Weekly Chronicle* 9 Mar. 1849; Minutes, Mar., Apr. 1849, NBEC, PANB
4 Documents, 1849, Saint John County Court, PANB
5 *Weekly Chronicle* 16 Mar. 1849
6 *Weekly Chronicle* 6 July 1849
7 Minutes Book, Wellington Orange Lodge, NBM
8 *Morning News* 13 July 1849
9 Head to Grey, 15 July 1849, CO 188. This question of the 'right' to public processions would become a hotly debated topic in the aftermath of the riot; it will be discussed below.
10 Thomas Paddock's testimony, Saint John Riot Trials, 1849, Records, NBEC, PANB; *Reporter* 13 July 1849
11 Head to Grey, 15 July 1849, CO 188
12 Francis Jones's testimony, Saint John Riot Trials, 1849, Records, NBEC, PANB

13 *Temperance Telegraph* 12 July 1849
14 *Morning News* 13 July 1849; *New-Brunswicker* 14 July 1849; *Courier* 14 July 1849; Francis Jones's testimony, Saint John Riot Trials, 1849, Records, NBEC, PANB
15 The question of whether the Orangemen were armed when they left Nethery's Hotel was to be of particular concern in the examinations after the riot. Although a few Orangemen, Mayor Wilmot, and Lieutenant-Governor Head had denied that arms were present, several brethren revealed that they had left their homes in the morning with swords, muskets, and pistols. See Squire Mank's, George McKelvey's, George Noble's, Jacob Allan's, and Charles Boyd's testimonies, Saint John Riot Trials, 1849, Records, NBEC, PANB; *Morning News* 13 July 1849; Head to Grey, 15 July 1849, CO 188.
16 George Noble's testimony, Saint John Riot Trials, 1849, Records, NBEC, PANB
17 Jacob Allan's testimony, Saint John Riot Trials, 1849, Records, NBEC, PANB; *Weekly Chronicle* 13 July 1849; *Sentinel* 3 July 1930
18 Head to Grey, 15 July 1849, CO 188; Josiah Wetmore's and Jeremiah McCarthy's testimonies, Saint John Riot Trials, 1849, Records, NBEC, PANB; *Sentinel* 3 July 1930
19 George Noble's and Jacob Allan's testimonies, Saint John Riot Trials, 1849, Records, NBEC, PANB; Head to Grey, 15 July 1849, CO 188
20 Samuel Gordon's, Charles Boyd's, Jacob Allan's, and Francis Jones's testimonies, Saint John Riot Trials, 1849, Records, NBEC, PANB
21 Head to Grey, 15 July 1849, CO 188; *Weekly Chronicle* 13 July 1849; *New-Brunswicker* 14 July 1849; *Sentinel* 3 July 1930; Jacob Allan's, George Mason's, Samuel Dalton's, Samuel Gordon's, and Francis Jones's testimonies, Saint John Riot Trials, 1849, Records, NBEC, PANB
22 James Gilbert's, Henry Gilbert's, and John Nixon's testimonies, Saint John Riot Trials, 1849, Records, NBEC, PANB; Head to Grey, 15 July 1849, CO 188
23 John Fitzpatrick's, Josiah Wetmore's, James Clark's, James Gilbert's, and Henry Gilbert's testimonies, Saint John Riot Trials, 1849, Records, NBEC, PANB
24 Jacob Allan's, Francis Jones's, and Squire Manks's testimonies, Saint John Riot Trials, 1849, Records, NBEC, PANB; Head to Grey, 15 July 1849, CO 188; *Sentinel* 29 Oct. 1891, 3 July 1930
25 This tactic, for example, was attempted at Woodstock in 1847. While it failed to prevent a riot, it was a bolder plan to defuse the situation. See chapter 5.
26 Head to Grey, 15 July 1849, CO 188; Jacob Allan's testimony, Saint John Riot Trials, 1849, Records, NBEC, PANB; *Morning News* 13 July 1849; *Temperance Telegraph* 19 July 1849
27 James McKenzie's, William Smith's, Francis Wilson's, and Francis Jones's testimonies, Saint John Riot Trials, 1849, Records, NBEC, PANB; *Temperance Telegraph* 19 July 1849; *Weekly Chronicle* 13 July 1849; *Morning News* 13 July 1849

28 Squire Manks's, James McKenzie's, William Smith's, Francis Wilson's, and Jeremiah Smith's testimonies, Saint John Riot Trials, 1849, Records, NBEC, PANB; *Morning News* 13 July 1849; *Christian Visitor* 14 July 1849; *Weekly Chronicle* 13 July 1849

29 Head to Grey, 15 July 1849, CO 188; Charles Boyd's testimony, Saint John Riot Trials, 1849, Records, NBEC, PANB; *Morning News* 13 July 1849; *New-Brunswicker* 14 July 1849; *Weekly Chronicle* 13 July 1849

30 Charles Boyd's and Jacob Allan's testimonies, Saint John Riot Trials, 1849, Records, NBEC, PANB; *Morning News* 13 July 1849; Head to Grey, 15 July 1849, CO 188

31 Jacob Allan's and Charles Boyd's testimonies, Saint John Riot Trials, 1849, Records, NBEC, PANB; *Morning News* 13 July 1849; Head to Grey, 15 July 1849, CO 188

32 Head to Grey, 15 July 1849, CO 188; *Morning News* 13 July 1849; *Weekly Chronicle* 13 July 1849

33 Head Letterbook, 13 July 1849, PANB; Head to Grey, 13 July 1849, CO 188; *Weekly Chronicle* 20 July 1849

34 Head to Grey, 15 July 1849, and L.A. Wilmot to R.D. Wilmot, 14 July 1849, CO 188; *Weekly Observer* 17 July 1849; *Weekly Chronicle* 20 July 1849; *Reporter* 20 July 1849; *Morning News* 13 July 1849

35 Head to Grey, 15 July 1849, CO 188

36 Jeremiah Smith's testimony, Saint John Riot Trials, 1849, Records, NBEC, PANB; *New-Brunswicker* 14 July 1849; *Weekly Observer* 17 July 1849; *Sentinel* 3 July 1930; *Morning News* 13 July 1849; *Weekly Chronicle* 13, 20 July 1849

37 Head to Grey, 15 July 1849, CO 188

38 *Morning News* 23 July 1849; *Courier* 21 July 1849; Head to Grey, 15 July 1849, CO 188

39 Kinnear to Head, 6 Sept. 1849, in Head to Grey, 7 Sept. 1849, CO 188; Miscellaneous Recognizances, Saint John Riot Trials, 1849, Records, NBEC, PANB; *Morning News* 30 July 1849

40 Kinnear to Head, 6 Sept. 1849, in Head to Grey, 7 Sept. 1849, CO 188; Miscellaneous Recognizances, Saint John Riot Trials, 1849, Records, NBEC, PANB

41 *Courier* 21, 28 July 1849

42 Documents, 1849, Saint John County Court, PANB; Testimony, Saint John Riot Trials, 1849, Records, NBEC, PANB; Kinnear to Head, 6 Sept. 1849, CO 188. Note especially the testimonies of Squire Manks, George Noble, and George McKelvey.

43 Records, 1849, NBSC, PANB

44 Kinnear to Head, 6 Sept. 1849, in Head to Grey, 7 Sept. 1849, CO 188; Documents, 1849, Saint John County Court, PANB

45 12 Victoria, c. 29, 1849, in *New Brunswick Statutes*

46 Head Correspondence, 1849, PANB; Kinnear to Head, 6 Sept. 1849, in Head to Grey, 7 Sept. 1849, CO 188

47 Judge Carter's charge to the jury, in *Royal Gazette* 17 Oct. 1849

48 Head to Grey, 7 Sept. 1849, Kinnear to Head, 6 Sept. 1849, CO 188; Documents, 1849, Saint John County Court, PANB; *Weekly Chronicle* 24 Aug. 1849; *Courier* 18, 25 Aug. 1849; *Carleton Sentinel* 28 Aug. 1849

49 *Courier* 25 Aug. 1849; *Temperance Telegraph* 23 Aug. 1849; *Reporter* 24 Aug. 1849; *Christian Visitor* 24 Aug. 1849; *Weekly Chronicle* 24 Aug. 1849; *Weekly Observer* 12, 28 Aug. 1849; *Morning News* 22 Aug. 1849; *Sentinel* 3 July 1930; Head Correspondence, 1849, PANB; Kinnear to Head, 6 Sept. 1849, in Head to Grey, 7 Sept. 1849, CO 188

50 12 Victoria, c. 29, chap. 5, art. 5, 1849, in *New Brunswick Statutes*; Kinnear to Head, 6 Sept. 1849, in Head to Grey, 7 Sept. 1849, CO 188; *Temperance Telegraph* 23 Aug. 1849

51 Grey to Head, 9 Sept. 1849, with enclosure from Q.C. Baldwin, CO 189; *Royal Gazette* 17 Oct. 1849; *Journal of the House Assembly*, 28 Feb. 1850

52 The legislature spent the next twenty-five years debating the fraternity's incorporation before giving its assent in 1875. See *Journal of the House Assembly*, 1850–1, 1853–4, 1857–60, 1867, 1872–5.

53 Kinnear to Head, 6 Sept. 1849, in Head to Grey, 7 Sept. 1849, CO 188

54 *Morning News* 22 Aug. 1849. Also see *Weekly Chronicle* 24 Aug. 1849; *Temperance Telegraph* 16 Aug. 1849.

55 John Haggerty's Petition to Head, Sept. 1849; Carter to Partelow, 31 Jan. 1850; Wilmot to Head, 3 Jan. 1850: Judicial Records, 1849, 1850, NBEC, PANB

56 W.S. MacNutt, *New Brunswick* (Toronto: Macmillan 1963) 347–9; MacNutt, 'The Coming of Responsible Government,' *CHR* 33 (1952) 127. MacNutt incorrectly argued that two Orangemen were sentenced, and implied that the organization suffered a general defeat.

57 Rev. J.W. Millidge, 'Reminiscences of St. John from 1849 to 1860,' *New Brunswick Historical Society Collections* 4 (1919): 8, 127

58 For details see chapter 10.

59 Acheson, *Saint John* (Toronto: U of Toronto P 1985) 111–12, 224–7

60 D.R. Jack, *Centennial Prize Essay on the History of the City and County of St. John* (Saint John: J. & A. McMillan 1883) 136–7

61 For standard Orange interpretations of the riot, consult *Sentinel* 3 July 1930, and 'The Battle of York Point,' Archives, Harriet Irving Library, U of New Brunswick.

62 Head to Grey, 15 July 1849, CO 188; Special Presentment of the Grand Jury, 21 Aug. 1849, in *Morning News* 24 Aug. 1849; Partelow to Grand Jury, 15 Sept. 1849, in *Royal Gazette* 19 Sept. 1849; *Courier* 25 Aug., 22 Sept. 1849; *Weekly Observer* 12 Aug. 1849; *Christian Visitor* 13 July 1849; *New-Brunswicker* 14 July 1849; *Morning News* 16 July 1849

63 Special Presentment of the Grand Jury, 21 Aug. 1849, in *Morning News* 24 Aug. 1849; Grand Jury to Partelow, in *Courier* 22 Sept. 1849; *Morning News* 13, 16 July, 24 Aug. 1849; *New-Brunswicker* 14 July 1849; *Courier* 25 Aug. 1849

64 *Weekly Chronicle* 13, 20 July 1849; Head to Grey, 15 July 1849, CO 188

65 *Morning News* 16 July 1849
66 Head to Grey, 15 July, 7 Sept. 1849, CO 188; Partelow to Grand Jury, 15 Sept. 1849, in *Courier* 22 Sept. 1849
67 Acheson, *Saint John* 227–9
68 George McKelvey's and George Noble's testimonies, Saint John Riot Trials, 1849, Records, NBEC, PANB; *Morning News* 23 July 1849; *Weekly Chronicle* 20 July 1849
69 *Weekly Chronicle* 20 July 1849
70 *Weekly Chronicle* 13, 20 July, 24, 31 Aug., 28 Sept. 1849; *Temperance Telegraph* 23 Aug. 1849; R.D. Wilmot's address, House of Assembly, in *Reporter* 1 Mar. 1850; Jacob Allan's testimony, Saint John Riot Trials, 1849, Records, NBEC, PANB
71 Acheson, *Saint John* 43
72 Minutes, 1848–60, SJCC, PANB; Documents, CP, PANB
73 Documents, CP, PANB; Acheson, *Saint John* 48–66
74 Minutes, 1848–60, SJCC, PANB
75 Special Presentment of the Grand Jury, 21 Aug. 1849, in *Morning News* 24 Aug. 1849. Italics in the original.
76 Judge Carter's charge to the jury, 1 Sept. 1849, in *Royal Gazette* 17 Oct. 1849; Grey to Head, 9 Sept. 1849, and enclosures, in *Royal Gazette* 17 Oct. 1849; Special Presentment of the Grand Jury, 21 Aug. 1849, in *Courier* 25 Aug. 1849; *Morning News* 16, 18, 21 July 1849
77 Head to Grey, 15 July 1849, CO 188
78 Head to Grey, 7 Sept. 1849; Kinnear to Partelow, 6 Sept. 1849: CO 188
79 *Morning News* 23 July 1849
80 See *Journal of the House Assembly* and Petitions, 1850–1, 1853–4, 1857–60, 1867, 1872–5, Documents, House of Assembly, PANB.
81 Head to Grey, 7 Sept. 1849, CO 188
82 *Courier* 19 July 1851; *Weekly Chronicle* 18 July 1851
83 *Morning News* 15, 20 July 1853; *Courier* 16, 23, 30 July, 6, 13 Aug. 1853; *Reporter* 15, 22 July 1853
84 *Freeman* 14 July 1855; McHarg Diary, NBM; *Sentinel* 3 July 1930
85 *Sentinel* 3 July 1930; *Morning News* 17 July 1876
86 Only two Orangemen were wounded, apparently by gunfire from their own ranks. See *Freeman* 13 July 1876.
87 *Freeman* 13, 15, 18 July 1876; *Morning News* 14, 17 July 1876; Millidge, 'Reminiscences' 127
88 *Morning News* 14 July 1876. See also Rev. Percival's address on 12 July 1876, in *Morning News* 17 July 1876

CHAPTER 9

1 For the growing phenomenon of using the Orange Order as an elective tool, see *Carleton Sentinel* 16, 23 July 1850, 22 July 1851, 17 July 1852, 9 July

1853; Circular from Amaranth Office, 14 Jan. 1850; Hill to Lenentine, 31 Aug. 1853; Resolutions from York County Lodge, 6 Feb. 1854; Circular from James S. Beek, 17 Mar. 1854: CP, PANB

2 William E. Perley letter, 1861, in Burpee Family Papers, PANB

3 Two studies that explore patronage and political linkages are Robert H. Babcock, 'The Orange Order and the Working Classes of Saint John, New Brunswick, 1870–1920,' unpublished paper, Joint Conference of Atlantic Canada Studies and Loyalist Studies, May 1983, Saint John, NB; and Peter M. Toner, 'Order and Occupation: The Orangemen of Saint Martin's, N.B.,' *Social Science Monograph Series* 4 (1981): 91–5. See also S.H. Gilbert's Address, 1853, York County Records, CP, PANB; *Reporter* 18 July 1856; *Freeman* 30 May 1876; Gordon to Campbell, 18 Dec. 1865, CO 188.

4 See T.W. Acheson, *Saint John* (Toronto: U of Toronto P 1985) 221–2.

5 Ibid., 214–16

6 Gordon to Cardwell, 18 Dec. 1865, CO 188

7 George F.G. Stanley, 'The Caraquet Riots of 1875,' *Acadiensis* 2 (1972); Arthur T. Doyle, *Front Benches and Back Rooms* (Toronto: Green Tree 1976) 10–16

8 This mirrors patterns of conflict elsewhere. See Charles Tilly, 'Collective Violence in European Perspective,' in *The History of Violence in America*, ed. H.D. Graham and T.R. Gurr (New York: Praeger 1969) 28–44.

CHAPTER 10

1 Many contemporaries rationalized that Irish 'party spirit' caused turmoil throughout the British Empire in the nineteenth century. For an example, see Grey to Colebrooke, 19 Jan. 1848, Immigration Papers, PANB.

2 For a discussion of the important contributions of ritual and symbolism to social movements, see E.J. Hobsbawm, *Primitive Rebels* (New York: W.W. Norton 1959) 150–67.

3 All the New Brunswick riots closely follow the pattern of expressive rioting to encourage group cohesiveness. See Michael Feldberg, *The Turbulent Era* (New York: Oxford UP 1980) 54–83, 128–9.

4 See, for example, Gregory Kealey's cogent description of ritualism and riots in Toronto during the nineteenth century in *Toronto Workers Respond to Industrial Capitalism* (Toronto: U of Toronto P 1980) 115–21.

5 Hannah Arendt called this phenomena the 'lawlessness inherent in uprooted peoples.' Although this was an oversimplification, it undeniably applied to the Irish experience in North America. See 'Lawlessness Is Inherent in the Uprooted,' *New York Times Magazine* 28 April 1968: 24.

6 R.S. Neale, *Class and Ideology in the Nineteenth Century* (London: Routledge & Kegan Paul 1972) 19–20. For a theoretical approach to Irish violence, see 'General Introduction' in *Irish Peasants*, ed. Samuel Clark and James S. Donnelly, Jr (Madison: U of Wisconsin P 1983) 3–21.

7 Allen D. Grimshaw, 'Interpreting Collective Violence: An Argument for the Importance of Social Structure,' in *Collective Violence*, ed. James F. Short, Jr, and Marvin E. Wolfgang (Chicago: Aldine-Atherton 1972) 36–46

8 Testimony from the Saint John and Fredericton riot trials clearly showed that victims of assault were routinely believed to be, even if they were not, members of the opposing crowd. See Saint John Riot Trials, 1845–9, Records, NBEC, PANB; and Fredericton Riot Trial, 1847, Records, NBSC, PANB.

9 This conclusion mirrors recent work on crowds and collective behaviour, which revises older interpretations of the 'irrational' and 'irritable' crowd. For examples of the latter, see Gustave LeBon, *The Crowd: A Study of the Popular Mind* (London: T. Fisher Unwin 1903) 26–36, 42, 133–41; and Hippolyte A. Taine, *The French Revolution*, 2 vols. (New York: Henry Holt 1881) 2:196–233. For the purposeful-crowd interpretations, see George Rudé, *The Crowd in History* (New York: John Wiley 1984); Rudé, 'The London "Mob" of the Eighteenth Century,' *Historical Journal* 2 (1959): 1–18; and Gordon S. Wood, 'A Note on Mobs in the American Revolution,' *William and Mary Quarterly* 23 (1966): 635–42. See also John Bohstedt's thoughtful critique of Rudé's tendency to find crowds too respectable, in *Riots and Community Politics* (Cambridge: Harvard UP 1983) 4–11.

10 Hugh Davis Graham, 'The Paradox of American Violence: A Historical Commentary,' *Annals of the American Academy of Political and Social Science* 391 (1970): 74–82; David Montgomery, 'The Shuttle and the Cross: Weavers and Artisans in the Kensington Riots of 1844,' *Journal of Social History* 5 (1972): 411–46; David Grimsted, 'Rioting in Its Jacksonian Setting,' *American Historical Review* 77 (1972): 361–97

11 Fredericton Riot Trials, 1847, Records, NBSC, PANB

12 Irish immigrants in the United States experienced a similar double standard. See Theodore M. Hammett, 'Two Mobs of Jacksonian Boston: Ideology and Interest,' *Journal of American History* 62 (1976): 866–7.

13 Woodstock Riot Trials, 1847, 1848, R&D, NBEC, PANB; Fredericton Riot Trials, 1847, Records, NBSC, PANB; Saint John Riot Trials, 1845–9, Records, NBEC, PANB

14 Colebrooke to Grey, 30 July 1847, CO 188; Colebrooke Correspondence, 1847, PANB

15 Head to Grey, 15 July 1849, CO 188; Grey to Head, 9 Sept. 1849, with enclosure from Q.C. Baldwin, CO 189; *Royal Gazette* 17 Oct. 1849; *Journal of the House of Assembly*, 28 Feb. 1850

16 Legislative Assembly Reports, 1847–9, PANB; Documents, R&D, NBEC, PANB

17 John Weaver effectively explored the distinction between cultural propensities and socio-economic conditions in 'Crime, Public Order, and Repression: The Gore District Upheaval, 1832–1851,' *Ontario History* 78 (1986): 188–204.

18 12 Victoria, c. 29, 1849, in *New Brunswick Statutes* (Fredericton: Queen's Printer); Peters to Odell, 18 July 1843, Legislative Assembly Papers, PANB

19 All of the above represent only the *known* Orangemen in the House of Assembly. It is entirely possible, indeed probable, that other Orangemen served throughout this period.

20 House of Assembly Records, 1840–60, PANB

21 David R. Facey-Crowther, 'The New Brunswick Militia: 1784–1871,' MA thesis, U of New Brunswick, 1965, 164–7; Colebrooke to Grey, 25 Nov. 1846, CO 188; Mary I. Langford, 'Sir Edmund Head's First Colonial Administration: New Brunswick 1848–1854,' MA thesis, U of Toronto, 1948, 130–4

22 Wright to Colebrooke, 29 Jan. 1848, Judicial Records, NBEC, PANB

23 11 Victoria, c. 12, 1848; 12 Victoria, c. 68, 1849; 13 Victoria, c. 1, 1850 (Local Acts): all in *New Brunswick Statutes* (Fredericton: Queen's Printer)

24 Note, for example, that the Portland Police Magistrate mustered his force from 'ten good Protestants.' See Allan to Saunders, 11 Nov. 1847, R&D, NBEC, PANB.

25 Each disturbance included a number of onlookers and bystanders who may have been swept into battle against their wills, such as at Fredericton in 1847, as well as people looking for fights rather than protecting their interests. These belated participants have been accounted for in the analysis; however, evidence suggests that they never reached significant numbers in any of the riots.

26 Crowd accounts were inevitably written by authorities and critics. See Richard A. Berk, 'The Controversy Surrounding Analyses of Collective Violence: Some Methodological Notes,' in *Collective Violence*, ed. Short and Wolfgang, 113–18; Rudé, *Crowd in History* 1–14.

27 Woodstock Riot Trials, 1847, 1848, R&D, NBEC, PANB; Fredericton Riot Trials, 1847, Records, NBSC, PANB; Saint John Riot Trials, 1845–9, Records, NBEC, PANB

28 Head to Grey, 31 July 1848, Kinnear to Partelow, 21 July 1848, CO 188; Judge Parker's address, in *Reporter* 4 Aug. 1848

29 Fredericton Riot Trials, 1847, Records, NBSC, PANB; *Royal Gazette* 17 Nov. 1847; Judge Carter's address to the Grand Jury, Fredericton Riot Trials, in *Reporter* 12 Nov. 1847

30 Saint John Riot Trials, 1845–9, Records, NBEC, PANB; R&D, NBEC, PANB; Kinnear to Head, 6 Sept. 1849, in Head to Grey, 7 Sept. 1849, CO 188

31 This conclusion corroborates analyses of crowds in Europe and North America. For example, see Rudé, *Crowd in History* 205–10; Leonard L. Richards, *'Gentlemen of Property and Standing'; Anti-Abolition Mobs in Jacksonian America* (New York: Oxford UP 1970) 130–55.

32 See Petitions for the Incorporation of the Orange Order, 1848–75, RGA, PANB.

33 Hereward Senior, *Orangeism: The Canadian Phase* (Toronto: McGraw-Hill Ryerson 1972); Cecil J. Houston and William J. Smyth, *The Sash Canada Wore* (Toronto: U of Toronto P 1980); Kealey, *Toronto Workers*

34 As Akenson pointed out, the demands for Canadian nationalism ultimately

led to 'an affirmation of a particularly opprobrious form of English-Canadian racism.' See *Being Had* (Port Credit, Ont.: Meany 1984) 142.

35 Tilly pursued the point about how notables tended to cope with substantial changes in *Big Structures* (New York: Russell Sage Foundation 1984) 10.

36 Kealey, *Toronto Workers*; Robert H. Babcock, 'The Orange Order and the Working Classes of Saint John,' unpublished paper, Joint Conference of Atlantic Canada Studies and Loyalist Studies, May 1983, Saint John

37 And yet perhaps not. Members of Ontario's practically moribund Orange Order at a recent gathering passed a resolution calling for a ban on all illegal immigrants. In language hauntingly reminiscent of their nineteenth-century nativist forebears, they called upon the government to 'encourage more immigration from such countries as the United Kingdom, the Commonwealth countries, the United States of America, the Northern European countries and others whose lifestyle is essentially similar to ours.' See *Globe & Mail* 11 July 1988.

38 For a discussion of the Irish communities along the Miramichi, see John J. Mannion, *Irish Settlements in Eastern Canada* (Toronto: U of Toronto P 1974)

39 For a succinct analysis of indigence and culture, see William M. Baker, '"God's Unfortunate People": Historiography of Irish Catholics in Nineteenth-Century Canada,' in *The Untold Story: The Irish in Canada*, 2 vols, ed. Robert O'Driscoll and Lorna Reynolds (Toronto: Celtic Arts of Canada 1988) 1:59–71.

40 Akenson's lively argument has been presented in several works, including *Small Differences* (Kingston: McGill-Queen's UP 1988) 15–48, 88–99; 'Data: What Is Known About the Irish in North America,' in *Untold Story*, ed. O'Driscoll and Reynolds, 1:15–25; *Being Had*; and *The Irish in Ontario* (Kingston: McGill-Queen's UP 1984).

41 Using census information, Peter Toner came to essentially the same conclusion: 'The Origins of the New Brunswick Irish,' *Journal of Canadian Studies* 23 (1988): 116; 'Another "New Ireland" Lost,' in *Untold Story*, ed. O'Driscoll and Reynolds, 1:233–5. See also Kerby Miller, *Emigrants and Exiles* (New York: Oxford UP 1985) 275.

42 Miller, *Emigrants and Exiles* 276. Bruce S. Elliott mounted an effective criticism of Miller's arguments in *Irish Migrants in the Canadas: A New Approach* (Kingston: McGill-Queen's UP 1988).

43 Acheson acknowledged this point: *Saint John* (Toronto: U of Toronto P 1985) 105–6.

44 James M. Whalen, 'New Brunswick Poor Law Policy,' MA thesis, U of New Brunswick, 1966, 36

45 For example, two researchers found that Irish-Catholics proved the only exception to groups that displayed a substantial degree of occupational mobility in Ontario during the 1860s. See A. Gordon Darroch and Michael D. Ornstein, 'Ethnicity and Class, Transitions Over a Decade: Ontario,

1861–1871,' Canadian Historical Association *Papers* (1984): 111–37; 'Ethnicity and Occupational Structure in Canada in 1871: The Vertical Mosaic in Historical Perspective,' *CHR* 61 (1980): 328–30.

46 Tilly, *Big Structures* 10–12, 53–6

47 As Akenson argued, Irish behaviour in Ontario can only be understood by exploring local factors rather than vague, and typically apocryphal, cultural propensities. See *Irish in Ontario* 45–7.

48 Bohstedt, *Riots and Community Politics* 26

49 Feldberg, *Turbulent Era* 80–3

50 Charles Tilly, 'Introduction,' *Class Conflict and Collective Action*, ed. Louise A. Tilly and Charles Tilly (Beverly Hills, Calif.: Sage 1981) 15–23

51 E.P. Thompson, 'The Moral Economy of the English Crowd in the Eighteenth Century,' *Past and Present* 50 (1971): 77–8; E.P. Thompson, *The Making of the English Working Class* (New York: Pantheon 1963) 62–5; Tilly, 'Collective Violence' 4–6

52 Michael Feldberg explored this 'preservatist' concept in *Turbulent Era* 5–8, 33–7, 126–8; and 'Urbanization as a Cause of Violence: Philadelphia as a Test Case,' in *The Peoples of Philadelphia: A History of Ethnic Groups and Lower-Class Life, 1790–1940*, ed. Allen F. Davis and Mark H. Haller (Philadelphia: Temple UP 1973) 56–9.

53 For discussions of vigilantism, see Richard M. Brown, 'The American Vigilante Tradition,' and 'Historical Patterns of Violence in America,' in *The History of Violence in America*, ed. H.D. Graham and T.R. Gurr (New York: Praeger 1969) 45–84, 154–217; Feldberg, *Turbulent Era* 73–5. See also Robert M. Senkewicz, *Vigilantes in Gold Rush San Francisco* (Stanford, Calif.: Stanford UP 1985).

54 For a discussion of rational violence, see Hannah Arendt, *On Violence* (New York: Harcourt Brace Jovanovich 1969) esp. 64–5.

55 Robert M. Brown, 'Vigilante Tradition' 188–201; Brown, *Strain of Violence* (New York: Oxford UP 1975) 103–8; Hobsbawm, *Primitive Rebels* 112–13

56 W.L. Morton, 'Victorian Canada,' in *The Shield of Achilles: Aspects of Canada in the Victorian Age*, ed. W.L. Morton (Toronto: McClelland & Stewart 1968) 314–16

57 William H. Elgee, *The Social Teachings of the Canadian Churches* (Toronto: Ryerson P 1964); Alexander Monro, *New Brunswick* (Halifax: Richard Nugent 1855) 258

58 Carl Wittke, *The Irish in America* (Baton Rouge: Louisiana State UP 1956) 10

59 Natalie Davis, 'The Rites of Violence,' *Past and Present* 59 (1973): 51–91

60 Tilly, 'Collective Violence' 12–15

61 For examples, see George Rudé, 'The Gordon Riots,' *Transactions of the Royal Historical Society* (1956): 93–114; John Stevenson, *Popular Disturbances in England* (London: Longman 1979) 137–42, 276–7.

62 See Sam Bass Warner, Jr, *The Private City: Philadelphia in Three Periods of Its*

*Growth* (Philadelphia: U of Pennsylvania P 1968) 125; Feldberg, *Turbulent Era.*

63 For examples, see E.J. Hobsbawm and George Rudé, *Captain Swing* (New York: Pantheon 1968); Malcolm I. Thomis, *The Luddites: Machine Breaking in Regency England* (London: David & Charles Archon 1970); David Williams, *The Rebecca Riots: A Study in Agrarian Protest* (Cardiff: U of Wales P 1955); Gwyn A. Williams, *The Merthyr Rising* (London: Croom Helm 1978).

64 George Rudó, 'The Study of Popular Disturbances in the "Pre-Industrial" Age,' *Historical Studies* 10 (1963) 457–60; Hobsbawm, *Primitive Rebels* 1–7, 108–14, 122–5

65 For an example of this phenomenon, consult Scott W. See, 'Polling Crowds and Patronage,' *CHR* 72 (1991). Also see Graeme Wynn, *Timber Colony* (Toronto: U of Toronto P 1981) 3–10, 130–7.

66 Wynn, *Timber Colony* 84–6, 166–7, 330; W.S. MacNutt, *New Brunswick* (Toronto: Macmillan 1963) 329; James Richard Rice, 'A History of Organized Labour in Saint John,' MA thesis, U of New Brunswick, 1968, 33–4

67 For example, see Akenson, *Small Differences* 101.

68 Note Acheson's assertions that the Orange Order tapped discriminatory strains in Saint John's society (*Saint John* 114).

69 Miller, *Emigrants and Exiles* 323

70 Notable exceptions to this point are Howard Palmer's 'Nativism in Alberta,' *Canadian Historical Association Papers* (1974) and *Patterns of Prejudice* (Toronto: McClelland & Stewart 1982).

71 'Orangemen in Canada,' in *Untold Story*, ed. O'Driscoll and Reynolds, 2:752.

72 See John Runcie, '"Hunting the Nigs" in Philadelphia: The Race Riot of August 1834,' *Pennsylvania History* 39 (1972): 187–218; Richards, *Anti-Abolition Mobs.*

73 Akenson, *Small Differences* 148

74 Heribert Adam argued this point in 'Combatting Racism,' *Queen's Quarterly* 89 (1982): 789–91; see also Akenson, *Being Had* 116, 141–2.

# Index